THE TINCTURE MASTER'S BIBLE

Your A-Z Guide to Craft DIY Herbal Healing Tinctures & Blends at Home and Protect Your Body, Mind, and Spirit Naturally

Rose Bradley

Table Of Contents

Introduction

Tinctures stand as one of the most ancient and revered methods of herbal extraction, esteemed for their ability to capture the essence and therapeutic benefits of plants in a highly concentrated form. They involve extracting the medicinal properties of herbs using alcohol, which acts as a solvent to pull out active ingredients from plant material. The resulting liquid offers a longer shelf life and can be administered in precise doses.

The origins of tinctures trace back to the earliest civilizations, where extracts of plants were preserved in alcohol to harness their medicinal properties for extended use. These potent extracts served not only as health remedies but also played a pivotal role in spiritual and ritual practices across various cultures. As we delve into the contemporary use of tinctures, we see that their relevance and efficacy remain undiminished, bridging the gap between ancient wisdom and modern health practices.

The preparation of a tincture involves steeping plant material—be it leaves, roots, bark, or berries—in alcohol, which serves as a solvent to extract soluble phytochemicals and as a preservative to extend the shelf life of the resulting solution. The choice of plant and alcohol type, the ratio of plant matter to solvent, and the duration of infusion are all critical factors that determine the quality and strength of a tincture.

Beyond their preparation, tinctures offer a versatile method of administration. They are typically taken orally, with the dosage easily controlled through the number of drops used. This allows for personalized adjustment to meet individual therapeutic needs, a flexibility that is less achievable with pre-formulated herbal capsules or tablets. Additionally, the rapid absorption of tinctures into the bloodstream makes them an efficient delivery system for herbal medicine, providing quick relief and action when needed most.

In this book, readers will find comprehensive profiles of numerous herbs, each detailed with its specific medicinal properties and how these can be best extracted and utilized through tinctures. We will explore both single-herb tinctures and formulations that combine multiple herbs for synergistic effects, expanding the healer's toolkit for addressing a wide range of physical ailments and wellness concerns.

As we embark on this exploration of tinctures, we aim not only to educate but also to inspire our readers to embrace the holistic benefits of herbal medicine. By returning to these roots, we reconnect with the natural world and access its profound capacity to heal and nourish. This book promises to be an invaluable resource for anyone seeking to deepen their understanding of herbal extracts and to incorporate the enduring power of tinctures into their health regimen.

Welcome to a journey of discovery, empowerment, and healing through the timeless art of tinctures.

Chapter 1

Tincture Preparation Process

A tincture is essentially a concentrated herbal extract crafted through the maceration of plant material in alcohol. The use of alcohol, typically ethanol, serves multiple purposes. It efficiently extracts active compounds from herbs, including alkaloids, flavonoids, oils, and other phytochemicals, which are often not fully soluble in water. Additionally, alcohol acts as a preservative, extending the shelf life of the herbal extract for several years. This dual role makes tinctures a preferred choice for herbalists seeking both potency and longevity in herbal remedies.

The process of making a tincture involves several steps, each critical to ensuring the quality and efficacy of the final product. Initially, the selected herbs are cleaned, chopped, and placed in an airtight container. Alcohol is then added, covering the herbs completely. This mixture is left to sit for a period ranging from two to six weeks, a crucial phase known as maceration. During this time, the container is kept in a cool, dark place to prevent degradation of the herbs' active ingredients. Regular shaking of the container helps to mix the contents and improve the extraction process.

Once maceration is complete, the liquid is strained to remove all solid plant parts, using fine mesh or cheesecloth. The resulting liquid, now rich in medicinal properties, is the tincture. It is stored in dark glass bottles to protect it from light, which can diminish its quality. Proper labeling is essential, noting the type of herb, alcohol percentage, and date of production, to ensure correct usage and potency over time.

Tinctures are particularly valued for their ease of use and rapid absorption. When administered sublingually—placed under the tongue—they are quickly absorbed into the bloodstream, bypassing the digestive system. This rapid action allows the effects of the medicinal compounds to manifest sooner than capsules or teas. Moreover, tinctures can be easily incorporated into daily routines; they can be added to water, tea, or juice, making them a convenient option for those seeking to integrate herbal remedies into their lives.

Overview of Tincture Preparation

Selection of Ingredients: The first step in tincture preparation is the selection of appropriate herbs. These are chosen based on their known medicinal properties, which are aligned with the patient's specific health needs. The quality of herbs is crucial; only well-dried, high-quality plant materials should be used to ensure the efficacy of the tincture.

Herb Preparation: Before extraction, herbs may need to be prepared to enhance the extraction process. This typically involves grinding or chopping herbs to increase the surface area, which facilitates a more complete extraction of medicinal compounds.

Extraction Process

Solvent Selection: Ethanol is the most commonly used solvent in tincture making due to its efficiency in extracting a wide range of water-soluble and fat-soluble compounds. The concentration of alcohol can vary, generally between 25% and 90%, depending on the nature of the substances being extracted and the intended use of the tincture.

Maceration: The prepared herbs are placed in an airtight container, and alcohol is added to cover the herbs completely. This mixture is left to macerate for several weeks, during which the alcohol dissolves the active components of the herbs. The container should be kept in a cool, dark place and shaken daily to ensure the herbs are consistently exposed to the solvent.

Straining and Storage

Straining the Mixture: After maceration, the mixture is strained using a fine mesh or cheesecloth to remove all solid particles. It's important to squeeze the soaked herbs to extract as much liquid as possible, maximizing the yield and potency of the tincture.

Storage: To preserve the integrity of the active compounds, tinctures should be stored in dark glass bottles, shielding them from light exposure. Bottles must be labeled clearly with the herb name, date of production, and alcohol strength. Stored properly, tinctures can be effective for up to five years.

Administration and Dosage

Dosage: Tinctures should be administered in small, controlled doses, usually a few drops to a teaspoon, taken two to three times per day. The exact dosage can vary based on the condition being treated, the age, and the health status of the patient.

Administration Tips

- Tinctures are usually taken diluted in water or tea to mitigate the strong taste of the alcohol.
- It is important to follow the practitioner's instructions regarding timing relative to meals, as some tinctures are absorbed better on an empty stomach while others may require ingestion with food.

Tips for Maximizing Effectiveness

- **Quality Control:** Always use the highest quality herbs and alcohol you can find. Organic herbs and grain alcohol are preferred for their purity and lack of contaminants.
- **Precise Labeling:** Detailed labeling helps in tracking the effectiveness and ensures the safe use of the tincture, particularly when multiple tinctures are being used.

TINCTURE PREPARATION FOR COMMON HERBS

HERB	HERB TO ALCOHOL RATIO	MACERATION TIME	PRIMARY BENEFITS
Echinacea	1:5	6-8 weeks	Boosts the immune system, fights infections
Valerian	1:5	4-6 weeks	Promotes relaxation, aids sleep, reduces anxiety
Passion Flower	1:5	4-6 weeks	Reduces anxiety, aids sleep
Arnica	1:10	3-4 weeks	Reduces inflammation, alleviates pain (external use)
Lavender	1:5	4-6 weeks	Calms nerves, soothes anxiety
Peppermint	1:5	4-6 weeks	Relieves nausea, improves digestion
Stinging Nettle	1:5	4-6 weeks	Detoxifies, reduces inflammation
Turmeric	1:5	4-6 weeks	Anti-inflammatory, supports liver health
Licorice Root	1:5	4-6 weeks	Soothes stomach, supports adrenal glands
Goldenseal	1:5	6-8 weeks	Antimicrobial, supports mucous membrane health
Chamomile	1:5	4-6 weeks	Calms anxiety, aids sleep, soothes digestive issues
Elderberry	1:4	4-6 weeks	Boosts immune system, fights colds and flu
Astragalus	1:5	6-8 weeks	Boosts immune system, supports cardiovascular health
Ginger	1:5	4-6 weeks	Reduces nausea, aids digestion, anti-inflammatory
Ginkgo Biloba	1:5	4-6 weeks	Enhances cognitive function, improves circulation
Hawthorn	1:3	4-6 weeks	Supports cardiovascular health, regulates blood pressure
Lemon Balm	1:5	4-6 weeks	Reduces anxiety, aids sleep, helps with digestive issues
Milk Thistle	1:5	4-6 weeks	Supports liver health, detoxifies the body
Saw Palmetto	1:5	6-8 weeks	Supports prostate health, may reduce inflammation
Ashwagandha	1:5	6-8 weeks	Reduces stress, boosts energy, improves concentration
St. John's Wort	1:5	4-6 weeks	Alleviates symptoms of depression, supports nerve health
Thyme	1:5	4-6 weeks	Antimicrobial, supports respiratory health
Comfrey	1:5	4-6 weeks	Promotes skin and bone healing, note: for external use only
Cat's Claw	1:5	6-8 weeks	Boosts immune system, anti-inflammatory
Calendula	1:5	4-6 weeks	Soothes skin irritations, promotes wound healing
Dandelion	1:5	4-6 weeks	Supports liver function, aids digestion
Ginseng	1:5	6-8 weeks	Enhances physical and mental endurance, boosts energy
Rosemary	1:5	4-6 weeks	Improves circulation, enhances memory and concentration
Sage	1:5	4-6 weeks	Supports digestive health, has antiseptic properties
Tulsi	1:5	4-6 weeks	Reduces stress, supports the immune system, has adaptogenic benefits

Determining the Right Dosage

In the realm of herbal medicine, the determination of appropriate dosages is paramount to both safety and efficacy. Unlike pharmaceuticals, which undergo rigorous testing for dosage accuracy, herbal preparations can vary significantly in concentration and potency. Therefore, understanding the principles that guide dosage in herbal medicine is essential for both practitioners and users.

One of the first steps in establishing a safe and effective dosage is understanding the specific properties of the herb being used. Herbs can range from mild to extremely potent, with some capable of causing significant harm if misused. For instance, herbs like St. John's Wort are widely used for their antidepressant qualities but can interact negatively with synthetic drugs. Similarly, the potent effects of herbs like foxglove, which contains digitalis, can be life-threatening if not dosed precisely, illustrating the fine line between medicine and toxin.

The method of delivery also influences the appropriate dosage of herbal remedies. Tinctures, teas, capsules, and powders each have different absorption rates and levels of efficacy. For example, tinctures may require smaller doses than teas due to higher concentration levels of active compounds. Understanding these differences is crucial for effective treatment planning.

Moreover, the individual characteristics of the patient play a significant role in dosage determination. Factors such as age, weight, metabolism, and overall health condition can affect how an individual responds to herbal treatment. Children, pregnant women, and the elderly, in particular, often require adjustments to standard dosages.

To navigate these complexities, practitioners of herbal medicine should adopt a cautious approach, starting with lower doses and gradually adjusting based on the patient's response. This method helps to minimize the risk of adverse reactions and side effects.

CORRECT DOSAGE OF TINCTURES FOR COMMON HERBS

HERB	ADULT DOSAGE	CHILDREN DOSAGE	CONSIDERATIONS
Echinacea	2-4 mL, 3 times daily	1-2 mL, 3 times daily (under supervision)	Use for up to 10 days. Not recommended for individuals with autoimmune diseases.
Valerian	2-3 mL, 3 times daily	Not recommended for children	May cause drowsiness. Avoid alcohol.
Passion Flower	1-2 mL, 3 times daily	0.5-1 mL, 3 times daily (under supervision)	Can cause drowsiness. Avoid with sedatives.
Arnica	Dilute with water 1:10 ratio, apply externally	Not recommended for children	
Lavender	1-2 mL, 3 times daily	0.5-1 mL, 3 times daily (under supervision)	Avoid with sedatives.
Peppermint	1-2 mL, 3 times daily	0.5-1 mL, 3 times daily (under supervision)	Can cause acid reflux in sensitive individuals.
Stinging Nettle	1-2 mL, 3 times daily	0.5-1 mL, 3 times daily (under supervision)	Monitor for allergic reactions, especially in those with plant allergies.
Turmeric	1-3 mL, 3 times daily	0.5-1.5 mL, 3 times daily (under supervision)	Avoid in pregnancy; can cause stomach upset.
Licorice Root	1-2 mL, 3 times daily	0.5-1 mL, 3 times daily (under supervision)	Should not be used in cases of hypertension or kidney disease.
Goldenseal	0.5-1 mL, 3 times daily	0.25-0.5 mL, 3 times daily (under supervision)	Short-term use only. Not recommended for pregnant or breastfeeding women.
Chamomile	2-4 mL, 3 times daily	1-2 mL, 3 times daily (under supervision)	
Elderberry	2-4 mL, 3 times daily	1-2 mL, 3 times daily (under supervision)	
Astragalus	2-4 mL, 3 times daily	1-2 mL, 3 times daily (under supervision)	Safe for long-term use. Avoid if fever is present.
Ginger	0.5-1 mL, 3 times daily	0.25-0.5 mL, 3 times daily (under supervision)	Avoid with blood thinners; can increase bile production.
Ginkgo Biloba	2-4 mL, 3 times daily	Not recommended for children	
Hawthorn	1-2 mL, 3 times daily	Not recommended for children	Generally safe for long-term use. Consult with a healthcare provider if on heart medications.
Lemon Balm	2-4 mL, 3 times daily	1-2 mL, 3 times daily (under supervision)	
Milk Thistle	2-4 mL, 3 times daily	1-2 mL, 3 times daily (under supervision)	

HERB	ADULT DOSAGE	CHILDREN DOSAGE	CONSIDERATIONS
Saw Palmetto	2-4 mL, 3 times daily	Not recommended for children	
Ashwagandha	2-4 mL, 3 times daily	1-2 mL, 3 times daily (under supervision)	Avoid during pregnancy; consult a doctor if taking thyroid medications.
St. John's Wort	2-4 mL, 3 times daily	Not recommended for children	
Thyme	1-2 mL, 3 times daily	0.5-1 mL, 3 times daily (under supervision)	
Comfrey	External use only	External use only	Do not apply to broken skin; not for internal use.
Cat's Claw	1-2 mL, 3 times daily	Not recommended for children	Can cause immune activation; avoid with autoimmune diseases.
Calendula	2-4 mL, 3 times daily	1-2 mL, 3 times daily (under supervision)	
Dandelion	2-5 mL, 3 times daily	1-2.5 mL, 3 times daily (under supervision)	Safe in most populations; may increase urine production.
Ginseng	1-2 mL, 3 times daily	Not recommended for children	May cause insomnia or palpitations; avoid with hypertension.
Rosemary	1-2 mL, 3 times daily	0.5-1 mL, 3 times daily (under supervision)	Avoid during pregnancy; can interfere with iron absorption.
Sage	1-2 mL, 3 times daily	0.5-1 mL, 3 times daily (under supervision)	Avoid during pregnancy; can lower seizure threshold.
Tulsi	2-4 mL, 3 times daily	1-2 mL, 3 times daily (under supervision)	Generally safe; monitor for possible blood sugar reductions.

Methods of Administration

Tinctures can be administered in several ways, each affecting the absorption rate and efficacy of the remedy.

- **Sublingual Application**: Placing a tincture under the tongue and holding it there for several seconds before swallowing allows for quick absorption through the mucous membranes into the bloodstream. This method circumvents the digestive system, providing rapid effects.

- **In Water or Juice**: Mixing tinctures with a small amount of water or juice can make ingestion easier, especially for those who find the alcohol content or the taste of the tincture challenging.

- **With Meals**: Taking tinctures with meals can help mitigate the potential for gastrointestinal upset, particularly with herbs known to irritate the digestive tract.

Timing for Optimal Effectiveness

The timing of tincture administration can significantly impact its effectiveness, depending on the intent of the remedy and the body's circadian rhythms.

- **Herbs for Sleep and Relaxation**: Administer calming tinctures, such as those containing lavender or chamomile, in the evening to promote restful sleep.

- **Digestive Remedies**: Tinctures aimed at aiding digestion, like ginger or peppermint, are most effective when taken before or with meals.

- **Adaptogens**: Herbs that support adrenal function and stress response, such as ashwagandha or rhodiola, are typically taken in the morning or early afternoon to support energy levels throughout the day.

Chapter 2

Safety and Efficacy

Factors Influencing Potency

The safety and efficacy of herbal remedies also hinge critically on their potency, which can vary widely.

The first major factor affecting the potency of herbal medicines is the source of the herb. The environment in which a plant grows has profound effects on its development and the concentration of its bioactive compounds. Soil quality, altitude, and climate all play pivotal roles. For instance, ginseng grown in its native Korean mountain soil tends to have higher levels of ginsenosides compared to those cultivated in less ideal conditions elsewhere. This variation underscores the importance of ethically sourcing herbs from environments conducive to their growth.

Another critical aspect is the timing of harvesting. The potency of an herb can vary significantly depending on the season and even the time of day it is collected. Many plants accumulate their active ingredients during specific phases of their growth cycle. For example, arnica flowers are most potent if harvested early in their blooming phase when their anti-inflammatory compounds are at their peak. Similarly, the medicinal quality of roots like dandelion is best just before the plant blooms, when energy stores are concentrated underground.

Processing methods also greatly impact the potency of herbal remedies. The way an herb is dried, stored, and extracted can either preserve or degrade its medicinal properties. Improper drying can lead to the degradation of essential oils and active constituents, while excessive heat during extraction can destroy sensitive compounds. Modern techniques like cold pressing and freeze-drying are often preferred to traditional methods because they better preserve the integrity of herbal constituents.

The form in which an herb is used—whether whole, cut, or ground—also affects its potency. Whole herbs generally maintain their effectiveness longer than those that are processed, as breaking down plant material can increase the rate of oxidative degradation. However, finely ground herbs are often more effective for immediate use in applications like poultices or teas, where quick release of active ingredients is desirable.

Storage conditions further influence herbal potency. Exposure to light, air, and moisture can lead to the rapid deterioration of herbal materials. Effective storage solutions involve airtight containers kept in cool, dark places to extend the shelf life and maintain the effectiveness of herbal remedies.

Common Interactions with Conventional Medications and Precautions

Herbal remedies are not inherently safe simply because they are natural. Many contain potent bioactive compounds that can interact with conventional medications, sometimes leading to adverse effects. For instance, St. John's Wort, commonly used for depression, can reduce the effectiveness of prescription drugs such as birth control pills, anticoagulants, and certain antiretroviral drugs through its induction of the cytochrome P450 enzyme system. This interaction can lead to therapeutic failure or unexpected side effects, highlighting the critical need for careful management of herbal and pharmaceutical regimens.

Another well-documented interaction involves the use of ginkgo biloba, popular for its memory-enhancing properties. When used with anticoagulants like warfarin or even over-the-counter non-steroidal anti-inflammatory drugs (NSAIDs), ginkgo can alter platelet function, increasing the risk of bleeding. Such interactions necessitate heightened vigilance and possibly adjustments in dosages of the conventional drugs involved.

The complexity of these interactions is further compounded by factors such as the patient's age, overall health condition, and the presence of chronic diseases. For example, elderly patients, who often take multiple medications, are at greater risk for adverse interactions. This population particularly requires careful monitoring and consultation with healthcare professionals when adding herbal remedies to their treatment plans.

The need for rigorous scrutiny extends to the way herbal products are marketed and sold. Unlike conventional medications, herbal remedies in many countries are not required to be tested for safety and efficacy before they reach the consumer. This lack of regulation can lead to inconsistencies in the quality and concentration of herbal products, making it difficult to predict their interaction with pharmaceutical drugs.

Precautionary measures include:

1. **Professional Consultation**: Always consult healthcare providers before starting any new herbal remedy, especially when taking other medications.

2. **Disclosure**: Inform all healthcare providers about every treatment being used, including all herbal and over-the-counter medications.

3. **Education**: Patients and healthcare providers should educate themselves about the potential interactions of herbs to better manage the risks involved.

4. **Monitoring**: Once an herbal remedy is integrated into a treatment plan, close monitoring for adverse effects and interactions is crucial. This can involve regular follow-ups and possibly blood tests to ensure that the treatment does not interfere with the efficacy of prescription medications.

Adequate knowledge, careful management, and open communication between patients and healthcare providers are essential to harness the benefits of combining herbal and conventional treatments. This careful approach ensures that patients receive the full benefits of both systems safely and effectively.

The Importance of Sourcing High-Quality Herbs

In the field of herbal medicine, the safety and efficacy of herbal treatments are profoundly influenced by the quality of the raw materials used. Poorly sourced herbs can lead to ineffective treatments at best, and at worst, they can pose serious health risks to consumers. This emphasis on quality not only pertains to the inherent properties of the herbs themselves but also to the sustainability and ethical considerations of their sourcing practices.

The primary concern in the sourcing of herbs revolves around the conditions under which they are grown. Herbs cultivated in suboptimal conditions or polluted environments can accumulate heavy metals, pesticides, and other contaminants. These substances can severely compromise the safety of the herb, and by extension, the health of the end-user. For instance, herbs grown alongside busy roads or in industrial areas may absorb significant levels of lead and other harmful pollutants, which are then transferred to consumers upon ingestion.

Furthermore, the efficacy of herbal medicine is directly tied to the potency and integrity of the herbs. Factors such as soil quality, climate, and harvesting methods play crucial roles in determining the levels of active constituents within each plant. For example, echinacea purpurea exhibits higher concentrations of active phytochemicals when grown in its native North American prairies under well-defined seasonal variations. Thus, sourcing herbs from their indigenous regions where they grow under optimal natural conditions can often guarantee higher efficacy in herbal preparations.

Additionally, the method and timing of harvesting are critical to preserving the beneficial properties of herbs. Herbs harvested at the wrong time in their growth cycle may have lower active constituent levels, reducing their therapeutic potential. Proper drying and storage are equally important; herbs must be dried quickly to prevent the growth of mold and degradation of essential oils, then stored in conditions that protect them from moisture and sunlight, which can further degrade their quality.

Sustainability is another significant aspect of sourcing quality herbs. Overharvesting and irresponsible cultivation practices can deplete natural resources and lead to the long-term unavailability of valuable medicinal plants. Sustainable sourcing practices, including the use of organically grown herbs and the support of fair trade suppliers, not only ensure the ongoing availability of these resources but also support ecological health and local communities involved in the cultivation of these herbs.

Given these factors, consumers and practitioners must diligently verify the source of their herbs. This involves purchasing from reputable suppliers who provide transparent information about the origin, growing conditions, and handling of their products. Certifications such as organic, wildcrafted, and fair trade can also serve as indicators of quality and ethical sourcing.

Principles of Sustainable Harvesting

Sustainable harvesting involves several key principles that balance the need for plant-based resources with the preservation of natural habitats. First and foremost is the understanding of the growth cycle of the plant species being harvested. Each species has a specific season or time when harvesting is least likely to harm the plant's long-term survival. For perennial plants, for instance, this might mean waiting for the end of the blooming period when the plant is at its most robust. Harvesting outside of these optimal periods can stress the plants, reduce their vitality, and diminish their ability to propagate.

Another crucial aspect is the quantity of the harvest. Ethical practices dictate that only a certain percentage of plants should be taken from any given area. This method, often referred to as the "rule of thirds," suggests that one third of the available plants may be harvested, one third should be left to regenerate, and one third left to support the local wildlife and maintain ecological balance. Such practices ensure that plant populations remain viable and ecosystems stay intact.

The technique of harvesting is equally important. Sustainable methods involve careful selection and extraction that minimize damage to the plant and its surroundings. This includes using tools that are appropriate for the specific type of plant and making clean cuts that help plants heal and regrow. For roots, it means replacing the soil and disturbed ground, thereby protecting the ecosystem's integrity.

Equally important is the consideration of local and indigenous rights. Many medicinal plants are found in regions inhabited by indigenous peoples, who may have used these resources for centuries. Sustainable harvesting practices must respect their knowledge, rights, and relationship with the land. This includes obtaining prior informed consent for access to these resources, respecting traditional practices and knowledge, and ensuring that benefits are shared with these communities.

Traceability and transparency in sourcing are also key components of sustainable harvesting. Suppliers of medicinal plants should be able to provide detailed information about where and how the plants were obtained, including the harvesting methods used. This transparency allows consumers to make informed choices, supporting companies that engage in ethical practices.

HERB	OPTIMAL GROWING CONDITIONS	IDEAL SOIL QUALITY	IDEAL CLIMATE	BEST METHODS AND TIMES TO HARVEST
Echinacea	Full sun to partial shade	Well-drained, loamy soil	Temperate regions, USDA zones 3-8	Harvest roots in the fall after 2-3 years of growth. Flowers and leaves can be harvested in the summer when the plant is in full bloom. Use a sharp knife or shears to cut the plant parts.
Valerian	Full sun to partial shade	Moist, well-drained soil	Temperate regions, USDA zones 4-9	Harvest roots in the fall of the second year when the plant is dormant. Dig up the roots carefully to avoid damage. Clean and dry the roots thoroughly before use.

HERB	OPTIMAL GROWING CONDITIONS	IDEAL SOIL QUALITY	IDEAL CLIMATE	BEST METHODS AND TIMES TO HARVEST
Passionflower	Full sun to partial shade	Well-drained, sandy or loamy soil	Warm climates, USDA zones 6-10	Harvest leaves and flowers during the blooming period in late spring to early summer. Cut the plant parts with sharp scissors or pruning shears. Ensure the plant has plenty of time to regrow for the next season.
Arnica	Full sun	Well-drained, slightly acidic soil	Cool, mountainous regions, USDA zones 4-9	Harvest flowers in the summer when they are fully open. Use scissors or pruning shears to cut the flowers, leaving some behind to allow for seed dispersal.
Comfrey	Full sun to partial shade	Moist, fertile, well-drained soil	Temperate regions, USDA zones 3-9	Harvest leaves throughout the growing season. Cut the leaves close to the base, allowing the plant to regrow. Roots can be harvested in the fall after the first frost.
Slippery Elm	Full sun to partial shade	Moist, well-drained, rich soil	Temperate regions, USDA zones 3-9	Harvest inner bark in the spring when the sap is rising. Use a sharp knife to carefully remove the bark from young branches, avoiding damage to the tree.
Aloe	Full sun to partial shade	Well-drained, sandy or loamy soil	Warm, arid to semi-arid regions, USDA zones 8-11	Harvest leaves as needed throughout the year. Cut mature, lower leaves close to the base with a sharp knife. Avoid over-harvesting to ensure continued growth.
Goldenseal	Partial to full shade	Moist, rich, well-drained soil	Woodland environments, USDA zones 4-8	Harvest roots in the fall of the third or fourth year. Carefully dig up the roots to avoid damage, then wash and dry them thoroughly. Leave some plants to flower and seed to ensure sustainability.
Stinging Nettle	Full sun to partial shade	Moist, well-drained, fertile soil	Temperate regions, USDA zones 3-10	Harvest young leaves in spring for the best flavor and potency. Use gloves to avoid stings, and cut the top 4-6 inches of the plant. Leaves can be harvested continuously throughout the growing season as the plant regrows.

HERB	OPTIMAL GROWING CONDITIONS	IDEAL SOIL QUALITY	IDEAL CLIMATE	BEST METHODS AND TIMES TO HARVEST
Chamomile	Full sun	Well-drained, sandy loam soil	Temperate regions, USDA zones 4-9	Harvest flowers in the morning after the dew has dried, usually from late spring to early summer. Use your fingers or a small rake to gently pull the flowers from the stems.
Lavender	Full sun	Well-drained, sandy or loamy soil	Mediterranean climates, USDA zones 5-9	Harvest flower spikes when the buds are just starting to open, usually in mid to late summer. Use pruning shears to cut the stems, and dry the flowers in a cool, dark place.
Peppermint	Full sun to partial shade	Moist, well-drained soil	Temperate regions, USDA zones 3-7	Harvest leaves just before flowering, usually in late spring to early summer. Use scissors or pruning shears to cut the stems. Peppermint can be harvested multiple times in a season as it regrows quickly.
Elderberry	Full sun to partial shade	Moist, well-drained, fertile soil	Temperate regions, USDA zones 3-8	Harvest berries when they are fully ripe, usually in late summer to early fall. Use pruning shears to cut the berry clusters. Flowers can be harvested in late spring to early summer.
Ginkgo	Full sun	Well-drained, sandy or loamy soil	Temperate to warm climates, USDA zones 4-9	Harvest leaves in the fall when they are at peak medicinal potency. Use pruning shears to cut the leaves from the branches. Ensure sustainable harvesting by not over-harvesting from a single tree.
Hawthorn	Full sun to partial shade	Well-drained, loamy soil	Temperate regions, USDA zones 4-7	Harvest berries in the fall when they are fully ripe. Use pruning shears to cut the berry clusters. Leaves and flowers can be harvested in the spring when they first bloom.
Lemon Balm	Full sun to partial shade	Well-drained, sandy or loamy soil	Temperate regions, USDA zones 4-9	Harvest leaves just before flowering, usually in late spring to early summer. Use scissors or pruning shears to cut the stems. Lemon balm can be harvested multiple times in a season as it regrows quickly.

HERB	OPTIMAL GROWING CONDITIONS	IDEAL SOIL QUALITY	IDEAL CLIMATE	BEST METHODS AND TIMES TO HARVEST
Milk Thistle	Full sun	Well-drained, sandy or clay soil	Warm climates, USDA zones 5-9	Harvest seeds in late summer to early fall when the flower heads have dried and turned brown. Use pruning shears to cut the flower heads, then allow them to dry further before extracting the seeds.
Saw Palmetto	Full sun to partial shade	Well-drained, sandy soil	Warm, humid climates, USDA zones 8-11	Harvest berries in the fall when they are fully ripe. Use gloves to protect hands from the sharp leaf edges and pruning shears to cut the berry clusters.
St. John's Wort	Full sun	Well-drained, sandy or loamy soil	Temperate regions, USDA zones 5-10	Harvest flowers and upper stems when the plant is in full bloom, usually in mid to late summer. Use scissors or pruning shears to cut the plant parts.
Turmeric	Full sun	Well-drained, fertile, sandy loam soil	Tropical to subtropical climates, USDA zones 8-11	Harvest rhizomes 8-10 months after planting, usually in late fall to early winter. Dig up the rhizomes carefully to avoid damage, then wash and dry them thoroughly.
Thyme	Full sun	Well-drained, sandy or loamy soil	Mediterranean climates, USDA zones 5-9	Harvest leaves just before the plant flowers, usually in late spring to early summer. Use scissors or pruning shears to cut the stems. Thyme can be harvested multiple times in a season as it regrows quickly.
Licorice Root	Full sun to partial shade	Well-drained, sandy or loamy soil	Warm climates, USDA zones 6-9	Harvest roots in the fall of the third or fourth year. Dig up the roots carefully to avoid damage, then wash and dry them thoroughly. Leave some plants to flower and seed to ensure sustainability.
Calendula	Full sun	Well-drained, fertile soil	Temperate regions, USDA zones 2-11	Harvest flowers in the morning after the dew has dried, usually from late spring to early summer. Use your fingers or a small rake to gently pull the flowers from the stems. Calendula can be harvested multiple times in a season as it regrows quickly.

Storing and Preserving Herbs

The proper storage and preservation of herbs are crucial to maintaining their medicinal properties, flavor, and overall quality. Whether used for culinary purposes, medicinal applications, or as part of holistic wellness practices, the way herbs are handled post-harvest can significantly impact their efficacy and shelf life.

So, delve into the best practices for storing and preserving herbs to ensure their optimal use:

Drying Herbs

Drying is one of the most common methods of preserving herbs. It reduces the moisture content, preventing mold and bacterial growth, and thus extends the shelf life of the herbs.

- **Air Drying**: This traditional method involves hanging small bunches of herbs upside down in a well-ventilated, dry, and dark space. Herbs like thyme, rosemary, and oregano are particularly well-suited to this method. The key is to ensure they are not exposed to direct sunlight, which can degrade their color and essential oils.

- **Dehydrators**: For a more controlled drying process, a food dehydrator can be used. This method is faster and allows for precise temperature settings, typically around 95-115°F (35-46°C), which helps retain the herbs' active compounds.

- **Oven Drying**: In the absence of a dehydrator, an oven can be used on its lowest setting. Spread the herbs on a baking sheet and keep the oven door slightly open to let moisture evaporate. Check frequently to avoid over-drying and potential burning.

Storing Dried Herbs

Once herbs are dried, proper storage is essential to maintain their quality.

- **Containers**: Store herbs in sealed containers, like glass jars with tight-fitting lids to protect them from air and moisture. Mason jars are an excellent choice, and dark-colored jars can help block light.

- **Location**: Store containers in a cool, dark place away from direct sunlight and heat sources. A pantry or a cupboard is ideal.

- **Labeling**: Always label containers with the herb's name and the date of storage. This practice helps in tracking the age of the herbs and ensuring they are used while still potent, typically within one year.

Freezing Herbs

Freezing is another effective method for preserving the freshness and flavor of herbs, particularly those with high moisture content, such as basil, cilantro, and parsley.

- **Blanching**: Briefly blanching herbs in boiling water and then plunging them into ice water can help retain their color and flavor. After blanching, pat them dry with a paper towel.

- **Freezing Whole**: Arrange the herbs in a single layer on a baking sheet and freeze them. Once frozen, transfer the herbs to airtight freezer bags or containers.

- **Ice Cube Trays**: Chop herbs finely and pack them into ice cube trays. Fill the trays with water or olive oil and freeze. These herb cubes can be added to stews, soups, and sauces.

Storing Fresh Herbs

For herbs that are used frequently, such as parsley, cilantro, and mint, storing them fresh can be practical.

- **Refrigeration**: Trim the stems and place the herbs in a jar with a small amount of water, much like a bouquet of flowers. Cover the herbs loosely with a plastic bag and store in the refrigerator. Change the water every couple of days to keep the herbs fresh.

- **Herb Keeper**: Specialized herb keepers are available that provide an optimal environment for storing fresh herbs, maintaining their freshness for longer periods.

Considerations for Preserving Medicinal Properties

When storing herbs for medicinal purposes, it is crucial to preserve their active compounds.

- **Herbal Oils and Tinctures**: Infusing herbs in oil or alcohol can extract and preserve their medicinal properties. Store these infusions in dark glass bottles away from light and heat.

- **Herbal Powders**: Grinding dried herbs into powder can be convenient for certain applications. Store powders in airtight containers, and use them within six months for best results.

Tools and Supplies Needed

1. Containers for Maceration

The choice of container is critical in the tincture-making process. Glass is the preferred material due to its non-reactive nature, which ensures that it does not interact chemically with the herbs or alcohol. Specifically, wide-mouthed glass jars are ideal as they facilitate easy insertion and removal of plant materials and simplify the stirring process during maceration.

- **Amber Glass Bottles**: These protect the tinctures from light, thus preserving their potency over time.
- **Mason Jars**: Commonly used for the initial maceration process, their airtight seals prevent evaporation and contamination.

2. Straining Tools

Once the maceration phase is complete, the next step is the separation of the solids from the liquid, for which specific tools are necessary:

- **Cheesecloth or Fine Mesh Strainer**: These are used to filter out the plant residues from the alcohol, ensuring a clear tincture.
- **Press**: For more efficiency in extracting every bit of liquid, a press, either manual or hydraulic, can be employed to squeeze out all viable extracts from the herb mass.

3. **Measuring Implements**

Precision in tincture making is not just advisable but necessary. The potency of the tincture heavily relies on the herb-to-solvent ratios used during preparation:

- **Measuring Cups and Spoons**: Glass or stainless steel measuring tools are recommended for accurate measurement of liquids.
- **Scales**: A high-quality digital scale is crucial for measuring herbs, especially when working with specific dosages and potent herbs.

4. **Labels and Marking Tools**

Organization and documentation are key in herbal preparations. Labeling each tincture with details about the contents, concentration, date of preparation, and expiration date ensures proper tracking and usage:

- **Waterproof Labels**: These should include the herb name, date, and alcohol percentage.
- **Permanent Markers**: Useful for writing directly on glass or labels, especially in environments where labels may come off.

Deciding Between Alcohol, Glycerin, and Vinegar as Solvents

When crafting tinctures, the choice of solvent is pivotal, as it affects the extraction efficiency of active compounds from herbs and their preservation. While alcohol is the most common solvent due to its excellent extraction capabilities and preservative properties, other solvents like glycerin and vinegar can also be used depending on the intended use and consumer preferences.

Alcohol as a Solvent

Alcohol is the most commonly used solvent in tincture making due to its efficiency in extracting a wide range of water-soluble and fat-soluble compounds. Here are key points to consider:

- **Efficiency**: Alcohol is highly effective at breaking down plant cells, releasing both polar (water-soluble) and non-polar (fat-soluble) substances.

- **Preservation**: It acts as a preservative, allowing tinctures to be stored for years without spoiling.

- **Versatility**: Alcohol can extract a wide array of phytochemicals, making it suitable for most herbs.

- **Considerations**: The typical concentration used ranges from 40% to 95% alcohol by volume, depending on the herb and desired strength. High-proof alcohol can be a safety hazard due to its flammability and should be handled with care.

Alcohol Safety

The use of high-proof alcohol, necessary for extracting the active compounds from herbs, requires careful handling due to its flammability and potency:

- **Ventilation:** Work in a well-ventilated area to avoid inhalation of fumes, especially when using high-proof spirits.

- **Flammability:** Keep alcohol away from open flames, stovetops, or any ignition sources due to its high flammability.

- **Storage:** Store alcohol in a cool, dark place away from direct sunlight and out of reach of children and pets.

Glycerin as a Solvent

Glycerin, a sweet-tasting syrupy liquid, is a non-alcohol-based solvent that is especially suitable for children, pets, and those avoiding alcohol for health or personal reasons.

- **Gentleness**: Glycerin is gentle and suitable for extracting milder tinctures, often used in pediatric formulations.

- **Extraction Capability**: While not as potent at extracting certain chemicals as alcohol, glycerin is excellent for tinctures meant for immediate use.

- **Shelf Life**: Tinctures made with glycerin have a shorter shelf life compared to those crafted with alcohol, typically lasting 1-2 years.

Vinegar as a Solvent

Vinegar is an excellent solvent for those looking for a completely food-based extraction, providing an acidic medium that extracts different compounds than alcohol or glycerin.

- **Acidity**: The acidic nature of vinegar helps to preserve tinctures while extracting nutrients and minerals from herbs effectively.

- **Flavor**: Vinegar imparts a distinct flavor, which may not be palatable to everyone and can alter the flavor profile of the herb.

- **Preservation**: While not as effective as alcohol, vinegar does offer antimicrobial properties that help extend the shelf life of tinctures.

Deciding on the Right Solvent

Choosing the right solvent depends on several factors:

- **Purpose of the Tincture**: Consider what the tincture is being used for. Alcohol is more suitable for extracting and preserving a broad range of compounds for long-term storage. Glycerin is ideal for non-alcoholic needs and pediatric uses, whereas vinegar might be preferred for its nutritional extractions.

- **Target Audience**: The intended user of the tincture can dictate the solvent choice. For instance, alcohol is unsuitable for children, whereas glycerin and vinegar provide safer alternatives.

- **Herb Properties**: Some herbs respond better to certain solvents based on the solubility of their active components.

Troubleshooting Common Issues in Tincture Making

1. Insufficient Extraction

Sometimes, the active constituents of the herbs may not extract as fully as desired, leading to a tincture that is less potent than intended.

- **Evaluate the Solvent Strength**: Ensure that the alcohol percentage is appropriate for the type of herb used. High resin or oil-containing herbs may require a higher percentage of alcohol to extract effectively.

- **Increase Maceration Time**: Allow the herbs more time to steep in the solvent. Extending the maceration period can enhance the extraction of active ingredients.

- **Agitate the Mixture**: Regular shaking of the tincture bottle can help distribute the solvent evenly and improve the extraction process.

2. Cloudiness or Sediment Formation

Cloudiness or sediment in tinctures can be concerning and may indicate contamination or incomplete filtration.

- **Filter Thoroughly**: Use a fine mesh or cheesecloth to filter the tincture multiple times until the liquid is clear. Ensure all plant material is completely removed.
- **Check for Contamination**: Ensure that all equipment is sterilized and that the herbs are clean and free from mold or decay before beginning the tincture-making process.
- **Store Properly**: Keep tinctures in dark, airtight containers in a cool, dry place to prevent degradation and microbial growth.

3. Altered or Unexpected Taste

The flavor of a tincture is a good indicator of its quality and potency. An off or unexpected taste can signal issues during the preparation or storage stages.

- **Assess Herb Quality**: Use high-quality, fresh or properly dried herbs. The taste of the tincture largely influenced by the quality of the initial ingredients.

- **Monitor Alcohol Quality**: Use only pharmaceutical or food-grade alcohol intended for tincture making. Avoid using denatured or low-quality alcohol.

4. **Tincture Too Weak or Too Strong**

   Adjusting the strength of a tincture to meet therapeutic needs is crucial for its effectiveness.

   - **Adjust Herb-to-Solvent Ratio**: If the tincture is too strong, it can be diluted with more solvent. If too weak, add more herb and allow further maceration.

   - **Reevaluate Extraction Method**: Some active compounds might extract better under different conditions, such as using a different solvent or altering the extraction temperature.

5. **Preservation Issues**

   Improperly preserved tinctures may lose potency over time or develop mold.

   - **Use Adequate Alcohol Content**: Ensure the alcohol content is sufficient to preserve the tincture. Typically, a minimum of 40% alcohol is necessary for effective preservation.

   - **Seal Containers Tightly**: Exposure to air can degrade the tincture and encourage the growth of mold and bacteria. Always use airtight containers for storage.

   - **Add Natural Preservatives**: In some cases, natural preservatives like vitamin E can be added to enhance shelf life.

Chapter 3

Herbs and Tincture Recipes

Arnica (Arnica montana)

- **Plant Description**: Arnica, a perennial plant, features vibrant yellow flowers that resemble daisies and sports a somewhat fuzzy stem.
- **Habitat**: Native to Europe and Siberia, Arnica grows in alpine meadows and well-drained, sandy soils.
- **Medicinal Properties**: Arnica has anti-inflammatory, analgesic, and antiseptic properties. It is used to treat bruises, sprains, muscle pain, and inflammation.
- **Traditional Uses**: Traditionally used to treat physical trauma and reduce inflammation. It has also been used to stimulate hair growth.
- **Preparation Methods**: Arnica is typically used topically in creams, gels, and ointments. It can also be used as a tincture for external application.
- **Precautions**: Arnica should not be ingested due to its toxicity. It can cause severe irritation and allergic reactions if applied to broken skin. Internal use should only be done under medical supervision.
- **How to Grow**: Arnica can be grown in pots or garden beds that receive full sun to partial shade. It needs light, loamy soil that is slightly moist. It is frost tolerant and requires regular watering without waterlogging.

HOMEMADE ARNICA TINCTURE RECIPE

PREPARATION TIME: 10 MINUTES

MACERATION TIME: 4 TO 6 WEEKS

YIELD: APPROXIMATELY 2 CUPS

INGREDIENTS

- Dried Arnica flowers: 1 cup (about 15 grams)
- High-proof alcohol (like vodka or grain alcohol, at least 40% alcohol by volume): 2 cups (480 milliliters)

TOOLS

- *Clean glass jar with a tight-fitting lid*
- *Cheesecloth or fine mesh strainer*
- *Dark glass bottle for storage*

INSTRUCTIONS

1. Place the dried arnica flowers in your clean glass jar.
2. Pour the high-proof alcohol over the flowers until fully submerged. Ensure that there are about 2-3 inches of alcohol above the level of the flowers to account for absorption.
3. Seal the jar tightly and shake it gently to mix the flowers with the alcohol.
4. Store the jar in a cool, dark place away from direct sunlight.
5. Shake the jar gently every few days to aid in the extraction process.
6. After 4 to 6 weeks, filter the mixture through a cheesecloth or fine mesh strainer into a clean bowl. Be sure to squeeze out as much of the alcohol as possible from the flowers to maximize your yield.
7. Store the tincture into a dark glass bottle. Label the bottle clearly with the date of finalization, and any other pertinent information.
8. Store the bottle in a cool, dark place. The tincture should be viable for up to 2 years if stored properly.

PREPARATION TIP:
- When handling the tincture and flowers, wear gloves to avoid skin irritation.

USAGE:
- Apply the tincture to the skin with a clean cloth or cotton ball for bruises, sprains, or muscle aches. Do not use on broken skin.

PRECAUTIONS:
- Arnica is highly potent and can cause irritation if not used correctly. Always conduct a patch test on a small area of skin first.
- If irritation or allergic reaction develops, stop using the product immediately and seek advice from a healthcare professional.

Ashwagandha (Withania somnifera)

- **Plant Description**: Ashwagandha, also known as Indian ginseng, is a small shrub with central branches that extend from a main root. It bears yellow flowers and is native to India and North Africa.
- **Leaves**: The leaves are dull green, elliptic, usually up to 10-12 cm long, and may have a rough texture. The plant is more recognized for its roots, which are used medicinally.
- **Habitat**: Although originally from India, ashwagandha can be grown in U.S. Zones 6-12. It adapts well to both high temperatures and cooler climates if protected from frost.
- **Medicinal Properties:** Adaptogen, stress relief, enhancing stamina, improving cognitive function.
- **Traditional Uses:** Used to balance energy, improve vitality, and support reproductive health.
- **Preparation Methods:** Powders, tinctures, capsules, and teas.
- **Precautions:** Possible interactions with thyroid medications and sedatives.
- **How to Grow:** Plant in full sun to partial shade in dry areas with sandy or well-draining soil. Water regularly but let the soil dry out between waterings to prevent root rot. Ashwagandha is drought-resistant once established.

ASHWAGANDHA ROOT TINCTURE RECIPE

PREPARATION TIME: 10 MINUTES

MACERATION TIME: 4 TO 6 WEEKS

YIELD: APPROXIMATELY 500 ML OF TINCTURE

INGREDIENTS

- Ashwagandha root, dried and chopped: 3.5 ounces/100 grams
- Vodka or grain alcohol (at least 40% alcohol by volume): 500 ml

TOOLS

- Glass jar with a tight-fitting lid
- Cheesecloth or fine mesh strainer
- Amber glass dropper bottles for storage

INSTRUCTIONS

1. Measure 100 grams of dried, chopped Ashwagandha root. Place the Ashwagandha roots into the jar.
2. Pour 500 ml of vodka or grain alcohol over the roots, ensuring the roots are completely submerged. If they float to the top, you might need to stir them down or add a bit more alcohol.
3. Close the jar tightly and label it with the date and contents. Store the jar in a cool, dark place.
4. Shake the jar daily for the first week to help the extraction process, then weekly thereafter.
5. After 4 to 6 weeks, filter the mixture using cheesecloth or a fine mesh strainer into a clean bowl. Squeeze or press the marc (the soaked roots) to extract as much liquid as possible.
6. Funnel the filtered liquid into amber glass bottles for easy use and storage. If possible, use bottles with droppers for easy dosage.
7. Label the bottles with the name, plant part used, alcohol used, date of completion, and any other pertinent information.

Astragalus (Astragalus membranaceus)

- **Plant Description**: Astragalus is a perennial herb with hairy stems, leaves with multiple leaflets, and yellow flowers.
- **Habitat**: Native to China, Mongolia, and Korea, Astragalus grows in grassy regions and open woodlands.
- **Medicinal Properties**: Astragalus is known for its immune-boosting, anti-inflammatory, and antioxidant properties. It supports cardiovascular health and helps manage stress.
- **Traditional Uses**: Traditionally used to strengthen the immune system, treat colds and upper respiratory infections, and support kidney function.
- **Preparation Methods**: Astragalus can be prepared as a tea by simmering the dried root in water, or taken as a tincture or supplement.
- **Precautions**: Generally safe for most people, but it should be avoided by individuals with autoimmune diseases and during pregnancy or breastfeeding without medical advice.
- **How to Grow**: Astragalus prefers full sun and well-draining, sandy soil. Once established, it is tolerant to drought conditions and needs only minimal watering. Seeds can be direct sown in fall or spring and benefit from occasional fertilization.

HOMEMADE ASTRAGALUS TINCTURE RECIPE

PREPARATION TIME: 10 MINUTES

MACERATION TIME: 6 TO 8 WEEKS

YIELD: APPROX 500 ML

INGREDIENTS

- Dried Astragalus root: 1 cup (about 30 grams)
- High-proof alcohol (60-70% alcohol by volume is ideal, such as grain alcohol): 500 milliliters (about 2 cups)

TOOLS

- Clean glass jar with a tight-fitting lid
- Cheesecloth or fine mesh strainer
- Amber glass bottle for storage

INSTRUCTIONS

1. Chop or break the dried astragalus root into small pieces to increase the surface area, which will enhance the extraction process.
2. Place the chopped astragalus into the clean glass jar.
3. Pour the high-proof alcohol over the roots, ensuring that the roots are completely submerged. Leave about an inch of alcohol above the root level to cover any swelling or absorption.
4. Seal the jar tightly with its lid and label it with the date and contents.
5. Store the jar in a cool, dark place, like a cupboard or a pantry, away from direct sunlight and heat.
6. Shake the jar every few days to mix the contents and facilitate the extraction.
7. After 6 to 8 weeks, filter the tincture using a cheesecloth or a fine mesh strainer into a clean bowl. Press or squeeze the marc (the soaked roots) to extract as much liquid as possible.
8. Transfer the strained liquid into an amber glass bottle to prevent light degradation.

9. Label the bottle clearly with the date of finalization, and any additional notes for future reference.
10. Store the bottle in a cool, dark place. Properly stored, the tincture should remain potent for up to 5 years.

PREPARATION TIP:

- Use gloves during this process to avoid contact with the potent extract.

USAGE:

- Dosage: Generally, 1-2 ml of the tincture can be taken up to three times daily, diluted in water or juice. Start with a low dose to assess tolerance.
- It's suitable for daily use to support immune function especially during the change of seasons or times of high stress.

PRECAUTIONS:

- Astragalus is typically safe, but as with any herb, monitoring for any adverse reactions is recommended when beginning treatment.

Baobab (Adansonia digitata)

- **Plant Description**: The Baobab tree, often called the "Tree of Life," is unmistakable with its thick trunk and sprawling branches. Baobab fruit is rich in vitamin C, calcium, and antioxidants. Its pulp, leaves, and seeds are all used for nutritional and medicinal purposes.
- **Habitat**: Native to Africa, baobab trees thrive in the arid, hot savannah regions of sub-Saharan Africa. They are extremely drought-resistant, capable of living for thousands of years.
- **Availability in the U.S.**: Baobab fruit powder is widely available in the U.S. in health food stores and online. It is often marketed as a superfood ingredient for smoothies and other health foods.
- **Medicinal Properties**: Rich in vitamin C, antioxidant, anti-inflammatory.
- **Traditional Uses**: Used to boost immune system, treat skin conditions, and improve digestive health.
- **Precautions:** Baobab has a high vitamin C content, which can potentially interact with certain medications, including chemotherapy drugs and blood thinners.
- **How to Grow:** Baobabs are best suited to hot, dry climates and do not tolerate cold weather. They are suitable for growing in USDA zones 10 and above. They require full sun and prefer well-drained sandy soil. Inadequate drainage may cause root rot.

HOMEMADE BAOBAB TINCTURE RECIPE

PREPARATION TIME: 10 MINUTES

MACERATION TIME: 4 WEEKS

YIELD: APPROX 500 ML

INGREDIENTS

- *Baobab fruit powder: 1/4 cup (about 60 grams)*
- *High-proof vodka or grain alcohol (60-70% alcohol by volume): 500 milliliters (about 2 cups)*

TOOLS

- *Clean glass jar with a tight-fitting lid*
- *Cheesecloth or fine mesh strainer*
- *Amber glass bottle for storage*

INSTRUCTIONS

1. Place the baobab powder into the clean glass jar.
2. Pour the alcohol over the powder, ensuring it is completely submerged with an extra inch of liquid on top to account for any absorption.
3. Securely seal the jar and label it with the date and contents.
4. Store the jar in a cool, dark cupboard away from direct sunlight.
5. Shake the jar every few days to agitate the mixture and promote extraction.
6. After 4 weeks, filter the mixture using a cheesecloth or fine mesh strainer into another clean bowl. Press the solids to extract as much liquid as possible.
7. Funnel the strained tincture into an amber glass bottle to prevent light from affecting the potency.
8. Label the bottle clearly with the date, and any other pertinent information.
9. Properly stored in a cool, dark place, the tincture should last up to 5 years.

SHOPPING TIP:

- Baobab powder can be purchased from health food stores or reputable online retailers that focus in organic and fair-trade products.

USAGE:

- Dosage: Typically, 1-2 ml of the tincture may be taken up to three times daily. Dilute in water or juice.
- Baobab tincture is particularly useful for its antioxidant benefits and can support daily immune function and promote skin health due to its high vitamin C content.

PREPARATION TIP:

- Wearing gloves can prevent any potential irritation from prolonged contact with the alcohol.

PRECAUTIONS:

- While baobab is generally considered safe, start with a lower dose to ensure compatibility.

Black Cohosh (Actaea racemosa)

- **Plant Description**: Black Cohosh is a tall, perennial herb with large, compound leaves and long, white flowering spikes.
- **Habitat**: Native to eastern North America, Black Cohosh grows in rich, moist soils of woodlands and shaded areas.
- **Medicinal Properties**: Known for its phytoestrogenic properties, Black Cohosh is used to balance hormones. It has anti-inflammatory and antispasmodic effects, making it useful for treating menopausal symptoms and menstrual discomfort.
- **Traditional Uses**: Traditionally used by Native Americans for women's health issues, rheumatism, and as a sedative. It is now commonly used to alleviate symptoms of menopause, such as hot flashes and night sweats.
- **Preparation Methods**: Black Cohosh is often taken as a supplement in capsule or tablet form. Tinctures and teas can also be made from the dried root, although the taste is quite bitter.
- **Precautions**: Long-term use of Black Cohosh should be monitored due to potential liver toxicity. It is not recommended for pregnant women, as it can stimulate uterine contractions.
- **How to Grow**: Black cohosh thrives in a woodland garden setting with partial shade and rich, moist, well-drained soil. It is a slow grower and may take several years to flower, so patience is necessary.

BLACK COHOSH TINCTURE RECIPE

PREPARATION TIME: 10 MINUTES   **MACERATION TIME:** 6 WEEKS   **YIELD:** APPROX 500 ML

INGREDIENTS

- Black Cohosh Root (freshly dug or dried): 100 grams (about 3.5 oz)
- Vodka or Brandy (at least 40% alcohol by volume): 500 milliliters (about 17 oz)

TOOLS

- Kitchen scale
- Clean jar with a tight-fitting lid (at least 1-liter capacity)
- Cheesecloth or fine mesh strainer
- Amber dropper bottles for storage

INSTRUCTIONS

1. If using fresh Black Cohosh root, wash it thoroughly under cold water. Chop the root into small pieces to increase the surface area, which aids in the extraction process. If using dried root, measure the required amount and ensure it is finely chopped or crushed.
2. Place the prepared Black Cohosh root into your clean jar.
3. Pour the vodka or brandy over the roots, ensuring the roots are completely submerged. The herb-to-alcohol ratio should be 1:5, meaning one part herb to five parts alcohol by volume.
4. Seal the jar tightly and shake it gently to mix the contents.
5. Store the jar in a cool, dark place such as a cupboard or pantry.

6. Allow the mixture to macerate for six weeks, shaking the jar every few days to mix the contents and promote extraction.
7. After six weeks, open the jar and filter the liquid using a cheesecloth or fine mesh strainer into a clean bowl. Press or squeeze the soaked Black Cohosh roots to extract as much liquid as possible.
8. Funnel the tincture into amber bottles. If possible, use bottles with droppers for easy dosage. Label each bottle with the date, and any other pertinent information.

USAGE:

- The typical dosage for Black Cohosh tincture is 1-2 milliliters (about 20-40 drops), taken 2-3 times daily.

Boswellia (Boswellia serrata)

- **Plant Description:** Boswellia, commonly known as Frankincense, is a genus of trees known for their ability to produce a resin rich in aromatic compounds. The trees have a thick, papery bark, and they can reach heights of up to 25 feet.
- **Leaves:** The leaves of the Boswellia tree are compound with a variable number of leaflets, which are typically lance-shaped and can be somewhat leathery.
- **Habitat:** Boswellia species are native to arid, mountainous regions in India, the Middle East, and Africa. They thrive in dry environments often found on rocky slopes and hillsides.
- **Availability in the U.S.:** While not native to the U.S., Boswellia trees can be grown in similar arid climates found in parts of the U.S. such as the southwestern states. They require a hot, dry climate and may not tolerate cold temperatures. Boswellia plants and seeds are available through specialty nurseries and online retailers that focus on medicinal plants or exotic botanicals.
- **Medicinal Properties**: Reduces inflammation, supports joint health.
- **Traditional Uses**: Used for arthritis, joint health, and reducing inflammation.
- **Precautions**: May cause digestive issues.
- **How to Grow:** Boswellia trees require well-drained soil, as waterlogging can be detrimental. Sandy or loamy soils that drain well are optimal. The ideal soil pH ranges from slightly acidic to neutral. If you are not in a climate that naturally supports Boswellia, you can grow it in a pot indoors or in a greenhouse. Ensure the pot has ample drainage holes.

BOSWELLIA TINCTURE RECIPE

PREPARATION TIME: 15 MINUTES   **MACERATION TIME:** 4-6 WEEKS   **YIELD:** APPROX 500 ML

INGREDIENTS

- *Boswellia Resin: 100 grams (about 3.5 oz)*
- *High-proof Ethanol (60-90% alcohol by volume, depending on availability): 500 milliliters (17 oz)*

TOOLS

- *Kitchen scale*
- *Glass jar with a tight-fitting lid (1-liter capacity)*
- *Cheesecloth or fine mesh strainer*
- *Amber glass dropper bottles for storage*

INSTRUCTIONS

1. Break the Boswellia resin into small, pea-sized pieces using a mortar and pestle.
2. Place the broken resin pieces into your clean jar.
3. Pour the ethanol over the resin until it is completely submerged. Maintain an herb-to-alcohol ratio of 1:5 for effective extraction.
4. Seal the jar tightly and shake it to ensure the resin is fully covered by the alcohol.
5. Store the jar in a cool, dark place, such as a cupboard away from direct sunlight and heat, to preserve the integrity of the tincture.

6. Let the mixture macerate for 4-6 weeks, shaking the jar every few days to agitate the mixture and promote extraction.
7. After the maceration period, filter the mixture using a cheesecloth or fine mesh strainer into a clean bowl. Press the resin pieces to extract as much liquid as possible. Discard the resin residues.
8. Funnel the liquid into amber bottles for long-term storage. If possible, use bottles with droppers for easy dosage. Label each bottle with the date, and any other pertinent information.

USAGE:

- Typical dosage of Boswellia tincture is 1-2 milliliters (about 20-40 drops), taken 1-3 times daily.

Calendula (Calendula officinalis)

- **Plant Description**: Calendula is an annual plant distinguished by its bright orange or yellow flowers.
- **Leaves**: The leaves are oblong-lanceolate, about 5-18 cm long, and are slightly hairy and sticky. They are arranged alternately along the stem.
- **Habitat:** Widely adaptable and can be found throughout the U.S., thriving in moderate climates.
- **Medicinal Properties:** Calendula is anti-inflammatory and antiseptic, making it excellent for soothing and healing wounds, burns, eczema, and other inflammatory skin conditions.
- **Traditional Uses:** Often used in creams and ointments to promote skin healing and reduce inflammation.
- **Precautions:** Calendula is generally safe, but individuals allergic to plants in the Asteraceae family should avoid it. Always use a filtered or refined product to avoid pollen and other potential allergens present in raw extracts.
- **How to Grow**: Calendula prefers full sun and well-drained soil. It can be easily grown in pots or garden beds. Sow seeds in spring in cooler climates or fall in warmer areas for winter blooms. Water regularly but avoid waterlogging.

CALENDULA TINCTURE RECIPE

PREPARATION TIME: 10 MINUTES   **MACERATION TIME:** 3-4 WEEKS   **YIELD:** APPROX 250 ML

INGREDIENTS

- *Dried Calendula Flowers: 50 grams (about 1.76 oz)*
- *High-proof Ethanol (60-90% alcohol by volume): 250 milliliters (about 8.5 oz)*

TOOLS

- *Kitchen scale*
- *Glass jar with a tight-fitting lid (500-milliliter capacity)*
- *Cheesecloth or fine mesh strainer*
- *Amber glass dropper bottles for storage*

INSTRUCTIONS

1. Make sure the calendula flowers are fully dry to avoid mold growth during maceration. If you've collected fresh flowers, let them dry in a warm, airy place away from direct sunlight until crispy.
2. Place the dried calendula flowers in your clean jar.
3. Pour the ethanol over the flowers until they are fully submerged. The ideal herb-to-alcohol ratio for calendula is 1:5.
4. Seal the jar tightly with its lid and shake it well to mix the ingredients thoroughly.
5. Store the jar in a cool, dark place, like a kitchen cabinet or a pantry, to protect it from light degradation.
6. Allow the flowers to macerate for 3-4 weeks, shaking the jar once every few days to ensure that the flowers are consistently exposed to the alcohol.

7. After the maceration period, filter the mixture using a cheesecloth or fine mesh strainer into another clean container.
8. Squeeze or press the flowers to extract as much liquid as possible.
9. Funnel the clear tincture into amber glass bottles. If possible, use bottles with droppers for easy dosage. Label each bottle with the date, and any other pertinent information.

USAGE:

- For skin application, apply a few drops of the tincture to the affected area 2-3 times daily. Always patch test on a small area first to ensure there is no allergic reaction.
- Consult a healthcare provider for advice on oral dosage for internal use, typically not exceeding 1-2 milliliters (20-40 drops) diluted in water 3 times daily.

California Poppy (Eschscholzia californica)

- **Plant Description**: This is a small to medium-sized herbaceous plant, recognized as the state flower of California. It features cup-shaped, orange-yellow blooms.
- **Leaves**: The leaves are finely divided and fernlike, lending a soft, lacy appearance to the plant.
- **Habitat**: Native to California but can be found in various parts of the U.S., particularly in sandy or rocky soils.
- **Medicinal Properties**: California Poppy has mild sedative effects, often used to enhance relaxation and ease anxiety. The plant possesses natural analgesic properties, and it can help relieve muscle spasms and cramps.
- **Traditional Uses**: Used to promote relaxation in cases of anxiety and insomnia. It acts as a mild pain reliever as well.
- **Precautions**: California Poppy is generally safe but consult a healthcare provider before use, especially if you are pregnant, nursing, or on medication. It should not be used with other sedative medications as it may enhance their effects.
- **How to Grow**: This drought-tolerant plant thrives in full sun and well-drained, poor soils. It is ideal for xeriscaping. Sow seeds in the fall or early spring directly where they are to grow, as they do not transplant well.

CALIFORNIA POPPY TINCTURE RECIPE

PREPARATION TIME: 10 MINUTES

MACERATION TIME: 4-6 WEEKS

YIELD: APPROX 60 SERVINGS

INGREDIENTS

- Fresh California Poppy flowers and leaves – 100 grams
- Vodka (40% alcohol by volume) – 500 milliliters (approximately 2 cups)

TOOLS

- Clean glass jar with a tight-fitting lid
- Cheesecloth or fine mesh strainer
- Amber glass dropper bottles for storage
- Label for marking

INSTRUCTIONS

1. Choose vibrant, fully bloomed California Poppy flowers early in the morning after the dew has evaporated.
2. Rinse the flowers gently under cool water to remove any dirt or small insects. Pat them dry with a clean towel. Roughly chop the flowers and leaves to increase the surface area, which will extract more active compounds.
3. Place the chopped flowers and leaves into your glass jar.
4. Pour the vodka over the poppies, ensuring the plant material is fully submerged to avoid mold formation.
5. Seal the jar tightly and shake it gently to mix the contents.

6. Store the jar in a cool, dark cupboard. The darkness and stable temperature will aid in the extraction process.
7. Shake the jar lightly every day for the first week to keep the herbs agitated, which enhances the infusion.
8. After 4-6 weeks, filter the tincture using a cheesecloth or fine mesh strainer into a clean bowl. Press or squeeze the plant material to extract as much liquid as possible.
9. Decant the strained tincture into amber glass bottles to protect from light. If possible, use bottles with droppers for easy dosage. Label each bottle clearly with the date of finalization, and any other pertinent information.

USAGE:

- For adults, use 15-30 drops (1-2 milliliters) in a small amount of water or juice, up to three times per day. Due to its sedative properties, it's best taken during times of stress or before bed.

STORAGE:

- Keep the bottles in a cool, dark place. Properly stored, the tincture can last for up to 5 years.

Cat's Claw (Uncaria tomentosa)

- **Plant Description**: The plant is named for its distinctive hooked thorns, which resemble the claws of a cat.
- **Habitat**: Cat's Claw is a vine commonly found in the rainforests of South America.
- **Medicinal Properties:** Anti-inflammatory, immune-enhancing, and antiviral activities.
- **Traditional Uses:** Used in South American traditional medicine, particularly in the Amazon, for wound healing and as a general health tonic.
- **Precautions:** Should be avoided during pregnancy and by those with autoimmune diseases, as it may stimulate the immune system.
- **How to Grow:** Cat's Claw is ideally suited to a tropical or subtropical climate, mimicking its native Amazonian environment. It thrives in humid environnement with indirect sunlight. The plant prefers well-draining soil rich in organic matter. It is relatively adaptable but performs best in slightly acidic to neutral pH levels.

CAT'S CLAW TINCTURE RECIPE

PREP TIME: 15 MINUTES   **MACERATION TIME:** 4-6 WEEKS   **YIELD:** APPROX 60 SERVINGS (1 DROPPERFUL EACH)

INGREDIENTS

- Cat's Claw bark, dried and shredded: 100 grams
- High-proof alcohol (e.g., vodka or grain alcohol at 40%-70%): 500 milliliters (about 2 cups)

TOOLS

- A clean, dry glass jar with a tight-fitting lid
- Cheesecloth or a fine mesh strainer
- Amber dropper bottles for storage

INSTRUCTIONS

1. Begin by ensuring your Cat's Claw bark is properly dried and shredded. If purchasing pre-packaged, check for any signs of moisture or mold. Place the Cat's Claw bark into the sterilized jar.
2. Pour the high-proof alcohol over the bark, ensuring it is completely submerged. The ideal herb-to-alcohol ratio is about 1:5, providing optimal extraction.
3. Tightly seal the jar with its lid. Shake the mixture vigorously for a minute.
4. Store the jar in a cool, dark cupboard.
5. Let the mixture macerate for 4-6 weeks. Shake the jar well every few days to mix the ingredients and aid the extraction process.
6. After the maceration period, open the jar and filter the liquid using a cheesecloth or fine mesh strainer into a clean bowl. Squeeze or press the bark in the cheesecloth to extract as much liquid as possible.
7. Funnel the tincture into amber bottles. If possible, use bottles with droppers for easy dosage. Label each bottle with the date of preparation, and any other pertinent information like expiration date (typically 3-5 years from bottling if stored properly).

USAGE: The typical dosage for Cat's Claw tincture is 1-2 milliliters (about 1 dropperful), taken 1-3 times daily. It can be mixed into water, tea, or juice for consumption.

Chamomile (Matricaria recutita)

- **Plant Description**: Chamomile is a low-growing perennial with daisy-like flowers.
- **Leaves**: Its leaves are delicate and feathery, with a fine texture that resembles that of ferns.
- **Habitat**: Grows throughout the U.S., particularly in cultivated gardens.
- **Medicinal Properties:** Known for its calming effects, Chamomile is a gentle sedative that helps reduce anxiety and promote better sleep.
- **Traditional Uses:** Used to soothe the nervous system, relieve anxiety, insomnia, and even mild depression. It is also used for its anti-inflammatory and anti-spasmodic properties.
- **Preparation Methods:** Typically consumed as tea. Steep 2-3 tablespoons of dried chamomile flowers in hot water for 5-10 minutes. It can also be used in tinctures or aromatherapy oils.
- **Precautions:** Chamomile is safe for most people but can cause allergic reactions in individuals sensitive to plants in the Asteraceae family, such as ragweed, chrysanthemums, and marigolds. Pregnant women should avoid excessive consumption as it can act as a uterine stimulant.
- **How to Grow**: Chamomile is easy to grow and does well in full sun to partial shade. It prefers light, well-draining soil and can even thrive in poor conditions. Sow seeds directly in the ground in spring.

CHAMOMILE RELAXATION TINCTURE

PREPARATION TIME: 10 MINUTES

MACERATING TIME: 4-6 WEEKS

YIELD: APPROX 30 SERVINGS

INGREDIENTS

- *Dried chamomile flowers, 50g*
- *Vodka (40% alcohol by volume), 500 ml*

INSTRUCTIONS

1. Fill a clean glass jar with the dried chamomile flowers.
2. Pour vodka over the flowers until completely submerged.
3. Seal the jar and store in a cool, dark place for 4-6 weeks, shaking occasionally.
4. Filter the tincture using a cheesecloth into a clean bottle.
5. Label your tincture with the date and contents.

TIPS:
- Chamomile can be used to help with sleep or anxiety.
- Take 1-2 ml of the tincture at night or when needed to help relax.

Chaste Tree (Vitex agnus-castus)

- **Plant Description:** The chaste tree is a shrub or small tree known for its aromatic, finger-shaped leaves and spikes of lavender flowers.
- **Leaves:** The leaves are palmate, resembling the hand with five pointed lobes, green on top and silvery underneath due to a fine layer of hair.
- **Habitat**: Thrives in the southern U.S. in warm climates.
- **Medicinal Properties:** Renowned for its capacity to balance hormones by affecting the pituitary gland, it can help regulate menstrual cycles and relieve PMS symptoms.
- **Traditional Uses:** Used to treat premenstrual syndrome (PMS), regulate irregular menstrual cycles, and ease menopausal symptoms. It is also used to treat certain fertility issues.
- **Preparation Methods:** Available in tincture, capsule, and tea forms. For tea, use 1 teaspoon of dried berries per cup of boiling water and steep for 15 minutes. Follow manufacturer's dosage instructions for tinctures and capsules.
- **Precautions:** May cause mild gastrointestinal disturbances and skin rash. It should not be used by pregnant or breastfeeding women without medical supervision. Those on hormone-related medications should consult with a healthcare provider before using Chaste Tree Berry.
- **How to Grow**: Chaste tree requires full sun and well-drained soil. It is drought-resistant once established and grows best in warm climates. It can be grown from seeds or cuttings and often blooms in the late summer.

CHASTE TREE BARK TINCTURE RECIPE

PREPARATION TIME: 10 MINUTES

MACERATION TIME: 4-6 WEEKS

YIELD: APPROX 60 SERVINGS (30 ML)

INGREDIENTS

- *Chaste Tree Bark, dried and chopped: 50 grams (about 1.76 oz)*
- *Vodka (80-100 proof): 500 mL (about 17 oz)*

TOOLS

- *Clean glass jar with a tight-fitting lid*
- *Cheesecloth or fine mesh strainer*
- *Amber glass dropper bottles for storage*

INSTRUCTIONS

1. Begin by sourcing high-quality, dried Chaste Tree bark from reputable health stores or herbalists. Ensure it is finely chopped.
2. Place the chopped bark into the clean glass jar.
3. Pour the vodka over the bark, ensuring it completely covers the bark by at least a couple of inches, as the bark will expand when soaked.
4. Tightly seal the jar with its lid. Label it with the date and contents. Store the jar in a cool, dark cupboard.

5. Allow the mixture to macerate for 4-6 weeks. Shake the jar well every few days to mix the ingredients and promote extraction.
6. After the maceration period, filter the tincture using a cheesecloth or fine mesh strainer into another clean jar. Press or squeeze the soaked bark to extract as much liquid as possible.
7. Funnel the tincture into amber glass bottles. If possible, use bottles with droppers for easy dosage. Label each bottle clearly with the date of finalization, and any other pertinent information.
8. Store the bottles in a cool, dark location. The tincture can be used for up to 3-5 years if stored properly.

USAGE:

- **Dosage:** Typically, 1-2 mL (about 30-40 drops) taken 1-2 times daily.
- **Application:** It can be taken directly under the tongue or diluted in a small amount of water or tea.

PREPARATION TIP:

- If sensitivity to alcohol is a concern, the tincture can be evaporated slightly under warm water to reduce the alcohol content before ingestion.

Cinnamon (Cinnamomum verum)

- **Plant Description**: Cinnamon is obtained from the inner bark of several tree species from the genus Cinnamomum. The trees are evergreen and can grow to be quite large under cultivation.
- **Leaves**: The leaves are ovate-oblong in shape, leathery in texture, dark green, and highly aromatic when crushed. They can grow quite large, up to 18 cm in length.
- **Habitat**: Not typically grown in the U.S. as it requires tropical conditions; mostly grown in greenhouses or as indoor plants.
- **Medicinal Properties**: Anti-inflammatory, antimicrobial, and antioxidant properties.
- **Traditional Uses**: Used for its antioxidant properties and to help reduce blood sugar levels, which is beneficial for people with diabetes.
- **How to Grow**: To grow cinnamon indoors, you need a high humidity environment and temperatures that do not drop below 60°F. It requires a well-draining, fertile soil mix and partial shade.

CINNAMON TINCTURE RECIPE

PREP TIME: 15 MINUTES   **MACERATION TIME:** 4 WEEKS   **YIELD:** APPROX 30 ML

INGREDIENTS

- *Cinnamon sticks, crushed: 100 grams (about 3.5 oz)*
- *High-proof vodka (at least 40% alcohol by volume): 500 mL (about 17 oz)*

TOOLS

- *Clean glass jar*
- *Cheesecloth or fine mesh strainer*
- *Amber glass dropper bottles*

INSTRUCTIONS

1. Start by sourcing high-quality, organic cinnamon sticks. Crush them lightly to help release the essential oils and increase the surface area for extraction.
2. Place the crushed cinnamon sticks into the clean glass jar.
3. Pour the vodka over the cinnamon, ensuring the sticks are completely submerged. Add more vodka if necessary to cover them by at least an inch to account for absorption.
4. Seal the jar tightly with its lid and label it with the date and contents. Store the jar in a cool, dark cupboard. Let the mixture sit for 4 weeks, shaking the jar gently every few days to mix the ingredients.
5. After maceration, filter the liquid using a cheesecloth or fine mesh strainer into another clean jar. Press the cinnamon sticks to extract as much liquid as possible.
6. Funnel the liquid into amber glass bottles. If possible, use bottles with droppers for easy dosage. Label each bottle clearly with the date of finalization, and any other pertinent information.
7. Keep the bottles in a cool, dark location. The tincture can be effectively used for up to 4 years.

USAGE: Typically, 1-2 mL (about 30-40 drops) can be taken up to 3 times daily, either directly under the tongue or diluted in water or tea.

PREPARATION TIP: You can evaporate it by mixing the tincture with hot water and letting it cool before consumption. This reduces the alcohol content while retaining the beneficial properties of cinnamon.

Cleavers (Galium aparine)

- **Plant Description**: Cleavers is an annual herb with slender, creeping stems covered with tiny hooked hairs, and small, white flowers.
- **Habitat**: Found in temperate regions of North America, Europe, and Asia, Cleavers thrives in hedgerows, fields, and woodland edges.
- **Medicinal Properties**: Cleavers is known for its diuretic, lymphatic, and anti-inflammatory properties. It is used to support the lymphatic system and treat skin conditions.
- **Traditional Uses**: Traditionally used to cleanse the lymphatic system, reduce swelling, and treat skin irritations such as eczema and psoriasis.
- **Preparation Methods**: Cleavers can be made into a tea by steeping the dried herb in hot water. It can also be taken as a tincture or used topically as a poultice.
- **Precautions**: Generally safe for most people, but it should be used with caution by individuals with diabetes or those taking diuretics.
- **How to Grow**: Cleavers prefer a partially shaded spot but can tolerate full sun in cooler climates. This plant thrives in moist, rich soil but can grow in a variety of soil types as long as they are well-drained. It's not particularly demanding regarding soil fertility.

CLEAVERS TINCTURE RECIPE

PREPARATION TIME: 20 MINUTES

MACERATION TIME: 6 WEEKS

YIELD: APPROX 60 SERVINGS (30 ML)

INGREDIENTS

- *Fresh cleavers herb: 200 grams (about 7 oz)*
- *High-proof vodka (at least 40% alcohol by volume): 1 liter (about 34 oz)*

TOOLS

- *Clean glass jar with a tight-fitting lid*
- *Cheesecloth or fine mesh strainer*
- *Amber glass dropper bottles for storage*

INSTRUCTIONS

1. Harvest fresh cleavers early in the morning when their medicinal qualities are most potent. Rinse gently to remove any dirt or debris.
2. Coarsely chop the cleavers to help release the essential oils and increase the surface area for extraction.
3. Place the chopped cleavers into the clean glass jar.
4. Pour the vodka over the cleavers, ensuring the herbs are completely submerged. If necessary, add more vodka to cover them by at least two inches to account for absorption and expansion.
5. Seal the jar tightly with its lid and label it with the date and contents. Store the jar in a cool, dark cupboard. Allow the mixture to macerate for 6 weeks, shaking the jar lightly every few days to aid the extraction process.
6. After the maceration period, filter the tincture using a cheesecloth or fine mesh strainer into another clean jar. Squeeze out as much liquid as possible from the herb pulp.

7. Funnel the liquid into amber glass bottles. If possible, use bottles with droppers for easy dosage. Label each bottle clearly with the date of finalization, and any other pertinent information.
8. Store the tincture bottles in a cool, dark location. Properly stored, the tincture can last up to 5 years.

USAGE:

- Take 2-3 mL (about 40-60 drops) of the tincture three times daily, either directly under the tongue or diluted in a small amount of water or tea.

PREPARATION TIP:

- The fresher the cleavers, the more potent your tincture will be, so try to use herbs harvested on the day of tincture making if possible.

Comfrey (Symphytum officinale)

- **Plant Description**: Comfrey is a perennial herb with large, hairy leaves and clusters of bell-shaped, purple or white flowers.
- **Habitat**: Native to Europe and parts of Asia, Comfrey prefers moist, fertile soils and is commonly found along riverbanks and in meadows.
- **Medicinal Properties**: Comfrey contains allantoin, which promotes cell regeneration and healing. It has anti-inflammatory and analgesic properties.
- **Traditional Uses**: Traditionally used to treat wounds, sprains, and fractures. It has been used as a poultice to reduce inflammation and promote healing.
- **Precautions**: Comfrey should not be taken internally due to the presence of pyrrolizidine alkaloids, which can cause liver damage. Topical use should be limited to intact skin and for short periods.
- **How to Grow**: Comfrey prefers full sun or partial shade and grows well in rich, moist soil. It is very hardy and can also be invasive. Frequent harvesting of leaves can help manage its growth. It's important to note that comfrey should only be used topically due to potential health risks when taken internally.

COMFREY TINCTURE RECIPE

PREPARATION TIME: 10 MINUTES **MACERATION TIME:** 6 WEEKS **YIELD:** APPROX 500 ML

INGREDIENTS

- Comfrey Leaves and Roots (fresh or dried): 100 grams
- Vodka (at least 40% alcohol by volume): 500 ml

TOOLS

- Clean glass jar with a tight-fitting lid (approximately 1-liter capacity)
- Cheesecloth or a fine mesh strainer
- Dark glass bottle with a dropper for storage
- Labels

INSTRUCTIONS

1. If using fresh comfrey, rinse the leaves and roots under cool water to remove any dirt or debris. Chop the comfrey into smaller pieces to help release the essential oils and increase the surface area for extraction. For dried comfrey, ensure the herb is well-crumbled. Whether fresh or dried, measure out about 100 grams of the plant material.
2. Place the comfrey pieces into the glass jar.
3. Pour the vodka over the comfrey, ensuring that it is completely submerged. The ideal herb-to-alcohol ratio is about 1:5, so adjust the volume of vodka accordingly.
4. Seal the jar tightly with its lid and shake gently to mix the ingredients.
5. Label the jar with the date and contents.
6. Store the jar in a cool, dark cupboard. The tincture should macerate for at least 6 weeks; however, shaking the jar gently every few days helps extract the active compounds more effectively.
7. After 6 weeks, filter the tincture using a cheesecloth or fine mesh strainer into another clean jar or bowl. Press or squeeze the plant material to extract as much liquid as possible.

8. Funnel the tincture into dark glass bottles to protect from light. A dropper bottle is convenient for topical application.
9. Label the bottles with the date of completion, and a reminder that it's for external use only.
10. Store the tincture in a cool, dark location. Properly stored, it should remain potent for up to a year.

USAGE:
- Apply the tincture directly to the skin over bruises, sprains, or other areas needing support. Remember, do not apply to open wounds.

PREPARATION TIP:
- Always wear gloves when handling comfrey to avoid skin irritation.

PRECAUTIONS:
- Comfrey contains pyrrolizidine alkaloids (PAs) which can be toxic if ingested. This tincture is strictly for external use only and should not be applied to open wounds.

Dandelion (Taraxacum officinale)

- **Plant Description**: Dandelion is a perennial herb with a rosette of leaves and bright yellow flowers that turn into white, fluffy seed heads.
- **Habitat**: Native to Europe and Asia, Dandelion is now widespread in temperate regions around the world. It grows in lawns, fields, and along roadsides.
- **Medicinal Properties**: Dandelion has diuretic, detoxifying, and anti-inflammatory properties. It supports liver health, digestion, and the urinary system.
- **Traditional Uses**: Traditionally used to treat liver and kidney disorders, improve digestion, and as a diuretic to reduce water retention.
- **Preparation Methods**: Dandelion leaves can be used in salads, brewed into tea, or taken as a tincture. The root is often roasted and used as a coffee substitute or made into a tincture.
- **Precautions**: Dandelion is generally safe but can cause allergic reactions in some individuals. It should be used with caution by individuals with gallbladder problems or those taking diuretics.
- **How to Grow**: Dandelions are extremely easy to grow. They can thrive in almost any kind of soil but prefer full sun or partial shade. Sow seeds directly in the garden in early spring. They are hardy and require minimal maintenance.

DANDELION ROOT TINCTURE

PREPARATION TIME: 10 MINUTES

MACERATION TIME: 4-6 WEEKS

YIELD: ABOUT 1 CUP (240 ML) OF TINCTURE

INGREDIENTS

- *1/4 cup dried dandelion root (25 grams)*
- *1 cup vodka (240 milliliters) (at least 40% alcohol by volume)*
- *Glass jar with a tight-fitting lid (250-300 milliliters)*
- *Cheesecloth or fine mesh strainer*
- *Dark glass dropper bottles for storage*

INSTRUCTIONS

1. Measure out 1/4 cup (25 grams) of dried dandelion root. Measure out 1 cup (240 milliliters) of vodka.
2. Place the dried dandelion root in a clean, dry glass jar. Pour the vodka over the dandelion root, ensuring the root is fully submerged.
3. Seal the jar tightly with its lid. Shake the jar well to mix the ingredients thoroughly.
4. Store the jar in a cool, dark cupboard. Shake the jar daily to help with the extraction process. Allow the mixture to infuse for 4-6 weeks.
5. After 4-6 weeks, filter the tincture using a cheesecloth or fine mesh strainer into a clean bowl to remove the solid particles. Squeeze the cheesecloth to extract as much liquid as possible from the dandelion root.
6. Store the tincture into dark glass bottles. If possible, use bottles with droppers for easy dosage. Label the bottles with the date and contents.

ADDITIONAL TIPS:

- <u>Storage</u>: Store the tincture in a cool, dark location. It can last for up to 2 years if stored properly.
- <u>Dosage</u>: The typical dosage is 20-30 drops (approximately 1 milliliter) diluted in water or juice, taken 2-3 times daily. Always consult with a healthcare provider before starting any new tincture.
- <u>Safety</u>: Dandelion root tincture should be used with caution by individuals with gallbladder problems or those taking diuretics. Always consult with a healthcare provider before use.

Devil's Claw (Harpagophytum procumbens)

- **Plant Description**: Devil's Claw is a perennial plant, known for its hook-like fruit. It is not a tree but rather grows somewhat horizontally, sprouting shoots and flowers above ground from a tuberous root system.
- **Leaves**: The leaves are large and roughly hairy, with an arrangement of spreading lobes.
- **Habitat**: Native to southern Africa, Devil's Claw is less common in the U.S. but can be grown in similar arid environments such as parts of the southern U.S.
- **Medicinal Properties**: Anti-inflammatory, pain relief, digestive aid.
- **Traditional Uses**: Used to treat arthritis, muscle pain, and digestive disorders.
- **Preparation Methods**: Teas, tinctures, and capsules.
- **How to Grow**: Devil's Claw requires sandy, well-draining soil and full sun, mimicking its native desert habitat. It is drought-tolerant once established. Start seeds indoors in a warm environment or direct sow outside after the last frost. Water sparingly.

DEVIL'S CLAW TINCTURE

PREPARATION TIME: 15 MINUTES

MACERATION TIME: 4-6 WEEKS

YIELD: APPROX 30 SERVINGS (1 MONTH SUPPLY)

INGREDIENTS

- *100 grams of dried Devil's Claw root*
- *500 ml of vodka (40% alcohol by volume) or another high-proof grain alcohol*

INSTRUCTIONS

1. If the dried Devil's Claw root isn't already chopped, chop it into small pieces using a sharp knife or a blender.
2. Place the chopped or ground Devil's Claw root into a clean, dry glass jar with a wide mouth.
3. Pour the vodka or grain alcohol over the Devil's Claw, ensuring that the roots are completely submerged. Add extra alcohol if necessary to cover the roots.
4. Tightly seal the jar with a lid. Shake the jar a bit to mix the contents. Store the jar in a cool, dark cupboard away from direct sunlight.
5. Let the mixture macerate for 4-6 weeks. Shake the jar every few days to mix the contents and promote extraction.
6. After the maceration period, filter the tincture using a fine mesh strainer or cheesecloth into another clean, sterilized jar. Squeeze or press the plant material to extract as much liquid as possible.
7. Funnel the tincture into dark glass bottles. If possible, use bottles with droppers for easy dosage.
8. Label the bottles with the date and contents.

USAGE: Take 1-2 ml of the tincture three times a day, diluted in water or tea.

HEALTH BENEFITS: Devil's Claw is used for its analgesic and anti-inflammatory properties, making it useful for those suffering from arthritis, back pain, or general muscle aches.

SERVING SUGGESTIONS: Incorporate the tincture into a daily regimen, ideally taken before meals to maximize absorption.

Dong Quai (Angelica sinensis)

- **Plant Description**: Dong Quai is a perennial plant native to China, belonging to the celery family.
- **Leaves**: The leaves are umbrella-like in shape, divided into leaflets with serrated edges, similar to other members of the Apiaceae family.
- **Habitat**: While not native to the U.S., Dong Quai is grown in herb gardens, particularly those that mimic its natural habitat of cool, damp high-altitude regions in Asia.
- **Medicinal Properties:** Dong Quai is renowned for its ability to balance estrogen levels, making it useful for menstrual and menopausal symptoms. It also improves blood circulation.
- **Traditional Uses:** Widely used in Traditional Chinese Medicine (TCM) to regulate menstrual cycles, relieve menstrual cramps, and alleviate menopausal symptoms.
- **Preparation Methods:** Commonly taken as a tea, tincture, or capsule. For tea, steep 1-2 teaspoons of dried root in boiling water for 15-20 minutes. It is also available in powder form to be added to smoothies or other beverages.
- **Precautions:** Dong Quai can increase sensitivity to sunlight and may increase the risk of bleeding. It should be avoided by pregnant women and those taking blood thinners. Always consult a healthcare provider before using Dong Quai, particularly if you have a history of hormone-sensitive conditions.
- **How to Grow**: Dong Quai can be grown in shady to partially shaded areas with rich, moist, well-draining soil. It's best to start from seed indoors and transplant outdoors in the spring. It requires patience as it may take a few years to establish and produce roots suitable for use.

DONG QUAI TINCTURE RECIPE

PREP TIME: 15 MINUTES   **MACERATION TIME:** 4 TO 6 WEEKS   **YIELD:** APPROX 500 ML

INGREDIENTS

- Dong Quai Root (dried and sliced): 100 grams
- High-proof vodka (at least 40% alcohol by volume, 80 proof): 500 ml

TOOLS

- Clean glass jar with a tight-fitting lid (1-liter capacity)
- Cheesecloth or fine mesh strainer
- Amber glass bottles with droppers for storage
- Labels

INSTRUCTIONS

1. Ensure the Dong Quai root is finely sliced to maximize the surface area exposed to the alcohol, enhancing the extraction process.
2. Measure out 100 grams of dried Dong Quai root.
3. Place the sliced Dong Quai into your clean glass jar.
4. Pour the vodka over the roots, ensuring the roots are completely submerged. The ideal ratio is about 1:5 by weight for dried roots.
5. Seal the jar tightly with its lid and shake it well to mix the roots with the alcohol.

6. Label the jar with the date and the name of the herb.
7. Store the jar in a cool, dark cupboard away from direct sunlight and heat sources. Allow the mixture to macerate for 4 to 6 weeks, shaking the jar every few days to agitate the contents and promote extraction.
8. After the maceration period, filter the tincture using cheesecloth or a fine mesh strainer into a clean bowl or another jar. Squeeze or press the soaked Dong Quai roots to extract as much liquid as possible.
9. Funnel the strained tincture into amber glass bottles.
10. Label each bottle clearly with the date of finalization, and any other pertinent information such as a reminder to check for contraindications.
11. Store the bottles in a cool, dark location. When stored properly, the tincture should remain potent for up to two years.

USAGE:

- Typically, the dosage for Dong Quai tincture is 1-2 ml, taken 2-3 times daily, unless otherwise directed by a healthcare provider.

PREPARATION TIP:

- If Dong Quai's strong aroma is too much, you can blend it with other herbs to create a more palatably scented tincture.

PRECAUTIONS:

- Dong Quai should not be used during pregnancy or by individuals taking blood thinners or those with hormone-sensitive conditions.

Echinacea (Echinacea spp.)

- **Plant Description**: Echinacea, commonly known as coneflower, features large, purple daisy-like flowers with a spiny central disk. It is a perennial plant that grows to a height of about 4 feet.
- **Habitat**: Native to North America, Echinacea thrives in prairies and open woodlands. It is commonly found in areas with well-drained soil and full sunlight.
- **Medicinal Properties**: renowned for its immune-boosting properties, Echinacea is rich in polysaccharides, flavonoids, and essential oils that enhance immune function and reduce inflammation.
- **Traditional Uses**: Traditionally used by Native American tribes to treat infections, wounds, and snakebites. It is now commonly used to prevent and treat the common cold and respiratory infections.
- **Preparation Methods**: Echinacea can be prepared as a tea by steeping the dried root or leaves in hot water for 10-15 minutes. It is also available in tincture form, which can be added to water or juice.
- **Precautions**: Echinacea is generally safe for short-term use. However, it may cause allergic reactions in individuals sensitive to plants in the daisy family. It is not recommended for people with autoimmune disorders or those on immunosuppressant medications.
- **How to Grow**: Echinacea prefers full sun and well-draining soil. Plant seeds in the spring or fall. It's drought-tolerant once established and requires minimal maintenance. Deadhead flowers to prolong blooming.

ECHINACEA TINCTURE RECIPE

PREPARATION TIME: 20 MINUTES   **MACERATION TIME:** 6-8 WEEKS   **YIELD:** APPROX 500 ML

INGREDIENTS

- Echinacea Root (dried and chopped): 100 grams
- High-proof vodka (at least 40% alcohol by volume, 80 proof): 500 ml

TOOLS

- Clean glass jar with a tight-fitting lid (1-liter capacity)
- Cheesecloth or fine mesh strainer
- Amber glass bottles with droppers for storage
- Labels

INSTRUCTIONS

1. Thoroughly clean and then chop the dried Echinacea root to help release the essential oils and increase the surface area for extraction.
2. Measure 100 grams of the prepared root.
3. Place the chopped Echinacea root into your clean glass jar.
4. Pour the vodka over the root, ensuring the root is completely submerged. Maintain an herb to alcohol ratio of about 1:5 by weight for dried roots.
5. Seal the jar tightly with its lid and shake the jar well to mix the ingredients thoroughly.
6. Label the jar with the date and the herb's name.

7. Store the jar in a cool, dark cupboard away from sunlight and heat, for 6 to 8 weeks. Shake the jar occasionally to help with the extraction process.
8. After the maceration period, filter the tincture using cheesecloth or a fine mesh strainer into another clean container. Press the marc (spent herb material) to extract as much liquid as possible.
9. Funnel the liquid into amber glass bottles for long-term storage.
10. Label each bottle clearly with the herb's name, the date of bottling, and storage instructions.
11. Store the bottles in a cool, dark location. Properly stored, the tincture can last up to two years.

USAGE:

- The typical dosage is 1-2 ml of the tincture, taken 2-3 times daily at the first sign of cold or flu symptoms. Consult with a healthcare professional before use, especially during pregnancy or while on medication.

PREPARATION TIP:

- Consider blending Echinacea with other immune-supportive herbs like goldenseal or elderberry for enhanced effects.

Elderberry (Sambucus nigra)

- **Plant Description**: Elderberry is a large shrub or small tree that produces clusters of small white or cream-colored flowers, followed by dark purple to black berries.
- **Leaves**: The leaves are compound with 5 to 9 leaflets, each leaflet being serrated and relatively symmetrical.
- **Habitat**: Commonly found in both wild and cultivated settings across the United States, particularly in moist, well-drained soil along riverbanks and near streams.
- **Medicinal Properties:** Elderberry is rich in antioxidants and vitamins, particularly vitamin C. It has antiviral, immune-boosting, and anti-inflammatory properties.
- **Traditional Uses:** Traditionally used to support the immune system and to treat cold and flu symptoms in children.
- **Precautions:** Raw elderberries can be toxic; always cook them before use. Elderberry products are generally safe for children but should be avoided in infants under one year due to honey content.
- **How to Grow**: Elderberry bushes prefer full sun or partial shade and thrive in moist, fertile soil. They can be grown from cuttings or seeds, and should be watered regularly.

ELDERBERRY TINCTURE RECIPE

PREPARATION TIME: 30 MINUTES   **MACERATION TIME:** 4-6 WEEKS   **YIELD:** APPROX 500 ML

INGREDIENTS

- Elderberries (dried): 100 grams
- Vodka (at least 40% alcohol by volume, 80 proof): 500 ml

TOOLS

- Clean glass jar with a tight-fitting lid (1-liter capacity)
- Cheesecloth or a fine mesh strainer
- Amber glass bottles with droppers for storage
- Labels

INSTRUCTIONS

1. Ensure the elderberries are fully ripe and dried. If you purchase them, choose organic berries from a reputable source to avoid pesticides and contaminants.
2. Measure 100 grams of the dried elderberries.
3. Place the dried elderberries in your clean glass jar.
4. Pour the vodka over the berries, ensuring they are completely covered. The herb to alcohol ratio should be about 1:5 by weight for dried berries.
5. Seal the jar tightly with its lid and shake well to mix the berries with the alcohol.
6. Label the jar with the date and the contents.
7. Store the jar in a cool, dark cupboard away from direct sunlight and heat, for 4 to 6 weeks. Shake the jar every few days to help with the extraction process.
8. After the maceration period, filter the tincture using cheesecloth or a fine mesh strainer into a clean container. Compress the berries to extract as much liquid as possible.

9. Funnel the strained tincture into amber glass bottles for storage.
10. Label each bottle clearly with the date of finalization, and any other pertinent information.
11. Store the bottles in a cool, dark location. The tincture will be potent and effective for up to two years if stored properly.

USAGE:

- The standard dosage is 1-2 ml of the tincture up to three times daily during flu season or at the first sign of symptoms. Always seek advice from a healthcare professional before beginning any new herbal treatment, especially for pregnant or nursing mothers and children.

PREPARATION TIP:

- Elderberry tincture can be combined with other immune-supporting tinctures like echinacea or astragalus to enhance its efficacy.

PRECAUTIONS:

- Unripe or raw elderberries are toxic; only ripe berries should be used for tinctures.

Elecampane (Inula helenium)

- **Plant Description**: Elecampane is a robust, perennial herb with a thick, branching, fibrous root and large, downy leaves. It produces yellow, daisy-like composite flowers.
- **Leaves**: The basal leaves are large, up to 12 inches long, and broadly ovate, with smaller, alternating leaves along the stem.
- **Habitat**: While native to Eurasia, Elecampane has naturalized in many parts of the United States, commonly found in meadows, fields, and along roadsides.
- **Medicinal Properties**: Expectorant and antibacterial properties.
- **Traditional Uses**: Traditionally used to treat respiratory conditions such as bronchitis and asthma due to its expectorant properties, helping to clear mucus from the lungs.
- **Precautions**: Elecampane should be used with caution in individuals with allergies to ragweed and related plants due to possible sensitivity.
- **How to Grow**: Plant Elecampane in full sun or partial shade in well-draining soil. It prefers a slightly damp location, so regular watering is important. It can be propagated from root cuttings or seeds in spring.

ELECAMPANE TINCTURE RECIPE

PREP TIME: 20 MINUTES   **MACERATION TIME:** 4-6 WEEKS   **YIELD:** APPROX 500 ML

INGREDIENTS

- *Elecampane Root (dried, sliced): 100 grams*
- *High-proof alcohol (vodka or brandy, at least 40% alcohol by volume, 80 proof): 500 ml*

TOOLS

- *Clean glass jar with a tight-fitting lid (1-liter capacity)*
- *Cheesecloth or a fine mesh strainer*
- *Amber glass bottles with droppers for storage*
- *Labels*

INSTRUCTIONS

1. Ensure dried elecampane root is properly dried and free from mold or dampness.
2. Measure 100 grams of the dried root and roughly chop if the slices are too large.
3. Place the chopped dried root into your clean glass jar. Pour the alcohol over the root, ensuring that it is completely submerged. Maintain an herb to alcohol ratio of about 1:5 by weight.
4. Seal the jar tightly with its lid and shake it to ensure the root is fully saturated with the alcohol.
5. Label the jar with the date and contents.
6. Store the jar in a cool, dark place, such as a cabinet away from light and heat, for 4 to 6 weeks. Shake the jar periodically to help with the extraction process.
7. After the maceration period, filter the tincture using cheesecloth or a fine mesh strainer into another clean jar, pressing the root material to extract as much liquid as possible.
8. Funnel the strained tincture into amber glass bottles for final storage.
9. Label each bottle clearly with the date of finalization, and any other pertinent information.
10. Store the bottles in a cool, dark location. Properly stored, the tincture should remain effective for up to two years.

USAGE: Typical use involves taking 1-2 ml of the tincture three times daily, especially during times of respiratory distress.

PREPARATION TIP: Consider blending your elecampane tincture with other respiratory-support herbs like mullein or licorice for enhanced effects.

Eyebright (Euphrasia officinalis)

- **Plant Description**: Eyebright is a small annual herb native to Europe, characterized by its tiny white flowers with purple streaks and a yellow spot on the lower lip.
- **Leaves**: The leaves are small and serrated, arranged in opposite pairs along the stem.
- **Habitat**: Eyebright is typically found in grassy meadows, pastures, and other open, well-drained areas across various parts of the United States. It prefers a cooler climate and is more commonly found in the northern states and mountainous regions.
- **Medicinal Properties:** Supporting eye health, offering a natural solution for maintaining optical wellness and combating daily eye fatigue.
- **Traditional Uses**: Traditionally used to relieve eye irritation and discomfort. Eyebright is often used in the form of eye drops or compresses to treat conjunctivitis and other inflammatory eye conditions.
- **Precautions**: Eyebright should be used with caution as it can cause sensitivity, especially in people with eye conditions.
- **How to Grow**: Eyebright thrives in well-drained, calcareous soil. It does not require fertile soil, often growing well in poor soils as long as they are not waterlogged. It prefers full sun to partial shade.

EYEBRIGHT TINCTURE RECIPE

PREP TIME: 15 MINUTES   **MACERATION TIME:** 4 WEEKS   **YIELD:** APPROX 300 ML

INGREDIENTS

- Eyebright Herb (dried): 50 grams
- High-proof alcohol (vodka or brandy, at least 40% alcohol by volume, 80 proof): 300 ml

TOOLS

- Clean glass jar with a tight-fitting lid
- Cheesecloth or a fine mesh strainer
- Amber glass bottles with droppers for storage
- Labels

INSTRUCTIONS

1. Measure 50 grams of the dried herb. Place the dried eyebright into your clean glass jar.
2. Pour the alcohol over the herbs, ensuring that the plant material is completely covered.
3. Seal the jar tightly with its lid and shake it well to mix the ingredients thoroughly.
4. Label the jar with the date and contents. Store the jar in a cool, dark cupboard for about 4 weeks. Shake the jar every few days to mix the herbs and aid in the extraction process.
5. After maceration, filter the tincture using cheesecloth or a fine mesh strainer into a clean jar. Press or squeeze the herb matter to extract as much liquid as possible.
6. Funnel the strained tincture into amber glass bottles for storage.
7. Label each bottle clearly with the date of production, expiration date, and any other pertinent information.
8. Store the bottles in a cool, dark location. When stored properly, the tincture should remain potent for up to two years.

USAGE: Typical dosage is 1-2 ml of the tincture diluted in water, taken 2-3 times daily, or as directed by a healthcare professional.

Feverfew (Tanacetum parthenium)

- **Plant Description**: Feverfew is a perennial herb with daisy-like flowers and pungent leaves. It reaches heights of typically 15–60 cm.
- **Leaves**: The leaves are arranged spirally, with a downy texture. They are light green in color and deeply lobed.
- **Habitat**: Common in gardens and escapes into wild road edges and fields.
- **Traditional Uses**: Traditionally used to prevent migraine headaches. It is also used for fever, irregular menstrual periods, arthritis, and other conditions.
- **Precautions**: Feverfew may interact with blood-thinning medications and is not recommended during pregnancy or breastfeeding.
- **How to Grow**: Prefers well-drained soil and can grow in full sun or partial shade. Sow seeds directly in the ground in spring or autumn.

FEVERFEW TINCTURE RECIPE

PREP TIME: 10 MINUTES   **MACERATION TIME:** 4 WEEKS   **YIELD:** APPROX 300 ML

INGREDIENTS

- Feverfew Leaves (fresh or dried): 100 grams
- High-proof alcohol (vodka or grain alcohol, 40%-50% alcohol by volume): 500 ml

TOOLS

- Clean glass jar with a tight-sealing lid
- Cheesecloth or fine mesh strainer
- Amber glass dropper bottles for storage
- Labels for marking

INSTRUCTIONS

1. If using dried leaves, ensure they are free from mold and debris. If using fresh leaves, rinse them well and gently pat dry. If fresh, chop the leaves finely to help release the essential oils and increase the surface area for extraction. Place the feverfew leaves into the clean glass jar.
2. Pour the alcohol over the leaves, ensuring they are completely submerged.
3. Seal the jar with its lid and shake lightly to settle the contents.
4. Label the jar with the date and contents for reference.
5. Store the jar in a cool, dark cupboard. Let it sit for 4 weeks, shaking the jar gently every few days to aid the maceration process.
6. After 4 weeks, filter the tincture using cheesecloth or a fine mesh strainer into another clean jar, squeezing the herb matter to extract as much liquid as possible.
7. Funnel the strained tincture into amber glass bottles.
8. Label each bottle clearly with the date of tincture preparation, and expiry date.
9. Store the bottles in a cool, dark location to preserve their potency, typically up to 2 years.

USAGE:

- Typical dosage for migraine prevention is 1-2 ml of the tincture, taken 2-3 times daily. Consult with a healthcare provider for personalized dosage recommendations.

Ginger (Zingiber officinale)

- **Plant Description**: Ginger is a tropical perennial that grows from a rhizome. It can stand about 2-4 feet in height.
- **Leaves**: Its leaves are long, narrow, and green, with a glossy texture, emanating directly from the rhizome at the base.
- **Habitat**: Typically grown indoors or in warm, moist climates.
- **Medicinal Properties**: Aids digestion, reduces nausea, anti-inflammatory.
- **Traditional Uses**: Used for digestive health, respiratory issues, and as a warming herb.
- **Precautions**: May cause heartburn in large doses.
- **How to Grow**: Requires warm and humid conditions. Plant ginger root sections in pots indoors in rich, well-draining potting soil.

GINGER DIGESTIVE TINCTURE

PREP TIME: 10 MINUTES   **MACERATION TIME:** 4-6 WEEKS   **YIELD:** APPROX 30 SERVINGS

INGREDIENTS

- Fresh ginger root, 100g (roughly chopped)
- Vodka (40% alcohol by volume), 500 ml
- Honey, 2 tbsp (optional, for flavor)

INSTRUCTIONS

1. Place the chopped ginger in a clean glass jar.
2. Pour vodka over the ginger until fully submerged.
3. Stir in honey if desired for additional flavor.
4. Seal the jar tightly with its lid and store in a cool, dark place for 4-6 weeks, shaking the jar every few days.
5. After maceration, filter the mixture using a cheesecloth into another clean glass container.
6. Label your tincture with the date and store in a cool, dark location.

TIPS:
- Use organic ginger to avoid pesticide residues.
- This tincture is great for aiding digestion and can be taken in doses of 1-2 ml before meals.

Ginkgo (Ginkgo biloba)

- **Tree Description**: Ginkgo biloba, also referred to as the maidenhair tree, stands alone as a distinct species without any closely related living counterparts. It can grow over 35 meters tall.
- **Leaves**: The leaves are distinctive, fan-shaped, and often split in the middle, resembling two lobes hence the name "biloba".
- **Habitat**: Commonly cultivated as an ornamental tree in urban areas.
- **Medicinal Properties:** Enhances cognitive function, improves circulation.
- **Traditional Uses:** Often taken for cognitive enhancement, to improve memory and attention. It is also used to treat circulatory disorders and to enhance blood flow to the brain.
- **Precautions:** May interact with blood thinners.
- **How to Grow**: Best grown from seed or young trees. Prefers full sun or partial shade and is tolerant of many soil types.

GINKGO BILOBA TINCTURE RECIPE

PREP TIME: 15 MINUTES   **MACERATION TIME:** 6 WEEKS   **YIELD:** APPROX 300 ML

INGREDIENTS

- Ginkgo Biloba Leaves (dried): 100 grams
- High-proof alcohol (vodka or grain alcohol, 45%-50% alcohol by volume): 500 ml

TOOLS

- Clean glass jar with a tight-fitting lid
- Cheesecloth or a fine mesh strainer
- Amber glass dropper bottles
- Labels for marking

INSTRUCTIONS

1. If using dried Ginkgo Biloba leaves, ensure they are free from contaminants. The leaves should be crumbled, not powdered. If fresh, gather leaves from unsprayed, healthy trees, wash them thoroughly, and dry them. Place the Ginkgo Biloba leaves into the clean glass jar.
2. Pour the alcohol over the leaves until they are fully submerged.
3. Seal the jar tightly with its lid and shake the jar well to mix the ingredients thoroughly.
4. Label the jar with the date and contents for reference.
5. Store the jar in a cool, dark cupboard. Allow the mixture to macerate for 6 weeks, shaking the jar lightly every few days to mix the contents and ensure optimal extraction.
6. After 6 weeks, filter the tincture using cheesecloth or a fine mesh strainer into another clean jar, pressing the leaves to extract as much liquid as possible.
7. Funnel the liquid into amber bottles. If possible, use bottles with droppers for easy dosage.
8. Label each bottle clearly with the date of finalization, and any usage notes.
9. Store in a cool, dark location. Tinctures can last up to 5 years if stored properly.

USAGE:

- For cognitive enhancement and circulatory support, a typical dose is 1-2 ml of the tincture, taken 1-3 times daily.

Ginseng (Panax ginseng)

- **Plant Description**: Ginseng is a slow-growing perennial plant with fleshy roots. It grows up to 60 cm tall.
- **Leaves**: Its leaves are compound with five or more leaflets arranged in a circular pattern.
- **Habitat**: Native to cooler climates in the eastern U.S., particularly in Appalachian and Ozark regions.
- **Medicinal Properties:** Boosts energy, supports immune function.
- **Traditional Uses:** Known for its ability to reduce stress, boost energy levels, and enhance mental clarity. Ginseng is also used to support the immune system and improve sexual dysfunction.
- **Preparation Methods:** Teas, tinctures, capsules.
- **Precautions:** Avoid in high blood pressure.
- **How to Grow**: Requires shaded areas, typically under the canopy of deciduous trees. Takes several years to mature.

GINSENG TINCTURE RECIPE

PREP TIME: 20 MINUTES   **MACERATION TIME:** 8 WEEKS   **YIELD:** APPROX 300 ML

INGREDIENTS

- Ginseng Root (dried and sliced): 100 grams
- High-proof alcohol (vodka or grain alcohol, 45%-50% ABV): 500 ml

TOOLS

- Clean glass jar with a tight-fitting lid
- Cheesecloth or a fine mesh strainer
- Amber glass dropper bottles for storage
- Labels for marking

INSTRUCTIONS

1. Slice the dried root thinly to increase the surface area, which aids in the extraction process.
2. Place the sliced ginseng root into the clean glass jar.
3. Pour the alcohol over the slices until they are completely submerged.
4. Seal the jar tightly and shake gently to mix.
5. Label the jar with the date of preparation and contents.
6. Store the jar in a dark, cool place for 8 weeks. Shake the jar once or twice a week to help the maceration process.
7. After 8 weeks, strain the mixture through cheesecloth or a fine mesh strainer into a clean jar. Press or squeeze the solids to extract maximum liquid.
8. Transfer the strained tincture into amber bottles for dosage control. If possible, use bottles with droppers. Label each bottle with the herb name, batch date, and storage instructions.
9. Store the bottles in a cool, dark location. Properly stored, ginseng tincture can remain potent for up to 5 years.

USAGE:

- The recommended dosage is 1-2 ml up to three times daily, either directly under the tongue or diluted in a small amount of water.

Golden Root (Rhodiola rosea)

- **Plant Description**: Golden Root, also known as Rhodiola, is a perennial herb with thick, fleshy roots and yellow flowers.
- **Habitat**: Native to the Arctic regions of Europe, Asia, and North America, Golden Root grows in cold, mountainous areas.
- **Medicinal Properties**: Golden Root is an adaptogen, renowned for its ability to enhance physical and mental performance and combat stress.
- **Traditional Uses**: Traditionally used to increase endurance, reduce fatigue, and promote longevity.
- **Preparation Methods**: Golden Root can be taken as a tea, tincture, or supplement. The dried root is steeped in hot water to make tea, or it can be added to alcohol for tinctures.
- **Precautions**: Generally considered safe, but it should be used under the guidance of a healthcare provider, especially for individuals with bipolar disorder or those on medication for mood disorders.
- **How to Grow**: Rhodiola rosea thrives in cool climates and can tolerate temperatures well below freezing. This plant prefers well-drained, sandy or loamy soil with a pH between 5.5 and 7.0. Good drainage is crucial to prevent root rot, as Rhodiola does not like waterlogged conditions.

GOLDEN ROOT TINCTURE RECIPE

PREPARATION TIME: 10 MINUTES (PLUS 4-6 WEEKS FOR TINCTURE TO INFUSE)

YIELD: ABOUT 1 CUP (240 MILLILITERS) OF TINCTURE

INGREDIENTS

- 1/4 cup dried golden root (Rhodiola rosea) (25 grams)
- 1 cup vodka (240 milliliters) (at least 40% alcohol by volume)

TOOLS

- Glass jar with a tight-fitting lid (250-300 milliliters)
- Cheesecloth or fine mesh strainer
- Dark glass dropper bottles for storage

INSTRUCTIONS

1. Measure out 1/4 cup (25 grams) of dried golden root (Rhodiola rosea). Measure out 1 cup (240 milliliters) of vodka.
2. Place the dried golden root in a clean, dry glass jar. Pour the vodka over the golden root, ensuring the root is fully submerged.
3. Seal the jar tightly with its lid. Shake the jar well to mix the ingredients thoroughly. Store the jar in a cool, dark place. Shake the jar daily to help with the extraction process. Allow the mixture to infuse for 4-6 weeks.
4. After 4-6 weeks, filter the tincture using a cheesecloth or fine mesh strainer into a clean bowl to remove the solid particles. Squeeze the cheesecloth to extract as much liquid as possible from the golden root.
5. Store the tincture into dark glass bottles. If possible, use bottles with droppers for easy dosage. Label the bottles with the date and contents. It can last for up to 2 years if stored properly.

ADDITIONAL TIPS:

- <u>Dosage</u>: The typical dosage is 20-30 drops (approximately 1 milliliter) diluted in water or juice, taken 2-3 times daily. Always consult with a healthcare provider before starting any new tincture.
- <u>Safety</u>: Golden root should be used with caution by individuals with bipolar disorder or those on medication for mood disorders. Always consult with a healthcare provider before use.

Goldenseal (Hydrastis canadensis)

- **Plant Description**: Goldenseal is a perennial herb with large, lobed leaves and small, greenish-white flowers. Its most notable feature is its bright yellow rhizome.
- **Habitat**: Native to the rich, shaded forests of North America, Goldenseal prefers moist, well-drained soils.
- **Medicinal Properties**: Goldenseal has antimicrobial, anti-inflammatory, and astringent properties. It is effective in treating infections, digestive issues, and skin conditions.
- **Traditional Uses**: Traditionally used by Native Americans to treat skin diseases, digestive disorders, and eye infections. It is now commonly used to boost the immune system and as a natural antibiotic.
- **Preparation Methods**: Goldenseal can be taken as a tea, tincture, or capsule. The dried root is steeped in hot water to make tea or added to alcohol for tinctures.
- **Precautions**: Goldenseal should not be used for extended periods due to potential toxicity. It is not recommended for pregnant or breastfeeding women. High doses can cause gastrointestinal distress.
- **How to Grow**: Requires rich, moist, well-drained soil and partial to full shade.

GOLDENSEAL TINCTURE RECIPE

PREPARATION TIME: 10 MINUTES (PLUS 4-6 WEEKS FOR TINCTURE TO INFUSE)

YIELD: ABOUT 1 CUP (240 MILLILITERS) OF TINCTURE

INGREDIENTS

- *1/4 cup dried goldenseal root (25 grams)*
- *1 cup vodka (240 milliliters) (at least 40% alcohol by volume)*

TOOLS

- *Glass jar with a tight-fitting lid (250-300 milliliters)*
- *Cheesecloth or fine mesh strainer*
- *Dark glass dropper bottles for storage*

INSTRUCTIONS

1. Measure out 1/4 cup (25 grams) of dried goldenseal root. Measure out 1 cup (240 milliliters) of vodka.
2. Place the dried goldenseal root in a clean, dry glass jar. Pour the vodka over the goldenseal root, ensuring the root is fully submerged.
3. Seal the jar tightly with its lid. Shake the jar well to mix the ingredients thoroughly.
4. Store the jar in a cool, dark place. Shake the jar daily to help with the extraction process. Allow the mixture to infuse for 4-6 weeks.
5. After 4-6 weeks, filter the tincture using a cheesecloth or fine mesh strainer into a clean bowl to remove the solid particles. Squeeze the cheesecloth to extract as much liquid as possible from the goldenseal root.
6. Storage the tincture into dark glass bottles. If possible, use bottles with droppers for easy dosage. Label the bottles with the date and contents. It can last for up to 2 years if stored properly.

DOSAGE: The typical dosage is 20-30 drops (approximately 1 milliliter) diluted in water or juice, taken 2-3 times daily. Always consult with a healthcare provider before starting any new tincture.

Gotu Kola (Centella asiatica)

- **Plant Description**: Gotu Kola is a small, perennial, creeper.
- **Leaves**: Its leaves are rounded, smooth, green, and kidney-shaped, forming in clusters at the stem nodes.
- **Habitat**: Best suited to warm, swampy areas in the Southeast.
- **Medicinal Properties**: Rejuvenating properties and support for mental clarity and circulation.
- **Traditional Uses**: Used to improve circulation, treat varicose veins, and enhance memory and cognitive function. It is also used in wound healing and to treat skin conditions like psoriasis and eczema.
- **Precautions:** Gotu Kola may interact with medications, especially those that affect the liver or sedatives. It may also interact with diabetes medications, causing blood sugar levels to drop too low.
- **How to Grow**: Thrives in wet, boggy conditions. Plant in partial shade and keep soil consistently moist.

GOTU KOLA TINCTURE RECIPE

PREPARATION TIME: 30 MINUTES

MACERATION TIME: 6 WEEKS

INGREDIENTS

- Fresh Gotu Kola Leaves: 100 grams
- High-Proof Alcohol (at least 40% alcohol by volume, such as vodka or grain alcohol): 500 milliliters

TOOLS

- Jar with a tight-fitting lid
- Strainer or cheesecloth
- Amber glass dropper bottles for storage
- Labels

INSTRUCTIONS

1. Rinse the leaves gently under cold running water. Pat them dry with a clean cloth or paper towels.
2. Finely chop the Gotu Kola leaves to help release the essential oils and increase the surface area for extraction.
3. Place the chopped leaves into the jar.
4. Pour the high-proof alcohol over the leaves, ensuring they are completely submerged. If using 40% alcohol, a 1:5 herb-to-alcohol ratio is adequate. Seal the jar tightly with its lid.
5. Store the jar in a cool, dark cupboard away from direct sunlight. The darkness prevents degradation of the herb's potent compounds.
6. Shake the jar daily for the first two weeks. This helps mix the plant material with the alcohol, ensuring a more uniform extraction. Let the mixture sit for a total of six weeks. This duration allows the alcohol to extract the active constituents effectively from the Gotu Kola.
7. After six weeks, filter the mixture using a cheesecloth or fine mesh strainer into a clean bowl. Press or squeeze the plant material to extract as much liquid as possible. Funnel the strained tincture into amber glass bottles for storage.
8. Label each bottle clearly with the date of finalization, and any other pertinent information. Tinctures can last up to 3-5 years if stored properly.

DOSAGE: Typically, 2-4 ml of the tincture can be taken up to three times a day, diluted in water or tea. Always start with the lower dose to assess tolerance.

PREPARATION TIP: If the tincture is too strong, it can be diluted with distilled water to reduce the alcohol strength, but this might shorten the shelf life.

Hawthorn (Crataegus spp.)

- **Plant Description**: Hawthorn is a small tree or shrub. It can grow up to 5-15 meters tall.
- **Leaves**: The leaves are typically lobed and toothed, varying somewhat between species. They are often dark green on top with a lighter underside.
- **Habitat**: Commonly found in wooded areas and along riverbanks across North America.
- **Medicinal Properties**: Heart health, blood pressure regulation, cholesterol control, antioxidant properties, digestive health, circulatory benefits.
- **Traditional Uses**: Often used to treat heart-related conditions such as high blood pressure, angina, and congestive heart failure. It is believed to improve heart function and circulation.
- **Precautions:** While generally safe for most adults when used correctly, some individuals might encounter side effects such as nausea, dizziness, and palpitations, especially with high doses.
- **How to Grow**: Thrives in full sun or partial shade. Plant in well-drained soil and water regularly. Hawthorn can be grown from seed but more commonly from cuttings or grafting.

HAWTHORN TINCTURE RECIPE

PREP TIME: 15 MINUTES   **MACERATION TIME:** 4 TO 6 WEEKS   **YIELD:** APPROX 500 ML

INGREDIENTS

- *Hawthorn berries, dried: 100 grams*
- *Vodka (40-50% alcohol by volume): 500 milliliters*

INSTRUCTIONS

1. If using fresh hawthorn berries, ensure they are fully ripe. Wash them thoroughly. If dried berries are used, ensure they are free from any mold or unpleasant smell.
2. Place the hawthorn berries into a sterilized jar.
3. Pour the vodka over the berries, ensuring they are completely submerged. If the berries absorb the vodka and rise above the level, add more vodka until they are covered.
4. Seal the jar tightly with its lid. Label the jar with the date and contents for reference.
5. Store the jar in a cool, dark cupboard. The ideal storage temperature is between 15-18°C (59-64°F).
6. Shake the jar gently every day for the first week to mix the contents and prevent clumping of the berries.
7. Let the mixture macerate for 4 to 6 weeks. This duration allows the alcohol to extract the active compounds from the hawthorn berries effectively.
8. After the maceration period, filter the mixture using a fine mesh strainer or cheesecloth into another clean, sterilized jar. Press or squeeze the berries to extract as much liquid as possible.
9. For a clearer tincture, strain a second time through a coffee filter or finer material.
10. Funnel the strained tincture into smaller, dark-colored glass bottles, preferably with dropper tops for easy use.
11. Label each bottle clearly with the date of finalization, and any other pertinent information.

DOSAGE:

- Typical dosage for an adult is 1-2 milliliters of tincture diluted in water or tea, taken 3 times per day.

Hops (Humulus lupulus)

- **Plant Description**: Hops are climbing plants known for their vigorous growth, climbing other plants or structures with the help of their sturdy stems.
- **Leaves**: Hops leaves are heart-shaped, lobed (typically with three to five lobes), and opposite with a coarse texture.
- **Habitat**: Native to the Northeastern United States, commonly cultivated in other parts for brewing use.
- **Medicinal Properties:** Promotes relaxation, aids in sleep. It also has antibacterial properties.
- **Traditional Uses:** Commonly known for its use in brewing beer, hops is also used for its sedative effects to treat anxiety, insomnia, and restlessness.
- **Preparation Methods:** Teas, tinctures.
- **Precautions:** May interact with sedatives.
- **How to Grow**: Requires a trellis or similar support structure for climbing. Plant in full sun and well-drained soil. It prefers a slightly acidic soil pH.

HOPS TINCTURE RECIPE

PREPARATION TIME: 10 MINUTES

MACERATION TIME: 4 TO 6 WEEKS

YIELD: APPROXIMATELY 500 ML

INGREDIENTS

- *Dried hops flowers: 100 grams*
- *Vodka (40-50% alcohol by volume): 500 milliliters*

INSTRUCTIONS

1. Ensure that the hops flowers are fully dried.
2. Break apart larger clumps to help release the essential oils and increase the surface area for extraction.
3. Place the prepared hops flowers into a sterilized jar.
4. Pour vodka over the flowers, ensuring that they are completely submerged. Top up with more vodka if the flowers absorb it and rise above the liquid level.
5. Tightly seal the jar and label it with the date and contents for reference.
6. Store the jar in a cool, dark cupboard. The temperature should ideally be around 15-18°C (59-64°F).
7. Shake the jar gently once daily for the first week to mix the hops and vodka thoroughly.
8. Allow the mixture to sit for 4 to 6 weeks, which permits adequate time for the alcohol to extract the sedative and other beneficial compounds from the hops.
9. After maceration, filter the tincture using a fine mesh sieve or cheesecloth into another clean, sterilized jar.
10. Funnel the strained tincture into dark-colored glass bottles equipped with droppers for easy administration.
11. Label each bottle clearly with the date of finalization, and any other pertinent information.

DOSAGE:

- A typical adult dosage is 1-2 milliliters, taken 2-3 times daily or as needed for relaxation or sleep support.

Horsetail (Equisetum arvense)

- **Plant Description**: Horsetail is a reed-like herbaceous perennial plant, known for its ability to absorb minerals from the soil. It has a hollow, jointed stem.
- **Leaves**: Technically, horsetail doesn't have true leaves but rather scales fused into a sheath around the stem at each joint.
- **Habitat**: Thrives in wet areas, often found near streams or in marshy fields throughout the Northern Hemisphere.
- **Medicinal Properties:** Supporting hair, skin, and bone health.
- **Traditional Uses:** Used to promote bone and tissue healing due to its high silica content. It is also used as a diuretic and to treat urinary tract infections.
- **Precautions:** Horsetail is not recommended for pregnant women due to potential risks, including stimulating uterine contractions. It's also advisable for breastfeeding mothers to avoid its use due to insufficient safety data.
- **How to Grow**: Prefers moist, sandy soil. It can be invasive, so it's often better to grow in containers to control spreading.

HORSETAIL TINCTURE RECIPE

PREP TIME: 10 MINUTES   **MACERATION TIME:** 4 WEEKS   **YIELD:** APPROXIMATELY 500 ML

INGREDIENTS

- *Dried horsetail herb: 100 grams*
- *Vodka (40-50% alcohol by volume): 500 milliliters*

INSTRUCTIONS

1. Ensure the horsetail herb is completely dried and free from impurities or moisture to prevent mold growth.
2. If using whole stems, chop them into smaller pieces to enhance the extraction process.
3. Place the dried horsetail herb into a sterilized jar.
4. Pour vodka over the herbs, ensuring they are fully submerged. Use additional vodka if necessary, as the herb will absorb some liquid and expand.
5. Securely close the jar with its lid and label it with the preparation date and contents for reference.
6. Store in a dark, cool cupboard away from direct sunlight and heat sources.
7. Shake the jar gently once a day for the first week to distribute the contents evenly.
8. Allow the tincture to sit undisturbed for the remaining three weeks to let the alcohol fully extract the silica and other beneficial compounds from the horsetail.
9. After four weeks, filter the tincture using a fine mesh strainer or cheesecloth into another sterilized glass jar. To ensure purity, you may strain a second time through a coffee filter.
10. Funnel the clear tincture into dark glass bottles with dropper lids for easy dosage.
11. Label each bottle clearly with the date of finalization, and any other pertinent information.

DOSAGE:
- For adults, the dosage is typically 1-2 milliliters, taken three times daily.

Hyssop (Hyssopus officinalis)

- **Plant Description**: Hyssop is a bushy herbaceous plant from the mint family, growing up to 60 cm tall.
- **Leaves**: The leaves are narrow, lanceolate, and slightly glossy with a strong, aromatic smell, similar to other members of the mint family.
- **Habitat**: Grows well in arid regions; often cultivated in herb gardens.
- **Traditional Uses:** Often used for its expectorant properties to relieve respiratory conditions, including coughs and congestion. It also has antiviral properties and is used to boost the immune system.
- **Precautions:** People who are allergic to plants in the Lamiaceae family, which includes mint and lavender, might also be allergic to hyssop. It's important to perform a patch test or start with a low dosage to monitor for allergic reactions.
- **How to Grow**: Plant in full sun and well-drained soil. Hyssop does well in poor soils and is drought-resistant once established. Propagate from seed or cuttings.

HYSSOP TINCTURE RECIPE

PREP TIME: 15 MINUTES   **MACERATION TIME:** 6 WEEKS   **YIELD:** APPROXIMATELY 500 ML

INGREDIENTS

- *Dried hyssop leaves and flowers: 100 grams*
- *Vodka or brandy (40-50% alcohol by volume): 500 milliliters*

INSTRUCTIONS

1. Ensure that the hyssop is completely dried to avoid any mold growth during maceration.
2. Crush the dried leaves and flowers slightly with a mortar and pestle to help release the essential oils and increase the surface area for extraction.
3. Place the crushed hyssop in a sterilized jar.
4. Pour the vodka or brandy over the hyssop, making sure that the herb is completely submerged. Add more alcohol if necessary.
5. Seal the jar tightly with its lid and label it with the date and contents for reference.
6. Store the jar in a cool, dark cupboard away from any direct sunlight or heat sources.
7. Shake the jar daily during the first week to mix the herbs and alcohol well.
8. Let the tincture sit for the remaining five weeks, shaking occasionally.
9. After six weeks, filter the mixture using a fine mesh sieve lined with cheesecloth into another sterilized glass container.
10. Press or squeeze the soaked hyssop to extract as much liquid as possible.
11. Funnel the strained tincture into dark glass bottles, preferably with dropper tops for easy use.
12. Label each bottle clearly with the date of finalization, and any other pertinent information.

DOSAGE:

- The typical dosage for adults is 1-2 milliliters, up to three times daily.

Juniper (Juniperus communis)

- **Plant Description**: Juniper is an evergreen shrub with needle-like leaves and blue-black berries. It grows up to 10 feet tall.
- **Habitat**: Native to Europe, Asia, and North America, Juniper thrives in well-drained, sandy soils and can be found in forests, rocky hills, and grasslands.
- **Medicinal Properties**: Juniper berries have diuretic, antiseptic, and anti-inflammatory properties. They are beneficial for urinary tract infections, digestive issues, and joint pain.
- **Traditional Uses**: Traditionally used by Native Americans for urinary tract health, respiratory infections, and digestive problems. Juniper is also used in purification rituals.
- **Preparation Methods**: Juniper berries can be used to make teas, tinctures, and infusions. They can also be incorporated into culinary dishes for flavor and medicinal benefits.
- **Precautions**: Juniper should be used in moderation due to its potent effects on the kidneys. It is not recommended for pregnant women or individuals with kidney disease.
- **How to Grow**: Prefers full sun and well-drained soil. Tolerates drought, poor soil conditions, and high altitudes. Can be grown from seed but is more commonly propagated from cuttings to ensure the characteristics of the parent plant are retained.

JUNIPER BERRY TINCTURE RECIPE

PREPARATION TIME: 20 MINUTES

MACERATION TIME: 4 TO 6 WEEKS

YIELD: APPROXIMATELY 500 ML

INGREDIENTS

- *Fresh juniper berries: 1 cup (about 100 grams)*
- *Vodka or grain alcohol (60% alcohol by volume): 500 milliliters*

INSTRUCTIONS

1. Select ripe, blue juniper berries that are firm to the touch. Ensure they are harvested from species known to be safe for culinary and medicinal purposes, primarily Juniperus communis.
2. Wash the berries gently under cold water. Pat them dry with a clean towel.
3. Place the juniper berries in your sterilized jar and lightly crush them with the back of a spoon or a muddler to release their oils.
4. Pour the vodka or alcohol over the berries, ensuring they are completely submerged. If necessary, add a bit more alcohol to cover them.
5. Seal the jar tightly with its lid and label it with the date and contents for reference.
6. Store the jar in a cool, dark cupboard away from direct sunlight and heat sources.
7. Shake the jar daily for the first week to mix the berries with the alcohol.
8. Allow the mixture to sit for the remaining weeks, shaking it once or twice a week.
9. After 4 to 6 weeks, filter the tincture using a fine mesh sieve or cheesecloth into another sterilized glass container. Press the berries to extract as much liquid as possible.
10. Funnel the strained tincture into dark glass bottles, preferably with dropper tops for easy dosage.
11. Label each bottle clearly with the date of finalization, and any other pertinent information.

DOSAGE: Typical adult dosage is 1-2 milliliters, taken 2-3 times daily.

Lavender (Lavandula spp.)

- **Plant Description**: Lavender is a small aromatic evergreen shrub of the mint family, known for its erect, flowering stalks. It typically grows to a height of 40 to 60 cm.
- **Leaves**: The leaves are narrow, long, and silvery-green, often covered with fine hairs. They are usually about 2 to 6 cm in length, with a somewhat lance-shaped appearance.
- **Habitat**: Thrives in full sun and well-drained soil, commonly found in home gardens and commercial lavender farms, particularly in regions with similar climates to the Mediterranean.
- **Medicinal Properties:** Lavender can help alleviate anxiety, insomnia, and stress for its calming and sedative effects. Lavender is also used topically for its antiseptic and anti-inflammatory properties.
- **Traditional Uses:** Widely used for anxiety relief, stress reduction, and sleep aid. Lavender is also applied topically for skin irritation and minor burns.
- **Precautions:** Some people may experience allergic reactions to lavender, especially those who are sensitive to plants in the Lamiaceae family (such as mint). Symptoms could include skin irritation, headache, or nausea. Always conduct a patch test before using lavender topically.
- **How to Grow**: Plant in loose, gravelly soil that is slightly alkaline. Lavender needs full sun and good air circulation. It is drought-resistant once established, making it suitable for xeriscaping. Hardy in USDA zones 5 through 9.

LAVENDER TINCTURE RECIPE

PREP TIME: 15 MINUTES   **MACERATION TIME:** 4 WEEKS   **YIELD:** APPROXIMATELY 500 ML

INGREDIENTS

- *Fresh lavender flowers: 1 cup (about 15 grams)*
- *High-proof vodka or ethanol (at least 40% alcohol by volume): 500 milliliters*

INSTRUCTIONS

1. Harvest lavender flowers when they are fully bloomed, preferably in the morning after the dew has evaporated.
2. Gently rinse the lavender flowers to remove any dust or insects, and pat them dry with a clean cloth.
3. Place the dried lavender flowers in a sterilized jar.
4. Pour the vodka or ethanol over the flowers, ensuring they are completely submerged. Add a bit more alcohol if necessary to cover them completely.
5. Seal the jar tightly with its lid and label it with the date and ingredients used.
6. Store the jar in a dark, cool cupboard away from direct sunlight and heat.
7. Shake the jar gently every day for the first week to ensure the flowers are well soaked.
8. Let the mixture sit for the remaining three weeks, shaking occasionally.
9. After four weeks, filter the tincture using a fine mesh sieve or cheesecloth into a clean glass bottle. Squeeze or press the flowers to extract as much liquid as possible.
10. Funnel the strained liquid into amber or dark-colored glass bottles. If possible, use bottles with droppers for easy dosage.

USAGE: Typical dosage is 1-2 milliliters of tincture, taken 2-3 times daily, or as needed.

Lemon Balm (Melissa officinalis)

- **Plant Description**: Lemon balm is a perennial herb from the mint family. It grows to a height of about 70 to 150 cm and spreads vegetatively as well as by seed.
- **Leaves**: The leaves are broadly ovate, toothed, and heart-shaped at the base, with a rough texture and a pronounced lemon scent when bruised.
- **Habitat**: Adaptable to many parts of the U.S., particularly thriving in temperate climates.
- **Medicinal Properties:** Eases stress and anxiety, helps with sleep disorders, and enhances mood.
- **Traditional Uses:** Has been used since the Middle Ages in Europe to reduce stress and anxiety, promote sleep, and improve appetite.
- **Preparation Methods:** Commonly prepared as tea, tinctures, or added to foods as a flavor enhancer.
- **Precautions:** Possible sedative effects if taken in large amounts; may interact with thyroid medications.
- **How to Grow**: Prefers well-drained clay or sandy loam and a sunny to partially shaded location. Lemon balm needs regular watering but can tolerate drought once established. It can spread vigorously, so some gardeners prefer to contain it in pots. Hardy in USDA zones 4 to 9.

LEMON BALM TINCTURE RECIPE

PREPARATION TIME: 20 MINUTES

MACERATION TIME: 4 TO 6 WEEKS

YIELD: YIELDS APPROXIMATELY 500 ML

INGREDIENTS

- Fresh lemon balm leaves: 1 cup (approximately 25 grams)
- Vodka or pure grain alcohol (60-70% alcohol by volume): 500 milliliters

INSTRUCTIONS

1. Choose fresh, vibrant lemon balm leaves, ideally harvested in the morning after the dew has evaporated and before the sun is at its peak.
2. Rinse the lemon balm leaves under cool water.
3. Pat the leaves dry gently with a clean towel or let them air dry on a clean surface for a few hours to reduce moisture (excess water can dilute the alcohol, which may affect preservation).
4. Roughly chop the lemon balm leaves to release their oils and place them into the sterilized glass jar.
5. Pour the vodka or alcohol over the leaves until they are completely submerged, leaving about an inch of space at the top of the jar.
6. Seal the jar tightly with the sterilized lid.
7. Store the jar in a cool, dark cupboard away from direct sunlight or heat.
8. Shake the jar gently every day for the first week to mix the lemon balm with the alcohol.
9. Let the tincture sit for a total of 4 to 6 weeks, shaking it occasionally to ensure maximum extraction.
10. After the maceration period, filter the tincture using a fine mesh sieve or cheesecloth into a clean bottle. Compress the plant material to extract as much liquid as possible.
11. Funnel the strained tincture into amber glass bottles, ideally with dropper tops for easy use. Label the bottles clearly with the date of finalization, and any other pertinent information.

USAGE: Typical use is 1-2 milliliters of tincture, taken up to 3 times daily.

Licorice Root (Glycyrrhiza glabra)

- **Plant Description**: Licorice, a leguminous plant native to Western Asia and Southern Europe, is a perennial that grows up to about 1 meter in height, with extensive root systems.
- **Leaves**: The leaves are compound, consisting of 4 to 7 pairs of leaflets plus an extra terminal leaflet. Each leaflet is oblong, ranging from 2 to 5 cm long.
- **Habitat**: Grows in certain regions, particularly where soils are deep and sandy.
- **Medicinal Properties:** Soothes gastrointestinal problems and can heal stomach ulcers. It is also used for heartburn, acid reflux, and gastritis.
- **Traditional Uses:** Widely used in traditional Chinese medicine and other herbal traditions for its protective effects on the stomach lining.
- **Precautions:** Excessive consumption can lead to high blood pressure, lower potassium levels, and may affect hormone levels. Not recommended for pregnant women and those with heart disease or hypertension.
- **How to Grow**: Requires well-drained soils in full sun, licorice root prefers loamy or sandy textures. Keep soil moist and fertile. It may require a long growing season, so starting indoors or in a greenhouse might be necessary in cooler climates. Hardy in USDA zones 7 to 10.

LICORICE ROOT TINCTURE RECIPE

PREP TIME: 15 MINUTES   **MACERATION TIME:** 4 WEEKS   **YIELD:** APPROXIMATELY 500 ML

INGREDIENTS

- *Dried licorice root: 100 grams (roughly 3.5 ounces)*
- *Vodka or grain alcohol (70-80% alcohol by volume): 500 milliliters*

INSTRUCTIONS

1. Cut or grind the dried licorice root into small pieces to help release the essential oils and increase the surface area, enhancing the extraction process. Ensure the pieces are uniform to ensure consistent maceration.
2. Place the cut licorice root into a sterilized glass jar.
3. Pour the alcohol over the root until it is fully submerged, leaving about an inch of space at the top.
4. Tightly seal the jar with the sterilized lid.
5. Store in a cool, dark cupboard away from direct sunlight to avoid degradation of the active compounds.
6. Allow the tincture to macerate for a minimum of 4 weeks, shaking the jar gently every few days to mix the contents and promote extraction.
7. After maceration, filter the tincture using a fine mesh sieve lined with cheesecloth into a clean bottle. Press the roots to extract as much liquid as possible.
8. Funnel the strained tincture into amber glass bottles with dropper tops for easy dispensing.
9. Label each bottle with the preparation date and ingredients for reference.

USAGE:

- The typical dosage is 1-2 milliliters, taken 2-3 times daily.

SHOPPING TIP:

- When buying licorice root, ensure it is specifically labeled for medicinal use and not just culinary purposes to guarantee therapeutic potency.

Linden (Tilia spp.)

- **Plant Description**: Linden trees, also known as basswood or lime trees, are deciduous trees that can grow up to 30 meters tall.
- **Leaves**: The heart-shaped, asymmetrical leaves are large, measuring 6 to 20 cm in diameter. They have serrated edges and are soft and downy when young.
- **Habitat**: Common as an ornamental and shade tree in urban areas across many U.S. regions.
- **Medicinal Properties:** Linden is traditionally used for its calming effects, to help reduce anxiety, and to promote a healthy sleep cycle.
- **Traditional Uses:** Linden helps with relaxation, reducing anxiety, and relieving tension headaches. It also has anti-inflammatory properties.
- **Precautions:** Individuals who have allergies to other plants in the Tiliaceae family may also be allergic to linden.
- **How to Grow**: Plant linden trees in full sun to partial shade in moist, well-drained soils. They are adaptable to a variety of soil conditions but prefer slightly acidic to neutral pH. Linden trees can grow large, so they need space to expand. Hardy in USDA zones 3 to 8.

LINDEN TINCTURE RECIPE

PREP TIME: 20 MINUTES   **MACERATION TIME:** 6 WEEKS   **YIELD:** APPROXIMATELY 500 ML

INGREDIENTS

- *Dried linden flowers: 100 grams (about 3.5 ounces)*
- *High-proof vodka or grain alcohol (70-80% alcohol by volume): 500 milliliters*

INSTRUCTIONS

1. Lightly crush the dried flowers between your fingers to slightly break them up, which helps release the active compounds during maceration.
2. Place the prepared linden flowers in a sterilized glass jar.
3. Pour the alcohol over the flowers until they are completely submerged. Leave about 2 cm (about 1 inch) of space at the top of the jar.
4. Tightly seal the jar with the sterilized lid.
5. Store the jar in a cool, dark cupboard.
6. Allow the tincture to macerate for 6 weeks, shaking the jar gently every few days to ensure that all parts of the flowers are exposed to the alcohol.
7. After 6 weeks, filter the tincture using a fine mesh sieve or cheesecloth into a clean bowl. Press on the solids to extract as much liquid as possible.
8. Funnel the strained tincture into amber glass bottles with dropper tops for easy dosage.
9. Clearly label each bottle with the herb, alcohol used, date of preparation, and expected expiration date (typically 3-5 years from preparation if stored properly).
10. Keep the tincture in a cool, dark location, away from direct sunlight.

USAGE: Standard dosage is 1-2 milliliters of tincture, taken up to 3 times a day.

Lobelia (Lobelia inflata)

- **Plant Description**: Lobelia is a small annual or biennial herb that grows about 15 to 100 cm tall. It features pale violet-pink flowers, with the plant often appearing slightly bushy.
- **Leaves**: The leaves are alternate, oval or lance-shaped, often irregularly toothed, and about 2.5 to 8 cm long. They are light green and sometimes hairy.
- **Habitat**: Native to Eastern North America, found in fields, gardens, and along roadsides.
- **Traditional Uses:** Traditionally used as a treatment for respiratory problems and as a muscle relaxant.
- **Precautions:** Caution is advised due to its potent effects and potential toxicity in high doses.
- **How to Grow**: Prefers moist, rich soil in partial shade. Lobelia seeds are tiny and require light to germinate, so they should not be covered with soil when planted. Water them regularly to keep the soil consistently moist. Tolerates USDA zones 3 to 9.

LOBELIA TINCTURE RECIPE

PREP TIME: 15 MINUTES   **MACERATION TIME:** 4-6 WEEKS   **YIELD:** APPROXIMATELY 500 ML (17 FL OZ)

INGREDIENTS

- *Dried lobelia herb: 100 grams (3.5 oz)*
- *Vodka or grain alcohol (50-60% alcohol by volume): 500 milliliters (17 fl oz)*

INSTRUCTIONS

1. Lightly crush the dried lobelia in a mortar and pestle or a similar tool to increase surface area, which will aid in the extraction process.
2. Place the crushed lobelia into a sterilized jar.
3. Pour the vodka or alcohol over the herbs, making sure the herbs are completely submerged. Leave about 2 cm (0.8 inch) of space at the top of the jar.
4. Seal the jar tightly with the sterilized lid.
5. Store the jar in a cool, dark cupboard or cellar to macerate. Light and heat can degrade the tincture.
6. Let the mixture sit for 4-6 weeks. Shake the jar every few days to mix the herbs and aid in the extraction process.
7. After the maceration period, filter the tincture using a fine mesh strainer or cheesecloth into another clean container.
8. Squeeze or press the herb pulp to extract as much liquid as possible.
9. Funnel the strained tincture into amber glass bottles equipped with droppers for easy use.
10. Label each bottle with the herb name, date of bottling, and expiration date (usually 4-5 years from the date of preparation).

USAGE:

- Typical use of lobelia tincture is 0.5-1 ml taken 2-3 times daily. Due to its potent nature, it is important to start with the lower end of the dosage range.

PREPARATION TIP:

- Due to lobelia's potent nature and potential toxicity in high doses, it is crucial to adhere to recommended dosages and consult with a healthcare professional before use.

Marshmallow (Althaea officinalis)

- **Plant Description**: Marshmallow is a perennial herb that is part of the mallow family. It typically grows to about 1.2 meters in height and has a soft, hairy stem.
- **Leaves**: The leaves are velvety due to a thick coating of hair. They are rounded, with irregular toothed edges, often 3 to 5 cm long.
- **Habitat**: Thrives in damp environments such as marshes and other wetlands across the United States.
- **Traditional Uses:** Traditionally used for its soothing properties on the digestive and respiratory tracts. The root and leaves are used to make teas and syrups to help with sore throats, coughs, and digestive issues.
- **Precautions:** Marshmallow root is generally safe, but it's best to confirm there are no contraindications with other conditions or medications, like chronic health issues or are pregnant or breastfeeding.
- **How to Grow**: Plant marshmallow in full sun to partial shade in rich, well-draining soil that retains moisture. It prefers a slightly acidic to neutral pH. Marshmallow needs regular watering to thrive, especially in dry conditions. Start seeds indoors before the last frost or sow directly in the ground in spring. Hardy in USDA zones 3-9.

MARSHMALLOW ROOT TINCTURE RECIPE

PREP TIME: 20 MINUTES   **MACERATION TIME:** 4-6 WEEKS   **YIELD:** APPROX 500 ML (ABOUT 17 FL OZ)

INGREDIENTS

- *Dried marshmallow root: 100 grams (3.5 oz)*
- *Vodka or grain alcohol (40-50% alcohol by volume): 500 milliliters (17 fl oz)*

INSTRUCTIONS

1. Gently chop the dried marshmallow root into small pieces with a sharp knife. This increases the surface area, enhancing the alcohol's ability to extract the active compounds.
2. Place the chopped marshmallow root into your sterilized jar.
3. Pour the alcohol over the root, ensuring it is completely submerged. Leave about an inch of space at the top of the jar.
4. Seal the jar tightly with its lid and store it in a cool, dark cupboard.
5. Allow the jar to sit for 4 to 6 weeks. Shake the jar lightly every couple of days to mix the roots with the alcohol and promote extraction.
6. After the maceration period, filter the liquid using a cheesecloth or fine mesh strainer into a clean bowl. Press or squeeze the root material to extract as much liquid as possible.
7. Funnel the strained tincture into amber bottles. If possible, use bottles with droppers for easy dosage.
8. Label each bottle clearly with the date of production, and expiry date (generally 3-5 years from preparation).

USAGE:
- Marshmallow root tincture can be taken orally. The usual dosage is 1-2 ml, up to three times daily.

SHOPPING TIP:
- When purchasing marshmallow root, ensure it's labeled as "Althaea officinalis," which is the botanical name, to avoid confusion with other similar herbs.

Milk Thistle (Silybum marianum)

- **Plant Description**: Milk thistle is either a biennial or a short-lived perennial that can reach heights of up to 2 meters. It has a stout, grooved, and branching stem.
- **Leaves**: The leaves are wide, glossy green with white veins, spiny-edged, and can be up to 50 cm long and 30 cm wide.
- **Habitat**: Commonly found in dry, rocky soils and can establish itself in waste areas. It is especially prevalent in California and other parts of the western U.S.
- **Medicinal Properties:** Known for its beneficial effects on liver health.
- **Traditional Uses:** It is often used to treat liver conditions such as hepatitis and cirrhosis, as well as to protect the liver from toxins and the effects of alcohol.
- **Precautions:** Milk thistle may interact with certain pharmaceuticals, especially those metabolized by the liver.
- **How to Grow**: Milk thistle prefers full sun and well-drained soil. It is drought-resistant and grows best in warm climates. Sow seeds in the spring in sandy or loamy soil. It can become invasive, so control is advised. Hardy in USDA zones 7-10.

MILK THISTLE TINCTURE RECIPE

PREP TIME: 20 MINUTES   **MACERATION TIME:** 6 WEEKS   **YIELD:** APPROX 500 ML (ABOUT 17 FL OZ)

INGREDIENTS

- Milk thistle seeds: 100 grams (3.5 oz)
- High-proof vodka or grain alcohol (40-50% alcohol by volume): 500 milliliters (17 fl oz)

INSTRUCTIONS

1. Using a mortar and pestle or a spice grinder, lightly crush the milk thistle seeds. This cracking open of the seeds aids in releasing the silymarin, the active compound, making it more available for extraction.
2. Place the crushed milk thistle seeds into your sterilized jar.
3. Pour the alcohol over the seeds, ensuring they are fully submerged. Leave about one inch of space at the top of the jar.
4. Seal the jar tightly with its lid and store it in a cool, dark cupboard or a cellar, to avoid light degradation.
5. Allow the jar to sit for 6 weeks. Shake the jar gently every few days to mix the seeds with the alcohol and promote the extraction of silymarin.
6. After 6 weeks, filter the tincture using a cheesecloth or a fine mesh strainer into another clean container. Press or squeeze the seed residue to extract as much liquid as possible.
7. Funnel the strained tincture into amber-colored bottles, which help protect the tincture from light. If possible, use bottles with droppers for easy dosage.
8. Label each bottle clearly with the date of finalization, and any other pertinent information.

USAGE:

- The standard dosage is 1-3 ml, taken 1-3 times daily.

Motherwort (Leonurus cardiaca)

- **Plant Description**: Motherwort is a perennial herb in the mint family, growing typically to about 60 to 90 cm tall. It has a square stem typical of the Lamiaceae family.
- **Leaves**: The leaves are deeply lobed, with the upper leaves being smaller and smoother than the lower leaves. They are rough and hairy.
- **Habitat**: Found in U.S. zones, particularly in disturbed areas like roadside ditches and vacant lots.
- **Medicinal Properties:** Motherwort is often used for its calming effects, especially to ease heart palpitations and reduce anxiety.
- **Traditional Uses:** Used primarily for heart conditions and as a tonic to improve heart function. It is also employed to ease stress and reduce symptoms of menopause and menstrual pain.
- **Precautions:** Always consult with a healthcare professional before starting any new herbal treatment, particularly if you are pregnant, nursing, or on medication, as motherwort can stimulate the uterus and affect other medications.
- **How to Grow**: Motherwort thrives in full sun to partial shade and tolerates a wide range of soil conditions but prefers moist, well-drained soil. Sow seeds directly outdoors in late fall or early spring. It can spread aggressively, so containment might be necessary. Hardy in USDA zones 4-8.

MOTHERWORT TINCTURE RECIPE

PREP TIME: 15 MINUTES   **MACERATION TIME:** 4-6 WEEKS   **YIELD:** 500 ML (17 FL OZ)

INGREDIENTS

- *Fresh motherwort herb: 150 grams (5.3 oz) or dried motherwort: 75 grams (2.6 oz)*
- *High-proof vodka or grain alcohol (at least 40% alcohol by volume): 500 milliliters (17 fl oz)*

INSTRUCTIONS

1. If using fresh motherwort, rinse the herb under cool water. Pat dry with paper towels. Chop the herb coarsely to increase the surface area for better extraction. If using dried motherwort, ensure the pieces are broken down adequately but not powdered.
2. Place the prepared motherwort herb into your sterilized jar.
3. Pour the alcohol over the herb until completely submerged. Ensure there is at least a couple of inches of alcohol above the level of the herbs to account for any absorption and swelling.
4. Tightly seal the jar with its lid and label it with the date and contents for reference.
5. Store the jar in a dark, cool cupboard.
6. Let the jar sit for 4 to 6 weeks, shaking it gently every few days to mix the herbs and the alcohol, which aids in the extraction process.
7. After the maceration period, filter the tincture using a cheesecloth or a fine mesh strainer into a clean bowl or container. Squeeze or press the herb pulp to extract as much liquid as possible.
8. Funnel the strained tincture into amber glass bottles equipped with dropper tops. Amber glass helps to block light, preserving the quality and effectiveness of the tincture.
9. Label each bottle clearly with the date of finalization, and any other pertinent information.
10. Store the bottles in a cool, dark location to maintain their potency.

USAGE: Typical dosage is 1-3 ml of the tincture taken 2-3 times daily.

SHOPPING TIP: When purchasing motherwort, always verify its botanical name (Leonurus cardiaca) to ensure you're getting the correct herb.

Mullein (Verbascum thapsus)

- **Plant Description**: Mullein is a biennial plant that can grow up to 2 meters tall, featuring a single, unbranched stem in its second year.
- **Leaves**: The leaves are large, up to 50 cm long, densely woolly, and oblong-spatulate. They are arranged in a basal rosette the first year and become alternately spaced up the stem in the second year.
- **Habitat**: Grows well in fields, pastures, and along roadsides, thriving in sandy or rocky soils with good sun exposure.
- **Medicinal Properties:** Soothes the bronchial tubes and reduces inflammation in the respiratory tract.
- **Traditional Uses:** Historically used to treat asthma, coughs, tuberculosis, and bronchial congestion.
- **Precautions:** Ensure tea is well-strained to avoid throat irritation. Consultation is recommended for pregnant and breastfeeding women.
- **How to Grow**: Mullein prefers full sun and sandy, well-drained soil. It is drought-tolerant and thrives in poor soil conditions. Sow seeds directly in the garden in late spring or start them indoors and transplant after the last frost. Hardy in USDA zones 4-9.

MULLEIN TINCTURE RECIPE

PREP TIME: 20 MINUTES   **MACERATION TIME:** 4-6 WEEKS   **YIELD:** APPROXIMATELY 500 ML (ABOUT 17 FL OZ)

INGREDIENTS

- *Fresh mullein leaves and flowers: 100 grams (3.5 oz) or dried mullein: 50 grams (1.7 oz)*
- *High-proof vodka or grain alcohol (at least 40% alcohol by volume): 500 milliliters (17 fl oz)*

INSTRUCTIONS

1. If using fresh mullein, gently wash the leaves and flowers to remove any dust or insects. Pat them dry with a clean towel. Chop the leaves and flowers coarsely to maximize surface area for better extraction. If using dried mullein, ensure it is crumbled into small, manageable pieces but not powdered.
2. Place the prepared mullein into your sterilized glass jar.
3. Pour the alcohol over the mullein until it is completely submerged. Ensure there's at least 2-3 inches of alcohol above the herb level.
4. Securely close the jar with its lid and label it with the date and herb type.
5. Store the jar in a cabinet or another cool, dark location to avoid light degradation.
6. Allow the jar to sit for 4 to 6 weeks. Shake the jar every few days to mix the contents and promote extraction.
7. After the maceration period, filter the tincture using cheesecloth or a fine mesh strainer into another clean container. Press the plant material to extract as much liquid as possible.
8. Funnel the strained tincture into dark amber glass bottles. If using dropper bottles, ensure they are clean and sterilized.
9. Label each bottle clearly with the date of finalization, and any other pertinent information.
10. Store in a cool, dark location such as a medicine cabinet.

USAGE: The typical dosage is 1-3 ml, up to three times per day.

Oregano (Origanum vulgare)

- **Plant Description**: Oregano, a perennial herb, is characterized by its purple blooms and spade-shaped, olive-green leaves. This herb is indigenous to the temperate zones of Western and Southwestern Eurasia as well as the Mediterranean area.
- **Leaves**: The leaves are slightly hairy, highly aromatic, and have a warm, slightly bitter taste. They typically measure 1 to 4 cm in length.
- **Habitat**: Oregano is commonly grown in home gardens throughout the U.S. It thrives in regions with warm, dry summers.
- **Medicinal Properties:** Strong antibacterial and antifungal effects, attributed primarily to its component carvacrol.
- **Traditional Uses:** Commonly used for its antibacterial and antioxidant properties. Oregano oil is often used to treat respiratory tract disorders, gastrointestinal (GI) disorders, menstrual cramps, and urinary tract infections.
- **Precautions:** Oregano oil may cause irritation to the skin and mucous membranes if not adequately diluted. Should be used cautiously in individuals with allergies to Lamiaceae family plants (mint, lavender, etc.).
- **How to Grow**: Oregano is a hardy perennial that prefers full sun and well-drained soil. It can be grown from seed, cuttings, or transplants. Oregano is drought-tolerant once established and does well in containers or in-ground gardens.

OREGANO TINCTURE RECIPE

PREP TIME: 15 MINUTES   **MACERATION TIME:** 4 WEEKS   **YIELD:** 300 ML (10 FL OZ)

INGREDIENTS

- *Fresh oregano leaves: 60 grams (2.1 oz) or dried oregano: 30 grams (1 oz)*
- *High-proof vodka or grain alcohol (at least 40% alcohol by volume): 300 milliliters (10 fl oz)*

INSTRUCTIONS

1. Rinse fresh oregano under cool water. Pat dry with a clean cloth. Roughly chop the leaves to help release the essential oils and increase the surface area for extraction. If using dried oregano, ensure the leaves are crumbled but not powdered. Place the prepared oregano into a sterilized glass jar.
2. Pour the alcohol over the oregano, ensuring the herb is completely submerged with a few inches of alcohol on top.
3. Seal the jar tightly with its lid and label it with the herb name, date, and alcohol used.
4. Store the jar in a dark, cool cupboard away from direct sunlight.
5. Let the mixture sit for 4 weeks, shaking the jar every few days to promote the extraction process.
6. After maceration, filter the mixture using a fine mesh sieve or cheesecloth into another sterilized jar. Press or squeeze the herb to extract as much liquid as possible.
7. Funnel the strained liquid into amber glass bottles. If possible, use bottles with droppers for easy dosage. Ensure the bottles are sterilized beforehand.
8. Label the bottles clearly with the date of finalization, and any other pertinent information.
9. Store the bottles in a cool, dark location to maintain potency.

USAGE: Typically, the dosage is 1-2 ml, taken 2-3 times daily.

Passionflower (Passiflora incarnata)

- **Plant Description**: Passionflower is a climbing vine with intricate, showy flowers that are usually purple, blue, or white, and deeply lobed leaves.
- **Habitat**: Native to the southeastern United States, Passionflower grows in fields, woodlands, and along fences and other structures.
- **Medicinal Properties**: Passionflower has sedative, anxiolytic, and antispasmodic properties. It is used to alleviate anxiety, insomnia, and mild pain.
- **Traditional Uses**: Traditionally used by Native Americans to treat wounds and boils. It later became popular in Europe for its calming effects.
- **Preparation Methods**: Passionflower can be used to make tea by steeping dried leaves and flowers in hot water. It is also available as tinctures, capsules, and extracts.
- **Precautions**: Passionflower is generally safe but may induce sleepiness and lightheadedness. It is not recommended for pregnant or breastfeeding women without medical advice and should not be combined with sedative medications.
- **How to Grow:** Plant passionflower in a sunny to partially shaded location with well-draining soil. It prefers a trellis or support to climb on. Water regularly but do not overwater. Passionflower is hardy and relatively easy to care for, but may require winter protection in cooler climates.

PASSIONFLOWER TINCTURE RECIPE

PREP TIME: 20 MINUTES   **MACERATION TIME:** 4 WEEKS   **YIELD:** APPROXIMATELY 300 ML (ABOUT 10 FL OZ)

INGREDIENTS

- *Fresh passionflower aerial parts (leaves, stems, flowers): 60 grams (2.1 oz) or dried passionflower: 30 grams (1 oz)*
- *High-proof vodka or grain alcohol (at least 40% alcohol by volume): 300 milliliters (10 fl oz)*

INSTRUCTIONS

1. Wash fresh passionflower gently under cold water. Pat dry thoroughly with a clean towel. Coarsely chop to increase surface area for better extraction. If using dried passionflower, ensure it is loosely broken up rather than finely powdered.
2. Place the prepared passionflower into a sterilized jar.
3. Pour the alcohol over the herb, ensuring all parts are submerged. Leave about an inch of alcohol above the herbs to allow for expansion.
4. Seal the jar tightly with its lid and label it with the date and any other pertinent information.
5. Store the jar in a dark, cool cupboard away from sunlight, to macerate.
6. Let the jar sit for 4 weeks. Shake the jar every few days to mix the contents and promote extraction.
7. After maceration, filter the liquid using a fine mesh strainer or cheesecloth into another sterilized jar. Press the herbs to extract as much liquid as possible.
8. Funnel the filtered tincture into dark, amber bottles to protect from light, ensuring the bottles are also sterilized. If possible, use bottles with droppers for easy dosage.
9. Clearly label the dropper bottles with the date of finalization, and any other pertinent information.
10. Store the tincture in a cool, dark location to preserve its medicinal qualities.

USAGE: Typical dosage is 1-2 ml up to three times a day.

Peppermint (Mentha piperita)

- **Plant Description**: Peppermint is a hybrid mint variety, resulting from a cross between watermint and spearmint. It spreads rapidly by underground rhizomes and can be invasive.
- **Leaves**: The leaves are dark green with reddish veins, and they are broad, lance-shaped, and sharply serrated. They are also highly aromatic.
- **Habitat:** Widely cultivated across the U.S., adaptable to various climates.
- **Medicinal Properties:** Contains menthol, a natural decongestant, and has antiviral and antibacterial properties.
- **Traditional Uses:** Relieves symptoms of the common cold and flu, such as nasal congestion, sinusitis, and throat irritations.
- **Precautions:** Avoid applying oil near the face of infants or young children. Those with GERD should avoid peppermint as it may worsen symptoms.
- **How to Grow:** Peppermint prefers moist, rich soils in partial shade. It can be invasive, so it's often grown in containers to control spreading. Plant in the spring and water consistently. Peppermint can also be propagated from cuttings.

PEPPERMINT TINCTURE RECIPE

PREP TIME: 10 MINUTES   **MACERATION TIME:** 4 WEEKS   **YIELD:** APPROX 500 ML

INGREDIENTS

- Fresh Peppermint Leaves: 1 cup (packed)
- High-proof alcohol (vodka or grain alcohol, at least 40% alcohol by volume): Approximately 500 ml

TOOLS

- A clean, dry glass jar with a tight-fitting lid
- Cheesecloth or fine mesh strainer
- Amber glass bottle for storage

INSTRUCTIONS

1. Wash the peppermint leaves. Pat them dry with a clean cloth to remove excess moisture.
2. Roughly chop the cleaned peppermint leaves to increase the surface area, which will enhance the extraction process. Place the chopped leaves into the glass jar.
3. Pour the alcohol over the peppermint leaves, ensuring they are completely submerged. The ideal herb to alcohol ratio is about 1:5 by weight.
4. Seal the jar tightly to prevent evaporation and contamination.
5. Store the jar in a cool, dark cupboard for about 4 weeks. This duration allows the alcohol to extract the essential oils, flavors, and medicinal compounds from the peppermint.
6. Shake the jar every few days to mix the contents and promote extraction.
7. After 4 weeks, filter the tincture using a cheesecloth or fine mesh strainer into a clean bowl. Squeeze or press the plant material to extract as much liquid as possible.
8. Funnel the strained liquid into an amber glass bottle to protect it from light.
9. Label the bottle clearly with the date of finalization, and any other pertinent information.

USAGE: Adults can take 1-2 milliliters of the tincture up to three times a day, mixed into a glass of water or tea. Start with a lower dose to gauge sensitivity.

Rosemary (Rosmarinus officinalis)

- **Plant Description**: Rosemary is a perennial, woody herb known for its aromatic, evergreen leaves that resemble needles. It is native to the Mediterranean region.
- **Leaves**: Rosemary leaves are long, narrow, and needle-like. They are dark green on the top and pale beneath, often with a leathery texture.
- **Habitat:** Commonly cultivated in gardens throughout the U.S., not native but adapts well to various climates.
- **Medicinal Properties:** Antibacterial and antioxidant properties.
- **Traditional Uses:** Often used for improving memory, aiding digestion, and enhancing hair growth.
- **Precautions:** In some people, rosemary can cause stomach upset, especially when taken in large amounts. Start with small doses to assess tolerance.
- **How to Grow:** Prefers full sun and well-drained, sandy soil. It is drought-resistant once established and can be grown from cuttings or seeds.

ROSEMARY COGNITIVE BOOST TINCTURE

PREP TIME: 10 MINUTES   **MACERATION TIME:** 4-6 WEEKS   **YIELD:** APPROX 30 SERVINGS

INGREDIENTS

- *Fresh rosemary leaves, 50g (finely chopped)*
- *Vodka (40% alcohol by volume), 500 ml*

INSTRUCTIONS

1. Place the finely chopped rosemary leaves in a clean glass jar.
2. Cover the leaves with vodka, ensuring they are completely submerged.
3. Seal the jar and place it in a cool, dark location for 4-6 weeks, shaking it occasionally.
4. Filter the liquid using a cheesecloth into a clean bottle.
5. Label the tincture with the date and details.

TIPS:

- Rosemary is great for enhancing memory and concentration.
- Use 1-2 ml of the tincture in the morning or before any activity that requires mental clarity.

Sage (Salvia officinalis)

- **Plant Description**: Sage is a perennial, evergreen subshrub, with woody stems and blue to purplish flowers.
- **Leaves**: The leaves are oblong, ranging from gray to green in color, often covered with fine, soft hairs. They are aromatic, with a textured surface.
- **Habitat:** Commonly cultivated in gardens across the U.S., particularly in temperate regions.
- **Traditional Uses:** Commonly used for digestive problems, including loss of appetite, gas, and stomach pain. It's also applied for throat infections, dental abscesses, and mouth ulcers.
- **Precautions:** Sage contains thujone, a compound that can stimulate menstrual flow, so it is advised that pregnant women avoid high doses of sage, especially in medicinal forms, to prevent the risk of miscarriage. While culinary amounts are generally safe, medicinal quantities should be avoided during breastfeeding as well, as it may reduce milk supply.
- **How to Grow:** Sage thrives in well-drained, sandy soil and full sun. Plant seeds or cuttings in the spring after the risk of frost has passed. It requires little water once established and is drought-tolerant.

SAGE TINCTURE RECIPE

PREP TIME: 15 MINUTES　　　　**MACERATION TIME:** 4 WEEKS　　　　**YIELD:** ABOUT 500 MILLILITERS

INGREDIENTS

- *Fresh Sage Leaves: 1 cup (packed)*
- *High-proof alcohol (at least 40% ABV, such as vodka or grain alcohol): Approximately 500 ml*

TOOLS

- *A clean, dry glass jar with a tight-fitting lid*
- *Cheesecloth or fine mesh strainer*
- *Amber glass dropper bottles for storage*

INSTRUCTIONS

1. Thoroughly rinse the sage leaves under cool water. Pat the leaves dry with a towel to remove excess moisture. Coarsely chop or bruise the sage leaves to release their essential oils.
2. Place the prepared leaves into your glass jar.
3. Pour enough alcohol over the sage leaves to completely submerge them. A good rule of thumb is to maintain a herb-to-alcohol ratio of about 1:5 by weight.
4. Secure the lid on the jar to prevent evaporation. Store the sealed jar in a cool, dark cupboard for 4 weeks to allow the alcohol to extract the active compounds from the sage.
5. Shake the jar lightly every few days to aid the extraction process.
6. After the maceration period, filter the tincture using cheesecloth or a fine mesh strainer into a clean bowl. Press the plant material to extract maximum liquid. Discard the plant remnants.
7. Funnel the strained tincture into amber glass bottles for storage. If possible, use bottles with droppers for easy dosage.
8. Label each bottle clearly with the date of finalization, and any other pertinent information.

USAGE: For adults, administer 1-2 milliliters of the tincture up to three times daily. Always start with a lower dose to assess tolerance.

Sarsaparilla (Smilax ornata)

- **Plant Description**: Sarsaparilla is a climbing vine with woody stems, heart-shaped leaves, and small, white flowers.
- **Habitat**: Native to Central and South America, Sarsaparilla grows in tropical forests.
- **Medicinal Properties**: Sarsaparilla has anti-inflammatory, diuretic, and detoxifying properties. It is used to treat skin conditions, arthritis, and to purify the blood.
- **Traditional Uses**: Traditionally used to treat skin diseases, arthritis, and as a general tonic for overall health.
- **Preparation Methods**: Sarsaparilla root can be brewed into a tea, or taken as a tincture or supplement. It is also commonly used in herbal tonic formulations.
- **Precautions**: Generally considered safe, but high doses can cause stomach irritation. It should be used cautiously by individuals with kidney problems.
- **How to Grow**: Sarsaparilla plants prefer a warm, humid climate but can also tolerate some shade. They are not frost-tolerant. These plants thrive in well-drained, slightly acidic to neutral soil. Rich, loamy soil that retains moisture without becoming waterlogged is ideal.

SARSAPARILLA TINCTURE RECIPE

PREP TIME: 20 MINUTES   **MACERATION TIME:** 6 WEEKS   **YIELD:** ABOUT 500 MILLILITERS

INGREDIENTS

- Dried Sarsaparilla Root: 100 grams
- High-proof alcohol (at least 40% ABV, such as vodka or grain alcohol): Approximately 500 ml

TOOLS

- A clean, dry glass jar with a tight-fitting lid
- Cheesecloth or fine mesh strainer
- Amber glass dropper bottles for storage

INSTRUCTIONS

1. If using whole dried roots, chop them into small pieces to help release the essential oils and increase the surface area for extraction. Place the chopped sarsaparilla root into your glass jar.
2. Pour the alcohol over the roots ensuring they are completely submerged. Aim for a herb-to-alcohol ratio of about 1:5.
3. Seal the jar tightly to prevent alcohol evaporation and contamination. Store the jar in a cool, dark cupboard for about 6 weeks. Shake the jar once or twice a week to help with the extraction process.
4. After the maceration period, filter the liquid using cheesecloth or a fine mesh into another clean glass container. Squeeze or press the herb residue to extract as much liquid as possible.
5. Funnel the strained tincture into amber bottles, which help preserve the tincture's potency by protecting it from light. If possible, use bottles with droppers for easy dosage.
6. Label each bottle clearly with the date of finalization, and any other pertinent information.

USAGE: The typical dosage for adults is 1-2 milliliters of the tincture up to three times per day. Always begin with the smaller dose to see how your body reacts.

PREPARATION TIP: Handle the sarsaparilla root with gloves if you have sensitive skin, as handling herbs can sometimes cause irritation.

Saw Palmetto (Serenoa repens)

- **Plant Description**: Saw palmetto is a small palm species that typically reaches a maximum height of approximately 7 to 10 feet.
- **Leaves**: The leaves are fan-shaped, stiff, and sharply serrated, which can cause skin abrasions if not handled carefully.
- **Habitat:** Native to the southeastern United States, particularly in Florida and parts of the Gulf Coast.
- **Traditional Uses:** Commonly employed to reduce symptoms associated with an enlarged prostate, it is also sometimes used to treat certain types of prostate infections and chronic pelvic pain, bladder disorders, reduced libido, hair loss, and hormone imbalances.
- **Precautions:** Avoid using saw palmetto during pregnancy and breastfeeding.
- **How to Grow:** Prefers sandy soil with good drainage and partial shade. It can be grown from seeds but may take a few years to establish fully and produce fruits.

SAW PALMETTO TINCTURE RECIPE

PREP TIME: 15 MINUTES   **MACERATION TIME:** 4 WEEKS   **YIELD:** ABOUT 500 MILLILITERS

INGREDIENTS

- *Dried Saw Palmetto Berries: 100 grams*
- *High-proof alcohol (at least 40% ABV, such as vodka or grain alcohol): 500 milliliters*

TOOLS

- *A clean, dry glass jar with a tight-fitting lid*
- *Cheesecloth or fine mesh strainer*
- *Amber glass dropper bottles for storage*

INSTRUCTIONS

1. If using whole berries, lightly crush them to open up the skins. This increases the surface area and enhances the extraction of active ingredients.
2. Place the crushed saw palmetto berries in the glass jar.
3. Pour the alcohol over the berries until fully submerged, maintaining a 1:5 herb-to-alcohol ratio by weight.
4. Seal the jar tightly with its lid to prevent evaporation and maintain purity.
5. Store the jar in a dark, cool cupboard for 4 weeks. This period allows for optimal extraction of the beneficial compounds from the berries.
6. Shake the jar every few days to help with the extraction process.
7. After the maceration period, filter the liquid using a cheesecloth or fine mesh strainer into a clean glass container. Press the berries to extract as much liquid as possible.
8. Funnel the strained tincture into amber glass bottles. If possible, use bottles with droppers for easy dosage.
9. Label each bottle clearly with the date of finalization, and any other pertinent information.

USAGE: Recommended adult dosage is 1-2 milliliters of tincture, taken 2-3 times daily.

Schisandra (Schisandra chinensis)

- **Plant Description**: Schisandra is a deciduous woody vine and it is famous for its clusters of bright red berries, which are traditionally used in both food and medicine. The plant is sometimes called the "five-flavor berry" because its berries possess all five basic flavors: sweet, sour, salty, bitter, and pungent.
- **Habitat:** Schisandra chinensis originates from the forests of Northern China and the Russian Far East. It thrives in temperate and subtropical regions and is particularly well-suited to the cool, damp environments found in these areas. Schisandra grows naturally under the canopy of deciduous forests, often climbing up trees or along the forest floor in rich, well-drained soils.
- **Medicinal Properties:** Boosts liver function, improves mental performance, and increases resistance to stress and disease.
- **Traditional Uses:** Used in Traditional Chinese Medicine to promote energy and alleviate fatigue. It is considered a harmonizing tonic.
- **Preparation Methods:** Typically available as dried berries, extracts, tinctures, and teas.
- **Precautions:** May exacerbate acid reflux or peptic ulcers; possible interactions with other drugs due to its effects on liver enzymes.
- **How to Grow:** Schisandra plants require a moist, well-drained soil and can be grown in partial shade to full sun. They are often trained on trellises in gardens and prefer a cool, temperate climate, making them suitable for cultivation in a variety of temperate regions.

SCHISANDRA TINCTURE RECIPE

PREP TIME: 10 MINUTES   **MACERATION TIME:** 4-6 WEEKS   **YIELD:** ABOUT 500 MILLILITERS

INGREDIENTS

- *Dried Schisandra Berries: 100 grams*
- *High-proof alcohol (40-50% ABV, such as vodka): 500 milliliters*

TOOLS

- *Clean, dry glass jar with a tight-fitting lid*
- *Cheesecloth or fine mesh strainer*
- *Amber glass dropper bottles for storage*

INSTRUCTIONS

1. Lightly crush the dried Schisandra berries to break their skins, which helps release their active compounds. Place the crushed berries into the glass jar.
2. Pour alcohol over the berries ensuring they are completely submerged. Maintain a 1:5 ratio of berries to alcohol by weight for optimal extraction. Secure the lid to prevent evaporation.
3. Store the jar in a cool, dark cupboard for 4 to 6 weeks. This duration allows the alcohol to extract the therapeutic compounds effectively. Shake the jar every few days to help with the extraction process.
4. After maceration, filter the tincture using a cheesecloth or fine strainer into another clean glass container. Squeeze out as much liquid as possible from the berries.
5. Funnel the liquid into amber glass bottles. If possible, use bottles with droppers for easy dosage.
6. Label each bottle clearly with the date of finalization, and any other pertinent information.

USAGE: The recommended adult dosage is 1-2 milliliters of tincture, up to three times daily.

Shatavari (Asparagus racemosus)

- **Plant Description:** Shatavari is a climbing plant that can grow up to one to two meters in height. It belongs to the Asparagus family and is characterized by its woody stems.
- **Leaves:** The leaves of Shatavari are small, uniform, and pine-needle-like. They are arranged in a uniform manner along the stem, giving the plant a dense, bushy appearance.
- **Flowers and Fruits:** The plant yields petite, white flowers with red berries that turn purple-black when ripe.
- **Habitat**: Shatavari is commonly found in India, Sri Lanka, Nepal, and the Himalayas. It thrives in rocky, gravelly soils and prefers areas that are slightly shaded. The plant is adaptable to various environmental conditions but favors moist, tropical climates. In the U.S., Shatavari is not typically found growing wild but is available for cultivation and purchase.
- **Medicinal Properties:** Supports female reproductive health, adaptogen, boosts immunity.
- **Traditional Uses:** Used in Ayurveda for female health, digestive issues, and general wellness.
- **Precautions:** Generally considered safe, but consult with a healthcare provider if pregnant or nursing.
- **How to Grow:** Shatavari prefers a humid, warm climate typical of tropical and subtropical regions. It can tolerate temperature variations if adequately mulched during colder months. The plant does best in well-draining, slightly alkaline soil. Rich, loamy soils with good organic content ensure healthy growth. The ideal pH should be between 6.5 and 8.

SHATAVARI TINCTURE RECIPE

PREP TIME: 15 MINUTES   **MACERATION TIME:** 4-6 WEEKS   **YIELD:** APPROX 500 ML

INGREDIENTS

- *Shatavari root powder: 100 grams*
- *High-proof alcohol (40-50% ABV, like vodka or brandy): 500 milliliters*

TOOLS

- *Airtight glass jar with a tight-fitting lid*
- *Cheesecloth or a fine mesh strainer*
- *Amber glass dropper bottles for storage*

INSTRUCTIONS

1. Place the Shatavari root powder into the clean, dry glass jar.
2. Pour the alcohol over the powder to submerge it fully, maintaining a ratio of 1:5 (herb to alcohol by weight). Seal the jar tightly to prevent evaporation.
3. Store the jar in a cool, dark cupboard for 4 to 6 weeks. Shake the jar every few days to enhance the extraction.
4. After the maceration period, filter the mixture using a cheesecloth or fine strainer into a clean container. Ensure all liquid is extracted from the powder.
5. Funnel the strained tincture into amber bottles. If possible, use bottles with droppers for easy dosage.
6. Label each bottle clearly with the date of finalization, and any other pertinent information.

USAGE: Typical adult dosage is 1-2 milliliters, taken up to three times daily.

Skullcap (Scutellaria lateriflora)

- **Plant Description**: Skullcap is a perennial herb.
- **Leaves**: The leaves are lanceolate to ovate, slightly serrated, and arranged oppositely along the stem.
- **Habitat:** Common in moist woodlands and meadows in the northern and eastern parts of the U.S.
- **Medicinal Properties:** Acts as a mild sedative and is used for nervous tension and sleep disorders.
- **Traditional Uses:** Historically used by Native Americans and in traditional herbal medicine as a nerve tonic to promote relaxation and emotional well-being.
- **Preparation Methods:** Typically prepared as a tea or tincture.
- **Precautions:** High doses may cause giddiness, stupor, confusion, and irregular heartbeat.
- **How to Grow:** Skullcap requires moist, rich soil in a partly shaded area. It can be propagated from seed or by dividing the roots in spring or fall.

SKULLCAP TINCTURE RECIPE

PREP TIME: 15 MINUTES   **MACERATION TIME:** 6 WEEKS   **YIELD:** APPROX 500 ML

INGREDIENTS

- *Dried Skullcap herb: 100 grams*
- *High-proof alcohol (40-50% ABV, such as vodka or grain alcohol): 500 milliliters*

TOOLS

- *Airtight glass jar with a tight-fitting lid*
- *Cheesecloth or fine mesh strainer*
- *Amber glass dropper bottles for storage*

INSTRUCTIONS

1. Thoroughly clean the dried Skullcap by checking for any impurities or debris.
2. Place the cleaned, dried Skullcap herb into a clean, dry glass jar.
3. Pour the alcohol over the herb ensuring it completely submerges the Skullcap, maintaining a herb to alcohol ratio of about 1:5 by weight.
4. Seal the jar securely to prevent any evaporation of alcohol.
5. Store the sealed jar in a cool, dark cupboard or a pantry, for 6 weeks. This duration allows the alcohol to effectively extract the medicinal components from the Skullcap.
6. Shake the jar once or twice a week to help with the extraction process.
7. After the maceration period, filter the mixture using a cheesecloth or a fine mesh strainer into another clean jar or container. Press or squeeze the plant material to extract as much liquid as possible.
8. Funnel the strained liquid into amber glass bottles. If possible, use bottles with droppers for easy dosage.
9. Label each bottle clearly with the date of finalization, and any other pertinent information.

USAGE: Typical adult dosage is 1-2 milliliters, taken 2-3 times daily or as needed for relaxation and nerve support.

Slippery Elm (Ulmus rubra)

- **Plant Description**: Slippery Elm is a deciduous tree with rough, reddish-brown bark and broad, serrated leaves.
- **Habitat**: Native to North America, Slippery Elm thrives in the damp, fertile soil found within woodlands and alongside streams.
- **Medicinal Properties**: Slippery Elm bark has mucilaginous, anti-inflammatory, and soothing properties. It is used to treat digestive issues, sore throats, and skin irritations.
- **Traditional Uses**: Traditionally used by Native Americans to treat wounds, gastrointestinal issues, and respiratory problems.
- **Precautions**: Slippery Elm is generally safe but should be taken with plenty of water. It could disrupt the uptake of other drugs if consumed at the same time.
- **How to Grow:** Prefers partial shade and fertile, well-drained soil. It is typically grown from seed but requires stratification for successful germination.

SLIPPERY ELM TINCTURE RECIPE

PREP TIME: 20 MINUTES   **MACERATION TIME:** 6 WEEKS   **YIELD:** APPROX 500 ML

INGREDIENTS

- *Slippery Elm bark powder: 100 grams*
- *High-proof alcohol (at least 50% ABV, such as vodka or brandy): 500 milliliters*

TOOLS

- *Airtight glass jar with a tight-fitting lid*
- *Cheesecloth or a fine mesh strainer*
- *Amber glass dropper bottles for storage*

INSTRUCTIONS

1. Ensure the Slippery Elm bark powder is finely ground to maximize the extraction surface area.
2. Place the Slippery Elm bark powder into your clean, dry glass jar.
3. Pour the alcohol over the powder, making sure it fully covers the herb with an extra inch of liquid on top, observing a ratio of about 1:5.
4. Seal the jar tightly to prevent evaporation.
5. Keep the jar in a cool, dark cupboard away from direct sunlight for 6 weeks. This allows the alcohol to extract the therapeutic properties effectively.
6. Shake the jar once a week to help the process.
7. After 6 weeks, filter the tincture using a cheesecloth or fine mesh strainer into another clean container. Compress the soaked powder to extract as much liquid as possible.
8. Funnel the strained tincture into amber glass bottles. If possible, use bottles with droppers for easy dosage.
9. Label each bottle clearly with the date of finalization, and any other pertinent information.

USAGE: The standard adult dosage is 2-3 milliliters, taken up to three times daily, mixed into water or tea. Always consult with a healthcare provider for personalized dosing.

St. John's Wort (Hypericum perforatum)

- **Plant Description**: St. John's wort is a perennial plant characterized by widespread, creeping rhizomes. The plant features upright stems that branch out in the upper section.

- **Leaves**: The leaves are small, oval, and have visible translucent dots when held up to the light, which appear as perforations.
- **Habitat:** Found in fields and along roadsides across the U.S., particularly in sunny, well-drained areas.
- **Medicinal Properties:** Known for its antidepressant and mood-stabilizing properties. It is believed to affect neurotransmitters in the brain that impact mood.
- **Traditional Uses:** Widely used to treat mild to moderate depression, anxiety, and seasonal affective disorder.
- **Preparation Methods:** Typically consumed as a tea, tincture, or in capsule form.
- Precautions: St. John's Wort may interact with various medications, such as antidepressants, birth control pills, and anticoagulants, potentially reducing their effectiveness. It can also increase sensitivity to sunlight. Consultation with a healthcare provider is recommended before starting use.
- **How to Grow:** Grows best in full sun and poor, well-drained soil. It can be invasive, so control is recommended by growing in containers or designated areas.

ST. JOHN'S WORT TINCTURE RECIPE

PREP TIME: 15 MINUTES   **MACERATION TIME:** 4-6 WEEKS   **YIELD:** APPROX 500 ML

INGREDIENTS

- *Fresh St. John's Wort flowers: 100 grams*
- *High-proof alcohol (at least 50% ABV, like vodka or grain alcohol): 500 milliliters*

TOOLS

- *Airtight glass jar with a tight-fitting lid*
- *Cheesecloth or a fine mesh strainer*
- *Amber glass dropper bottles for storage*

INSTRUCTIONS

1. Harvest the St. John's Wort flowers when they are fully bloomed, which is typically around midsummer.
2. Clean the flowers gently to remove any dirt or insects, and slightly chop them to increase the extraction surface.
3. Place the prepared flowers in your clean, dry glass jar.
4. Pour the alcohol over the flowers, ensuring they are completely submerged with an extra inch of liquid on top, maintaining a ratio of about 1:5. Seal the jar securely.
5. Store the jar in a cool, dark cupboard away from direct sunlight, for 4-6 weeks. This duration allows for optimal extraction of the active compounds.
6. Shake the jar every few days to help with the extraction process.
7. After the maceration period, filter the tincture using cheesecloth or a fine mesh strainer into a clean container. Press or squeeze the soaked flowers to extract as much liquid as possible.

8. Funnel the strained tincture into amber glass bottles to minimize light exposure. If possible, use bottles with droppers for easy dosage.
9. Label each bottle clearly with the date of finalization, and any other pertinent information.

USAGE:

*   Typically, the dosage for adults is 1-2 milliliters of the tincture, taken three times daily. It can be administered directly under the tongue or diluted in a small amount of water or juice.
*   Consult a healthcare provider before starting any new treatment, especially if you are currently taking medications, as St. John's Wort can interact with various drugs.

Stinging Nettle (Urtica dioica)

- **Plant Description**: Stinging Nettle is a perennial herb with serrated, heart-shaped leaves covered in stinging hairs, and small, greenish flowers.
- **Habitat**: Native to Europe, Asia, and North America, Stinging Nettle grows in moist, nutrient-rich soils in forests, grasslands, and along stream banks.
- **Medicinal Properties**: Stinging Nettle has anti-inflammatory, diuretic, and antihistamine properties. It is used to treat allergies, arthritis, and urinary issues.
- **Traditional Uses**: Traditionally used to treat joint pain, seasonal allergies, and as a general tonic for overall health.
- **Preparation Methods**: Nettle leaves can be brewed into tea, taken as a tincture, or cooked and eaten like spinach. The root is often used supplements for prostate health.
- **Precautions**: Fresh nettle can cause skin irritation. It should be avoided by pregnant women and individuals with kidney problems or heart conditions without medical advice.
- **How to Grow**: Nettle prefers partial shade but can grow in full sun if the soil is kept moist. It thrives in rich soil with good water retention. Can be propagated from seed in spring or by dividing plants in fall or spring. Handle with gloves to avoid stinging hairs.

STINGING NETTLE TINCTURE RECIPE

PREP TIME: 20 MINUTES   **MACERATION TIME:** 4-6 WEEKS   **YIELD:** APPROX 500 ML

INGREDIENTS

- *Fresh stinging nettle leaves: 100 grams (ensure to handle with gloves to avoid irritation)*
- *High-proof alcohol (40-50% ABV, such as vodka): 500 milliliters*

TOOLS

- *Airtight glass jar with a tight-fitting lid*
- *Cheesecloth or a fine mesh strainer*
- *Amber glass dropper bottles for storage*

INSTRUCTIONS

1. Collect fresh stinging nettle leaves, preferably in the spring when they are most tender. Wear gloves to avoid stings.
2. Rinse the leaves under cool water to clean them. Pat dry with a towel and chop them coarsely to help release the essential oils and increase the surface area for extraction.
3. Place the chopped nettle leaves in your clean, dry glass jar.
4. Pour the alcohol over the leaves until fully submerged, with an extra inch of liquid on top, maintaining a ratio of about 1:5. Seal the jar tightly. Store the jar in a cool, dark cupboard for 4-6 weeks.
5. Shake the jar once or twice a week to encourage the extraction.
6. After the maceration period, use cheesecloth or a fine mesh strainer to filter the tincture into a clean container. Compress the leaves to extract maximum liquid.
7. Funnel the tincture into amber glass bottles. If possible, use bottles with droppers for easy dosage.
8. Label each bottle clearly with the date of finalization, and any other pertinent information.

USAGE: For adults, the typical dosage is 1-2 milliliters of the tincture up to three times daily. It can be administered directly under the tongue or diluted in water or tea.

Thyme (Thymus vulgaris)

- **Plant Description**: Thyme is a low-growing, woody perennial. It forms dense, spreading mats up to 12 inches high.
- **Leaves**: The leaves are small, about 1/4 inch long, aromatic, and usually gray-green. They are ovate to elliptical in shape with a slightly curved edge.
- **Habitat:** Thyme grows wild in many parts of the U.S., especially in sunny, dry, and rocky areas.
- **Medicinal Properties:** Contains thymol, which has demonstrated strong antimicrobial activity against a variety of pathogens.
- **Traditional Uses:** Historically used for respiratory infections, and for its antiseptic properties.
- **Precautions:** Not recommended for pregnant women, those with high blood pressure, or epilepsy.
- **How to Grow:** Plant thyme in well-drained soil with plenty of sunshine. It is drought-tolerant and grows well in gardens or as a potted plant. Thyme spreads easily, so it works well as ground cover or in rock gardens.

THYME TINCTURE RECIPE

PREP TIME: 15 MINUTES   **MACERATION TIME:** 4-6 WEEKS   **YIELD:** APPROX 500 ML

INGREDIENTS

- *Fresh thyme: 100 grams (For a potent tincture, the fresher the herb, the better.)*
- *High-proof alcohol (40-50% ABV, such as vodka or brandy): 500 milliliters*

TOOLS

- *Airtight glass jar with a tight-fitting lid*
- *Cheesecloth or a fine mesh strainer*
- *Amber glass dropper bottles for storage*

INSTRUCTIONS

1. Select fresh thyme, ideally harvested just before the plant flowers to ensure the highest concentration of essential oils. Wash the thyme under cool water. Pat dry with a clean cloth.
2. Coarsely chop the thyme to increase the surface area, which will facilitate better alcohol extraction.
3. Place the chopped thyme into your glass jar.
4. Pour the alcohol over the thyme until it is completely submerged, with an inch of liquid above the top of the herbs. Seal the jar tightly to prevent evaporation.
5. Store the jar in a cool, dark cupboard or a cellar where it's away from direct sunlight for 4-6 weeks.
6. Shake the jar every few days to help with the extraction process.
7. After the infusion period, use cheesecloth or a fine mesh strainer to filter out the plant material from the alcohol. Ensure to squeeze out as much liquid as possible from the thyme.
8. Transfer the strained liquid into another clean jar.
9. Use a funnel to pour the tincture into amber bottles, which help maintain the tincture's potency by protecting it from light. If possible, use bottles with droppers for easy dosage.
10. Label each bottle clearly with the date of finalization, and any other pertinent information.

USAGE: Adult dosage is generally 1-2 milliliters of the tincture three times per day, either taken directly under the tongue or diluted in a small amount of water or tea.

Tulsi or Holy Basil (Ocimum sanctum)

- **Plant Description**: Tulsi is a fragrant, small, and branched perennial herb, originates from the Indian subcontinent. It can grow up to 2 feet tall.
- **Leaves**: The leaves are green or purple, simple, and ovate with a slightly toothed margin. They are highly aromatic and have a slightly sweet, clove-like scent.
- **Habitat:** Not native but can be grown in the U.S. as an annual or indoors where winters are harsh.
- **Medicinal Properties**: Adaptogen, anti-inflammatory, immune booster.
- **Traditional Uses**: Used for respiratory health, stress relief, and immune support.
- **Preparation Methods**: Teas, fresh leaves, and tinctures.
- **Precautions**: Generally considered safe, but avoid in large amounts during pregnancy.
- **How to Grow:** Tulsi prefers warm temperatures and lots of sunlight. Plant in pots or in a garden with rich, fertile soil and ensure it gets at least six hours of sunlight daily. Keep the soil moist but not soggy.

AYURVEDIC TULSI TINCTURE RECIPE

PREP TIME: 15 MINUTES

MACERATION TIME: 4 TO 6 WEEKS

YIELD: ABOUT 250 ML

INGREDIENTS

- Fresh Tulsi Leaves: 1 cup (about 30 grams)
- Vodka or Brandy: 500 ml (80-proof to extract the herbal constituents effectively)
- Glass Jar: 1 liter capacity with a tight-fitting lid

INSTRUCTIONS

1. Wash the Tulsi leaves thoroughly to remove any dirt or debris. Pat them dry gently.
2. Roughly chop the Tulsi leaves to increase their surface area, enhancing the extraction process.
3. Place the chopped Tulsi leaves into the glass jar.
4. Pour the vodka or brandy over the leaves until they are completely submerged. Ensure there is about 2-3 cm of alcohol above the level of the leaves.
5. Close the jar tightly and shake it a bit to mix the leaves with the alcohol. Store the jar in a cool, dark cupboard.
6. Shake the jar once a day for the first week to promote the extraction.
7. Allow the mixture to infuse for 4 to 6 weeks. The more time it spends infusing, the more potent your tincture will be.
8. Once the infusion time is complete, filter the tincture using a cheesecloth or fine strainer into another clean, dry glass jar. Press the plant material to extract as much liquid as possible.
9. Transfer the strained tincture into dark glass bottles.

Turmeric (Curcuma longa)

- **Plant Description**: Turmeric is a perennial herbaceous plant. It typically grows to about 3 feet in height.
- **Leaves**: The leaves are large, oblong to lanceolate, and arranged in a rosette pattern. They are bright green and can grow up to 2 feet long. The leaves emerge from rhizomes, which are the primary source of turmeric's medicinal and culinary uses.
- **Habitat:** Best suited to tropical and subtropical climates and is often grown in the southern parts of the U.S. or in greenhouses.
- **Medicinal Properties**: Anti-inflammatory, antioxidant, antimicrobial.
- **Traditional Uses**: Used for skin health, wound healing, and as an anti-inflammatory.
- **Precautions**: High doses of turmeric may cause gastrointestinal issues. It can also interact with blood thinners and medications for diabetes, so consultation with a healthcare provider is advised before starting supplementation.
- **How to Grow:** Turmeric requires warm temperatures (above 68°F) and high humidity. Plant rhizomes in well-draining, fertile soil. It can be grown outdoors in summer in cooler climates but needs to be moved indoors for the winter.

TURMERIC TINCTURE RECIPE

PREP TIME: 20 MINUTES   **MACERATION TIME:** 4-6 WEEKS   **YIELD:** APPROX 500 ML

INGREDIENTS

- *Fresh turmeric root: 200 grams (Fresh root ensures a higher concentration of curcumin, the active compound.)*
- *High-proof alcohol (at least 50% ABV, such as vodka or grain alcohol): 500 milliliters*

TOOLS

- *Airtight glass jar with a tight-fitting lid*
- *Cheesecloth or a fine mesh strainer*
- *Amber glass dropper bottles for storage*

INSTRUCTIONS

1. Thoroughly wash the turmeric roots.
2. Peel the roots with a vegetable peeler to expose the fresh, vibrant inner material.
3. Grate the turmeric roots coarsely or chop finely to maximize the surface area exposed to the alcohol.
4. Place the prepared turmeric into your glass jar.
5. Pour the alcohol over the turmeric until fully submerged, with an extra inch of liquid above the turmeric. Securely close the jar to prevent any alcohol evaporation.
6. Store the jar in a cupboard away from direct sunlight. Allow it to sit for 4-6 weeks; this duration allows the curcumin and other beneficial compounds to leach into the alcohol.
7. Shake the jar every few days to help with the extraction process.
8. After the maceration time, use cheesecloth or a fine mesh strainer to filter the turmeric particles from the alcohol. Press or squeeze the turmeric pulp to extract as much liquid as possible.
9. Dispose of the solid material and transfer the tincture into a clean glass jar.
10. Use a funnel to decant the tincture into amber-colored bottles. If possible, use bottles with droppers for easy dosage. Label each bottle clearly with the date of finalization, and any other pertinent information.

USAGE: Typical adult dosage is about 1-2 milliliters of tincture three times daily, either taken directly or mixed into a small amount of water or juice.

Valerian (Valeriana officinalis)

- **Plant Description**: Valerian is a perennial herb that can grow up to 5 feet tall.
- **Leaves**: The leaves are arranged in opposite pairs, compound, and pinnate with lance-shaped leaflets that have serrated edges.
- **Habitat:** Common in temperate regions and often found growing wild in damp grasslands.
- **Medicinal Properties:** Acts as a sedative and anti-anxiety agent, helping to improve sleep quality and reduce nervous tension.
- **Traditional Uses:** Used for insomnia, anxiety, and stress-related conditions.
- **Preparation Methods:** Commonly taken as a capsule or as a tincture. For tea, steep 1 teaspoon of dried root in hot water for 10 minutes.
- **Precautions:** Valerian root is generally safe for short-term use, but it can cause drowsiness and impairments in coordination, especially at higher doses. It should not be used when operating heavy machinery or driving. Valerian should not be combined with alcohol or other sedative medications.
- **How to Grow:** Plant valerian in well-drained soil in a sunny location. This perennial loves moist conditions but is quite hardy and tolerates cold well. It can be propagated from seed or by division in the spring.

VALERIAN TINCTURE RECIPE

PREP TIME: 15 MINUTES   **MACERATION TIME:** 4-6 WEEKS   **YIELD:** APPROX 500 ML

INGREDIENTS

- *Dried valerian root: 100 grams (Dried root is preferred for its concentrated properties and extended shelf life.)*
- *High-proof alcohol (at least 40-50% ABV, such as vodka or brandy): 500 milliliters*

TOOLS

- *Airtight glass jar with a tight-fitting lid*
- *Cheesecloth or a fine mesh strainer*
- *Amber glass dropper bottles for storage*

INSTRUCTIONS

1. If using whole dried roots, chop them into smaller pieces to help release the essential oils and increase the surface area for extraction. Ensure that the roots are completely dry and free from any mold or unpleasant odor.
2. Place the chopped valerian root into your glass jar.
3. Pour the alcohol over the roots until they are fully submerged, with an inch of liquid above the top of the roots.
4. Seal the jar tightly to prevent evaporation and ensure a potent tincture.
5. Store the jar in a dark, cool cupboard or a pantry, away from direct sunlight and significant temperature changes.
6. Shake the jar every couple of days to mix the roots with the alcohol and promote extraction.

7. After 4-6 weeks, filter the mixture using cheesecloth or a fine mesh strainer into a clean bowl. Squeeze or press the root matter to extract as much liquid as possible. Discard the solid material.
8. Using a funnel, decant the tincture into amber-colored bottles, which help protect the contents from light. If possible, use bottles with droppers for easy dosage.
9. Label each bottle clearly with the date of finalization, and any other pertinent information.

USAGE:
- The typical adult dosage is about 1-2 milliliters of the tincture taken with water 30 minutes before bedtime or during periods of increased anxiety.

White Willow (Salix alba)

- **Plant Description**: White Willow is a large tree that can reach up to 80 feet in height.
- **Leaves**: The leaves are elongated, narrow, and finely toothed. They are light green above and silvery beneath due to a fine layer of hairs, which give the tree its name.
- **Habitat:** Commonly found near streams, rivers, and moist locations throughout the eastern United States.
- **Medicinal Properties:** Contains salicin which the body converts to salicylic acid, providing anti-inflammatory and pain-relieving effects similar to aspirin.
- **Traditional Uses:** Used throughout history as a natural remedy for pain and inflammation.
- **Preparation Methods:** Typically taken as an extract, tincture, or tea.
- **Precautions:** Should not be used by those allergic to aspirin or who are taking blood thinners. Additionally, its use is not recommended for children due to the potential risk of Reye's syndrome.
- **How to Grow:** Plant white willow in wet or moist soil in a sunny area. It thrives in deep, fertile, slightly acidic to neutral soil. Regular watering and full sun exposure help promote healthy growth. It can be propagated from cuttings taken in late winter or early spring.

WHITE WILLOW TINCTURE RECIPE

PREP TIME: 20 MINUTES   **MACERATION TIME:** 4 WEEKS   **YIELD:** APPROX 500 ML

INGREDIENTS

- *Dried white willow bark: 100 grams (Ensure the bark is finely chopped for better extraction.)*
- *High-proof alcohol (at least 40-50% ABV, such as vodka or brandy): 500 milliliters*

TOOLS

- *Airtight glass jar with a tight-fitting lid*
- *Cheesecloth or a fine mesh strainer*
- *Amber glass dropper bottles for storage*

INSTRUCTIONS

1. Ensure that the white willow bark is finely chopped or ground to enhance the surface area for optimal extraction. Check the bark for any mold or impurities before use.
2. Place the prepared bark into the glass jar.
3. Pour enough alcohol over the bark to completely cover it by about an inch to account for absorption and evaporation. Seal the jar tightly.
4. Keep the jar in a cool, dark cupboard away from direct sunlight and fluctuating temperatures.
5. Shake the jar daily for the first week, then weekly thereafter to promote the extraction of salicin from the bark.
6. After 4 weeks, filter the mixture using cheesecloth or a fine mesh into a clean bowl, pressing the bark to extract as much liquid as possible. Dispose of the bark responsibly.
7. Using a funnel, transfer the liquid into amber glass bottles, which help preserve the integrity of the tincture by protecting it from light. If possible, use bottles with droppers for easy dosage.
8. Label each bottle clearly with the date of finalization, and any other pertinent information.

USAGE: The typical adult dosage is 1-2 milliliters up to three times daily. It can be diluted in water or tea.

Wild Cherry Bark (Prunus serotina)

- **Plant Description**: Wild Cherry is a deciduous tree with dark, shiny bark and clusters of white flowers that develop into small, dark cherries.
- **Habitat**: Native to North America, Wild Cherry is found in forests and along stream banks, preferring well-drained soils.
- **Medicinal Properties**: Wild Cherry Bark has antitussive, expectorant, and astringent properties. It is effective in soothing coughs, reducing inflammation, and aiding digestion.
- **Traditional Uses**: Traditionally used by Native Americans and early settlers to treat coughs, colds, and bronchitis. It is also used to soothe digestive issues.
- **Preparation Methods**: The bark can be brewed into a tea or used to make a syrup by simmering with water and honey. Tinctures are another common preparation method.
- **Precautions**: Wild Cherry Bark contains cyanogenic compounds, which can be toxic in large amounts. It should be used in recommended doses and avoided during pregnancy.
- **How to Grow**: Wild cherry trees are hardy and adaptable, thriving in USDA zones 3 through 9. They prefer temperate climates with well-defined seasons. These trees are not overly picky about soil but perform best in deep, fertile, moist, well-draining soil. They can tolerate a range from sandy to clay soils with a slightly acidic to neutral pH.

WILD CHERRY BARK TINCTURE RECIPE

PREP TIME: 15 MINUTES   **MACERATION TIME:** 6 WEEKS   **YIELD:** APPROX 500 ML

INGREDIENTS

- *Wild cherry bark: 100 grams (chopped finely to maximize extraction)*
- *High-proof alcohol (40-50% ABV, such as vodka or grain alcohol): 500 milliliters*

TOOLS

- *Airtight glass jar*
- *Cheesecloth or fine mesh strainer*
- *Amber glass dropper bottles for storage*

INSTRUCTIONS

1. Thoroughly inspect and clean the wild cherry bark, ensuring it is free from dust and other contaminants. Chop the bark finely to enhance the extraction process.
2. Place the chopped bark in the airtight glass jar.
3. Cover completely with alcohol, ensuring there is at least one inch of alcohol above the bark to allow for expansion and absorption. Secure the lid tightly.
4. Store the jar in a cool, dark cupboard, away from direct sunlight and heat, which could degrade the active compounds. Shake the jar every day for the first week, then occasionally for the remainder of the maceration period to promote thorough extraction.
5. After six weeks, filter the liquid using a cheesecloth or fine mesh strainer into a clean bowl, pressing the bark to extract as much tincture as possible. Compost the used bark appropriately.
6. Funnel the strained tincture into amber glass bottles. If possible, use bottles with droppers for easy dosage.
7. Label each bottle clearly with the date of finalization, and any other pertinent information.

USAGE: Standard adult dosage is 1-2 milliliters, up to three times daily. Mix with water or juice for ease of use.

Wood Betony (Stachys officinalis)

- **Plant Description**: Wood Betony is a perennial herb. It forms clumps and generally grows up to 1 to 2 feet tall.
- **Leaves**: The leaves are heart-shaped at the base and lanceolate towards the tip, with a somewhat wrinkled texture and a coarse, hairy surface.
- **Habitat:** Often found in open fields, meadows, and along roadsides, primarily in the northeastern U.S.
- **Traditional Uses**: Used in traditional medicine for nervous system ailments including anxiety and headaches. It is also used for gastrointestinal and respiratory issues.
- **Precautions**: Wood betony might interact with medications. It has sedative properties, so it should be used with caution if you are taking sedatives or central nervous system depressants as it may enhance their effects.
- **How to Grow:** Wood betony prefers well-drained soil and full sun to partial shade. It is drought-resistant once established and can be propagated from seeds or by dividing the roots in spring or fall.

WOOD BETONY TINCTURE RECIPE

PREP TIME: 15 MINUTES   **MACERATION TIME:** 6 WEEKS   **YIELD:** APPROX 500 ML

INGREDIENTS

- *Wood betony (dried aerial parts): 100 grams*
- *High-proof alcohol (45-60% ABV, such as vodka or brandy): 500 milliliters*

TOOLS

- *Airtight glass jar*
- *Cheesecloth or fine mesh strainer*
- *Amber glass dropper bottles for storage*

INSTRUCTIONS

1. Ensure the wood betony is clean and free from any debris or impurities.
2. Chop or grind the dried herb to help release the essential oils and increase the surface area for extraction.
3. Place the prepared wood betony in the airtight glass jar.
4. Pour alcohol over the herbs, making sure they are completely submerged with about an inch of alcohol covering the top to account for absorption.
5. Store the jar in a dark, cool cupboard away from direct sunlight.
6. Shake the jar daily for the first week to mix the contents, then shake once a week for the remainder of the maceration period.
7. After six weeks, filter the tincture using a cheesecloth or fine mesh strainer into a clean container. Squeeze or press the herbs to extract as much liquid as possible. Dispose of the spent herbs responsibly.
8. Funnel the strained tincture into amber glass bottles to minimize light exposure, which helps preserve the tincture's potency. If possible, use bottles with droppers for easy dosage.
9. Label each bottle clearly with the date of finalization, and any other pertinent information.

USAGE: Typical dosage is 1-2 milliliters, taken 2-3 times daily or as needed. It can be taken directly under the tongue or diluted in a small amount of water or tea.

Yarrow (Achillea millefolium)

- **Plant Description**: Yarrow is a perennial herb with feathery, aromatic leaves and clusters of small, white to pink flowers.
- **Habitat**: Native to temperate regions of the Northern Hemisphere, yarrow thrives in meadows, grasslands, and open woodlands.
- **Medicinal Properties**: Yarrow has anti-inflammatory, antiseptic, astringent, and hemostatic properties. It is effective in reducing fever, treating wounds, and relieving digestive issues.
- **Traditional Uses**: Traditionally used to stop bleeding, yarrow is also employed to treat colds, flu, and digestive problems. It is valued for its ability to support wound healing and reduce inflammation.
- **Preparation Methods**: Yarrow can be prepared as a tea by steeping dried flowers and leaves in hot water for 10-15 minutes. It can also be used in tinctures or applied topically as a poultice.
- **Precautions**: Yarrow should be used cautiously by individuals with allergies to the Asteraceae family. In addition, it should be avoided by pregnant women as it may induce uterine contractions.
- **How to Grow:** Yarrow is easy to cultivate and can be grown from seed or by dividing existing plants in spring or fall. It prefers full sun and tolerates drought well, making it suitable for xeriscaping. Plant in well-drained soil and water regularly until established.

YARROW TINCTURE RECIPE

PREP TIME: 15 MINUTES   **MACERATION TIME:** 4-6 WEEKS   **YIELD:** APPROX 500 ML

INGREDIENTS

- *Yarrow flowers and leaves (freshly harvested or dried): 100 grams*
- *High-proof alcohol (45-60% ABV, such as vodka or grain alcohol): 500 milliliters*

TOOLS

- *Airtight glass jar*
- *Cheesecloth or fine mesh strainer*
- *Amber glass dropper bottles for storage*

INSTRUCTIONS

1. If using fresh yarrow, ensure the flowers and leaves are free from dirt and insects.
2. Roughly chop the fresh or dried yarrow to help release the essential oils and increase the surface area for extraction. Place the chopped yarrow in the airtight glass jar.
3. Cover completely with alcohol, ensuring there is at least an inch of alcohol above the herb level to cover any swelling or absorption.
4. Seal the jar tightly with its lid and store it in a cool, dark cupboard to prevent the degradation of medicinal properties.
5. Shake the jar daily for the first week to promote extraction, then once weekly thereafter.
6. After 4-6 weeks, filter the tincture using a cheesecloth or fine mesh strainer into a clean bowl. Compress the plant material to extract maximum liquid.
7. Funnel the strained tincture into amber glass bottles. If possible, use bottles with droppers for easy dosage. Label each bottle clearly with the date of finalization, and any other pertinent information.

USAGE: Recommended dosage is 1-2 milliliters, taken 2-3 times daily. It can be administered directly under the tongue or diluted in a little water or tea.

Chapter 4

Tincture Recipe Formulas

Anti-Inflammatory

TURMERIC AND GINGER POWER BLEND

This tincture is ideal for daily use, with a recommended dosage of 5 milliliters once or twice a day, ideally before meals to aid absorption.

PREP TIME: 15 MINUTES   **MACERATION TIME:** 4-6 WEEKS   **YIELD:** APPROX 500 ML

INGREDIENTS

- Turmeric Root: 30 grams (dried, finely chopped)
- Ginger Root: 30 grams (dried, finely chopped)
- High-proof Alcohol (vodka or brandy, 40-50% alcohol by volume): 500 milliliters

TOOLS

- Glass jar with a tight-fitting lid
- Kitchen scale
- Measuring cup
- Fine mesh sieve or cheesecloth
- Dark-colored glass dropper bottles for storage

INSTRUCTIONS

1. Using a kitchen scale, measure the dried Turmeric and Ginger. Make sure the herbs are finely chopped to help release the essential oils and increase the surface area for extraction.
2. Place the chopped herbs in your clean glass jar. Pour over enough vodka or brandy to cover the herbs by about two to three inches, ensuring all plant material is submerged.
3. Secure the lid tightly and shake the jar to help with the extraction process. Store the jar in a dark, cool cupboard, away from direct sunlight, for 4-6 weeks. Shake the jar every few days.
4. After the maceration period, filter the tincture using a fine mesh sieve or cheesecloth into another clean jar. Compress the herbs to extract as much liquid as possible.

5. Funnel the filtered tincture into dark-colored glass bottles. If possible, use bottles with droppers for easy dosage. Sterilize the bottles beforehand to ensure they are free from contaminants.
6. Clearly label each bottle with the expiration date (typically one year from the preparation date) and any other pertinent information.

PREPARATION TIPS: Ensure herbs are completely dried and finely chopped to enhance the extraction process.

ANTI-INFLAMMATORY HERBAL HARMONY

This anti-inflammatory tincture is perfect for daily use, especially beneficial before bedtime to leverage Chamomile's soothing effects. Suggested dosage is 5 milliliters in the evening or as needed for pain relief.

PREP TIME: 20 MINUTES   **MACERATION TIME:** 4-6 WEEKS   **YIELD:** APPROX 500 ML

INGREDIENTS

- *Chamomile Flowers: 20 grams (dried)*
- *Boswellia Resin: 20 grams (finely ground)*
- *High-proof Alcohol (vodka or brandy, at least 40-50% alcohol by volume): 500 milliliters*

TOOLS

- *Glass jar with a tight-fitting lid*
- *Kitchen scale*
- *Measuring cup*
- *Fine mesh sieve or cheesecloth*
- *Amber glass dropper bottles for storage*

INSTRUCTIONS

1. Weigh the dried Chamomile and finely ground Boswellia using a kitchen scale to ensure accuracy.
2. Place the herbs in your clean glass jar. Pour the high-proof alcohol over the herbs until they are completely submerged, with an extra inch of liquid above the top of the herbs.
3. Tighten the lid on the jar and shake well to mix the ingredients thoroughly. Store the jar in a cool, dark cupboard to macerate. Shake the jar every few days to mix the herbs and aid in the extraction process.
4. After 4-6 weeks, filter the mixture using a fine mesh sieve or cheesecloth over another clean jar. Press or squeeze the soaked herbs to extract as much liquid as possible.
5. Funnel the strained tincture into amber glass bottles, which have been sterilized to prevent contamination. If possible, use bottles with droppers for easy dosage.
6. Label each bottle with the expiry date (one year from making) and any other pertinent information.

PREPARATION TIPS: Grinding Boswellia resin before maceration can enhance the extraction of its active components.

ANTI-INFLAMMATORY TRIO BLEND

This tincture is particularly effective when used daily, with a dosage of 5 milliliters in water or tea. It's designed for those seeking natural ways to manage conditions like arthritis, sports injuries, or chronic inflammation.

PREP TIME: 40 MINUTES   **MACERATION TIME:** 6 WEEKS   **YIELD:** APPROX 500 ML

INGREDIENTS

- *Turmeric Root: 25 grams (freshly grated)*
- *Ginger Root: 25 grams (freshly grated)*
- *Boswellia Resin: 15 grams (finely powdered)*
- *High-proof Alcohol (such as vodka or ethanol, 95% alcohol by volume): 500 milliliters*

TOOLS

- *Kitchen scale*
- *Grater*
- *Mortar and pestle (for Boswellia resin)*

- *Mixing bowl*
- *Fine mesh sieve or cheesecloth*

- *Dark glass bottles with droppers for storage*

INSTRUCTIONS

1. Grate the fresh Turmeric and Ginger roots. Use a mortar and pestle to finely powder the Boswellia resin.
2. In a sterilized mixing bowl, combine the grated Turmeric, Ginger, and powdered Boswellia.
3. Transfer the herbal mixture into a clean glass jar. Pour the high-proof alcohol over the herbs, ensuring the liquid covers them by at least two inches to allow for expansion.
4. Tightly seal the jar and place it in a dark, cool cupboard. Let the tincture macerate for 6 weeks, shaking the jar lightly every few days to enhance the extraction process.
5. After 6 weeks, filter the tincture using a fine mesh sieve or cheesecloth into another clean jar, pressing firmly on the solids to extract as much liquid as possible.
6. Funnel the final tincture into sterilized dark glass bottles. Label each bottle with the tincture details, production date, and suggested expiration date (typically one year from the date of preparation).

SHOPPING TIPS:
- If Boswellia resin is not available in powdered form, purchase in chunks and grind manually.

PREPARATION TIPS:
- For those sensitive to alcohol, glycerin can be used as an alternative solvent, though it may result in a less potent tincture.

SOOTHING HERBAL BLEND

DOSAGE: Take 5 milliliters of the tincture diluted in water or a warm beverage, up to three times daily.

PRECAUTIONS: This tincture is not recommended for pregnant or breastfeeding women due to the potent effects of the herbs involved.

PREP TIME: 30 MINUTES　　　**MACERATION TIME:** 4 WEEKS　　　**YIELD:** APPROX 500 ML

INGREDIENTS

- *Chamomile Flowers: 20 grams (dried)*
- *Rosemary Leaves: 20 grams (fresh or dried)*
- *Lavender Flowers: 10 grams (dried)*
- *High-proof Alcohol (such as vodka or grain alcohol, 40-50% alcohol by volume): 500 milliliters*

TOOLS

- *Kitchen scale*
- *Clean dry jar with a tight-fitting lid*
- *Fine mesh sieve or cheesecloth*

- *Dark glass bottles with droppers for storage*

INSTRUCTIONS

1. If using fresh rosemary, finely chop the leaves. For dried chamomile and lavender, ensure they are free from any impurities.
2. Place the chamomile, rosemary, and lavender in a clean, dry jar.
3. Pour the alcohol over the herbs, making sure they are completely submerged with a few centimeters of alcohol on top to account for absorption.
4. Seal the jar tightly with its lid and store it in a dark, cool cupboard. Allow the mixture to macerate for 4 weeks, shaking the jar every few days to mix the herbs and alcohol.
5. After maceration, filter the mixture using a fine mesh sieve or cheesecloth into another clean jar. Squeeze or press the herb pulp to extract as much liquid as possible.
6. Funnel the strained tincture into dark glass bottles, label them with the ingredients, date of production, and expiry date (typically one year from making).

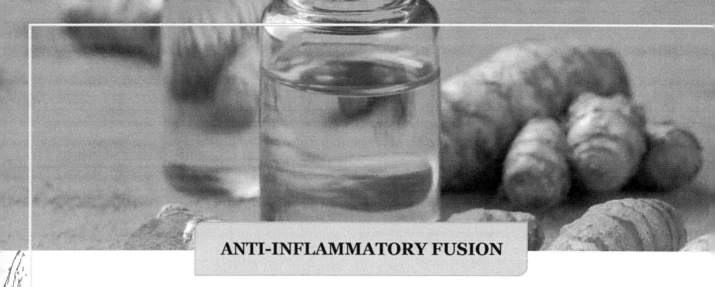

ANTI-INFLAMMATORY FUSION

DOSAGE: Consume 5 milliliters of the tincture diluted in water or juice, up to three times daily.

PRECAUTIONS: This tincture is not recommended during pregnancy or breastfeeding due to the potent nature of the ingredients.

PREP TIME: 20 MINUTES   **MACERATION TIME**: 6 WEEKS   **YIELD:** APPROX 500 ML

INGREDIENTS

- *Turmeric Root: 30 grams (freshly grated or dried and powdered)*
- *Ginger Root: 20 grams (freshly grated)*
- *Black Pepper: 5 grams (freshly ground)*
- *High-proof Alcohol (such as vodka or grain alcohol, 40-50% alcohol by volume): 500 milliliters*

TOOLS

- *Kitchen scale*
- *Clean dry jar with a tight-fitting lid*
- *Fine mesh sieve or cheesecloth*
- *Dark glass bottles with droppers for storage*

INSTRUCTIONS

1. If using fresh turmeric and ginger, wash, peel, and grate finely. Ensure black pepper is freshly ground to maintain potency.
2. In a clean, dry jar, combine the grated turmeric, grated ginger, and ground black pepper.
3. Pour the alcohol over the herbs until they are fully submerged with a couple of centimeters to spare at the top to allow for expansion.
4. Tightly seal the jar and store it in a dark, cool cupboard. Let the herbs macerate for 6 weeks, shaking the jar every few days.
5. Use a fine mesh sieve or cheesecloth to filter the mixture into a clean jar, pressing the herbs to extract maximum liquid.
6. Funnel the strained tincture to dark glass bottles. Label them clearly with ingredients, production date, and expiry date (usually one year from the date of production).

PREPARATION TIPS: Handle turmeric and ginger with gloves.

WHITE WILLOW AND CHAMOMILE BLEND

DOSAGE: Take 5 milliliters of the tincture mixed in water or tea, up to three times daily, especially when experiencing inflammation or pain.

PRECAUTIONS: This tincture combines herbs known for their medicinal properties but can interact with certain medications or conditions.

PREP TIME: 15 MINUTES   **MACERATION TIME:** 4-6 WEEKS   **YIELD:** APPROX 500 ML

INGREDIENTS

- *White Willow Bark: 40 grams (dried and chopped)*
- *Chamomile Flowers: 20 grams (dried)*
- *Licorice Root: 10 grams (dried and sliced)*
- *High-proof Alcohol (at least 40% alcohol by volume, such as vodka or grain alcohol): 500 milliliters*

TOOLS

- *Kitchen scale*
- *Clean, dry jar with a tight-fitting lid*
- *Fine mesh sieve or cheesecloth*
- *Dark glass bottles with droppers for storage*

INSTRUCTIONS

1. Measure and mix the dried white willow bark, chamomile flowers, and licorice root. Ensure all components are free from any debris or impurities.
2. Place the mixed herbs in a clean, dry jar.
3. Pour the alcohol over the herbs to cover them completely by several centimeters to allow for expansion and shaking.
4. Seal the jar tightly with its lid and store it in a cool, dark cupboard. Allow the mixture to macerate for 4 to 6 weeks, shaking the jar every few days to help the extraction process.
5. After the maceration period, filter the tincture using a fine mesh sieve or cheesecloth into another clean jar. Press or squeeze the herbs to extract as much liquid as possible.
6. Funnel the strained tincture into dark glass bottles. Label each bottle with the name, ingredients, production date, and recommended expiration date (typically one year from making).

PREPARATION TIPS: Use gloves when handling white willow bark to avoid irritation from any residual salicin.

DEVIL'S CLAW AND TURMERIC BLEND

DOSAGE: Administer 5 milliliters of the tincture diluted in water or juice, up to three times daily, particularly when experiencing joint pain or inflammation.

PRECAUTIONS: This tincture is intended for adult use and should be used with caution due to the potent nature of the ingredients.

PREP TIME: 20 MINUTES   **MACERATION TIME**: 4-6 WEEKS   **YIELD:** APPROX 500 ML

INGREDIENTS

- *Devil's Claw Root: 30 grams (dried and chopped)*
- *Turmeric Root: 30 grams (dried and finely powdered)*
- *Black Pepper: 5 grams (finely ground)*
- *High-proof Alcohol (at least 40% alcohol by volume, such as vodka or grain alcohol): 500 milliliters*

TOOLS

- *Kitchen scale*
- *Clean, dry jar with a tight-fitting lid*
- *Fine mesh sieve or cheesecloth*
- *Amber glass dropper bottles for storage*

INSTRUCTIONS

1. Measure and combine the dried devil's claw root, turmeric powder, and ground black pepper.
2. Transfer the herb mixture into a clean, dry jar.
3. Pour the alcohol over the herbs, ensuring they are fully submerged by several centimeters to accommodate swelling and agitation.
4. Tightly seal the jar with its lid and place it in a cool, dark area. Let the mixture sit for 4 to 6 weeks, shaking the jar every few days to distribute the contents and promote extraction.
5. Once maceration is complete, filter the tincture using a fine mesh sieve or cheesecloth into a clean jar, squeezing the herbs to extract maximum liquid.
6. Funnel the strained liquid into amber glass bottles. Clearly label each bottle with the ingredients, date of production, and expiration date (usually one year from the date of creation).

PREPARATION TIPS: Handling turmeric and devil's claw can stain; use gloves and protective equipment as needed.

Immune Boosting

ECHINACEA AND ELDERBERRY TINCTURE

This Echinacea and Elderberry tincture serves as an excellent preventive measure during flu seasons and can also be used to boost overall immune response.

DOSAGE: It's recommended to take 5 milliliters daily during high-risk times or when feeling under the weather.

PREP TIME: 30 MINUTES   **MACERATION TIME**: 4-6 WEEKS   **YIELD:** APPROX 500 ML

INGREDIENTS

- Echinacea: 30 grams (dried root)
- Elderberry: 30 grams (dried berries)
- Alcohol (vodka or brandy, 40-60% alcohol by volume): 500 milliliters (approximately 17 ounces)

TOOLS

- Glass jar with a tight-fitting lid
- Kitchen scale (for precise herb measurement)
- Measuring cup or jug
- Fine mesh strainer or cheesecloth
- Dark glass dropper bottles for storage

INSTRUCTIONS

1. Using a kitchen scale, measure the dried Echinacea root and Elderberry. Combine them in your glass jar.
2. Pour vodka or brandy over the herbs to submerge them completely, covering them by at least 2-3 inches because the herbs will swell as they soak.
3. Tightly seal the jar and shake it slightly to ensure the herbs are well mixed with the alcohol. Store the jar in a dark, cool cupboard, away from direct sunlight.
4. Allow the herbs to macerate for 4-6 weeks, shaking the jar every few days to mix the herbs and alcohol.
5. After the maceration period, filter the tincture using a fine mesh strainer or cheesecloth into a clean glass jar, making sure to remove all solid particles.
6. Decant the clear tincture into dark glass bottles for. If possible, use bottles with droppers for easy dosage.
7. Label each bottle with the herb names, date of preparation, and expiration date (usually one year from the making date).

PREPARATION TIPS: Handling Elderberry with care is recommended as it can stain surfaces and clothing.

ASTRAGALUS AND ECHINACEA IMMUNE BOOST

This blend is perfect for preparing the body for cold and flu season or for general immune support.

DOSAGE: Take 5 milliliters of the tincture up to three times per day in water or tea, particularly during times when immune support is needed.

PREP TIME: 15 MINUTES   **MACERATION TIME**: 4-6 WEEKS   **YIELD:** APPROX 500 ML

INGREDIENTS

- *Astragalus Root: 40 grams (sliced dried root)*
- *Echinacea Root: 20 grams (dried and chopped)*
- *High-proof Alcohol (at least 40% alcohol by volume, such as vodka or grain alcohol): 500 milliliters*

TOOLS

- *Kitchen scale*
- *Clean, dry jar with a tight-fitting lid*
- *Fine mesh sieve or cheesecloth*

- *Amber glass dropper bottles for storage*

INSTRUCTIONS

1. Measure the astragalus and echinacea using a kitchen scale. Place the herbs in a clean, dry jar.
2. Pour enough alcohol over the herbs to completely cover them by at least 2-3 inches, ensuring good immersion as the herbs will expand slightly when soaked.
3. Seal the jar tightly with its lid and store it in a cool, dark cupboard. Allow the herbs to macerate for 4 to 6 weeks, shaking the jar daily to help with the extraction process.
4. After maceration, filter the mixture using a fine mesh sieve or cheesecloth into another clean jar. Press or squeeze the herbs to extract as much liquid as possible.
5. Funnel the strained tincture into amber glass bottles. If possible, use bottles with droppers for easy dosage. Label each bottle with the herb names, preparation date, and any other pertinent information.

PREPARATION TIPS: If you have a sensitivity to alcohol, glycerin can be used as an alternative solvent, though it may not extract certain constituents as effectively.

CAT'S CLAW AND GINGER IMMUNE TINCTURE

DOSAGE: Dosage suggestion is 5 milliliters of the tincture up to three times daily, diluted in water or juice as preferred. This is particularly effective during cold and flu season or whenever immune support is needed.

PREP TIME: 20 MINUTES   **MACERATION TIME**: 4-6 WEEKS   **YIELD:** APPROX 500 ML

INGREDIENTS

- Cat's Claw Bark: 30 grams (dried and finely chopped)
- Ginger Root: 20 grams (freshly grated)
- High-proof Alcohol (at least 60% alcohol by volume, such as vodka or grain alcohol): 500 milliliters

TOOLS

- Kitchen scale
- Clean, dry jar with a tight-fitting lid
- Fine mesh sieve or cheesecloth
- Amber glass dropper bottles for storage

INSTRUCTIONS

1. Weigh the Cat's Claw and Ginger accurately using a kitchen scale to ensure the correct ratio.
2. Place both the dried Cat's Claw and freshly grated Ginger in your clean, dry jar.
3. Pour the alcohol over the herbs, ensuring they are completely submerged by at least 2-3 inches to accommodate for expansion.
4. Seal the jar tightly with its lid and place it in a cool, dark cupboard to macerate. Shake the jar once daily to facilitate extraction.
5. After the maceration period, filter the tincture using a fine mesh sieve or cheesecloth, compressing the herbs to extract as much liquid as possible.
6. Funnel the strained liquid into amber glass bottles. If possible, use bottles with droppers for easy dosage. Label each bottle clearly with the date of finalization, and other relevant details.

PREPARATION TIPS: For those sensitive to alcohol, a non-alcoholic version can be made using vegetable glycerin, though the extraction will differ slightly.

OREGANO AND ECHINACEA IMMUNE BOOSTER

DOSAGE: Suggested use is 5 milliliters of the tincture up to three times a day, taken with water. Begin use at the first sign of immune weakness or exposure to illness.

PREP TIME: 15 MINUTES   **MACERATION TIME:** 4-6 WEEKS   **YIELD:** APPROX 500 ML

INGREDIENTS

- Oregano Leaves: 20 grams (freshly picked and dried)
- Echinacea Root: 30 grams (dried and coarsely chopped)
- High-proof Alcohol (at least 60% alcohol by volume, such as vodka or grain alcohol): 500 milliliters

TOOLS

- Kitchen scale
- Clean, dry jar with a tight-fitting lid
- Fine mesh sieve or cheesecloth
- Amber glass dropper bottles for storage

INSTRUCTIONS

1. Weigh out the Oregano and Echinacea using a kitchen scale.
2. Place the dried Oregano and Echinacea into your clean jar.
3. Pour enough alcohol into the jar to cover the herbs completely, ensuring they are submerged by at least two inches to allow for expansion.
4. Secure the lid tightly and place the jar in a cool, dark cupboard. Shake the jar daily to promote extraction.
5. After 4-6 weeks, filter the mixture using a sieve or cheesecloth into a clean bowl, squeezing the herbs to extract as much liquid as possible.
6. Funnel the strained tincture into amber bottles. If possible, use bottles with droppers for easy dosage. Label each bottle with the herb names, date, and batch number.

Tonifying

DANDELION AND NETTLE TONIFYING TINCTURE

This tincture blends the cleansing properties of Dandelion with the nutrient-rich benefits of Nettle to create a tonic that supports liver function, detoxification, and overall vitality.

DOSAGE: Take 5 milliliters of the tincture three times daily, diluted in water or tea, especially beneficial during changes of seasons or when additional detoxification is needed.

PRECAUTIONS: This tincture is generally safe but monitor for any allergic reactions, particularly if you are sensitive to other Asteraceae or Urticaceae family plants.

PREP TIME: 20 MINUTES   **MACERATION TIME:** 4-6 WEEKS   **YIELD:** APPROX 500 ML

INGREDIENTS

- *Dandelion Root: 25 grams (dried and chopped)*
- *Nettle Leaves: 25 grams (dried)*
- *High-proof Alcohol (at least 40% alcohol by volume, such as vodka): 500 milliliters*

TOOLS

- *Kitchen scale*
- *Clean, dry jar with a tight-fitting lid*
- *Fine mesh sieve or cheesecloth*
- *Amber glass dropper bottles for storage*

INSTRUCTIONS

1. Weigh the Dandelion root and Nettle leaves accurately using a kitchen scale to ensure the correct ratio.
2. Combine the Dandelion and Nettle in your sterilized jar.

3. Pour alcohol over the herbs until completely submerged, with an extra two inches of liquid above to allow for expansion.
4. Seal the jar tightly with its lid and store it in a dark, cool cupboard. Shake the jar daily to help with the extraction process.
5. After 4-6 weeks, filter the tincture using a fine mesh or cheesecloth into a clean vessel. Compress the herbs to extract maximum liquid.
6. Funnel the strained tincture into amber bottles equipped with droppers. Label each bottle clearly with the date of finalization, and any other pertinent information.

GINSENG AND ASTRAGALUS VITALITY TINCTURE

DOSAGE: Consume 5 milliliters of the tincture up to three times daily, diluted in water or juice, especially during times of stress or when extra immunity support is needed.

PRECAUTIONS: Monitor for any possible side effects, as Ginseng and Astragalus can interact with some medications and may affect blood pressure and blood sugar levels.

PREP TIME: 15 MINUTES   **MACERATION TIME**: 6-8 WEEKS   **YIELD:** APPROX 500 ML

INGREDIENTS

- *Ginseng Root: 30 grams (sliced)*
- *Astragalus Root: 30 grams (sliced)*
- *High-proof Alcohol (at least 40% alcohol by volume, such as vodka or grain alcohol): 500 milliliters*

TOOLS

- *Kitchen scale*
- *Clean, dry jar with a tight-fitting lid*
- *Fine mesh sieve or cheesecloth*
- *Amber glass dropper bottles for storage*

INSTRUCTIONS

1. Weigh both the Ginseng and Astragalus roots using a kitchen scale to maintain accuracy for optimal benefits.
2. Place the sliced roots into your sterilized jar.
3. Pour the alcohol over the roots until they are fully submerged, with an extra two inches of liquid on top to allow for expansion.
4. Seal the jar tightly with its lid and store it in a dark, cool cupboard. Shake the jar daily to help with the extraction process.
5. After 6-8 weeks, filter the tincture using a fine mesh or cheesecloth into another clean container, ensuring all liquid is extracted.
6. Funnel the liquid to amber glass bottles. If possible, use bottles with droppers for easy dosage. Label each bottle clearly with the date of finalization, and any other pertinent information.

GOLDEN ROOT AND SIBERIAN GINSENG VITALITY BOOST

DOSAGE: Take 5 milliliters of the tincture up to three times daily, preferably in the morning or early afternoon to support energy levels throughout the day.

PRECAUTIONS: Siberian Ginseng and Golden Root are known for their adaptogenic properties but they might induce symptoms such as restlessness or insomnia in those who are sensitive, particularly if taken late in the day.

PREP TIME: 20 MINUTES

MACERATION TIME: 4 TO 6 WEEKS

YIELD: APPROX 500 ML

INGREDIENTS

- Golden Root Powder: 25 grams
- Siberian Ginseng Root: 25 grams, finely chopped
- 100-proof Vodka: 500 milliliters

TOOLS

- Precision scale
- Clean, dry glass jar with airtight lid
- Cheesecloth or a fine mesh strainer
- Amber glass bottles with droppers for storage

INSTRUCTIONS

1. Use a precision scale to measure out the Golden Root powder and Siberian Ginseng root to ensure accuracy and optimal dosage.
2. Combine both herbs in the clean glass jar.
3. Pour the vodka over the herbs, ensuring they are completely submerged by about two inches of liquid to allow for expansion and agitation.
4. Tightly seal the jar with its lid and store it in a cool, dark cupboard. Shake the jar daily to mix the contents and aid in the extraction process.
5. After 4-6 weeks, filter the tincture using cheesecloth or a fine mesh strainer into a clean jar, pressing the herbs to extract as much liquid as possible.
6. Funnel the strained tincture into amber glass bottles. If possible, use bottles with droppers for easy dosage. Label each bottle clearly with the date of finalization, and any other pertinent information.

SCHISANDRA AND ASHWAGANDHA VITALITY TINCTURE

DOSAGE: Consume 5 milliliters of the tincture twice daily, preferably in the morning and early afternoon to support day-long vitality without disturbing sleep patterns.

PREP TIME: 15 MINUTES

MACERATION TIME: 6 WEEKS

YIELD: APPROX 500 ML

- Schisandra Berries: 30 grams, dried
- Ashwagandha Root: 30 grams, dried and powdered
- 190-proof Ethanol: 500 milliliters (or a suitable high-proof spirit available in your region)

TOOLS

- Precision scale for accurate measurement
- Clean, dry glass jar with airtight lid (1-liter capacity)
- Cheesecloth or a fine mesh strainer
- Amber glass dropper bottles for final storage

INSTRUCTIONS

1. Measure the dried Schisandra berries and Ashwagandha root powder using a precision scale to ensure correct dosage. Place the Schisandra berries and Ashwagandha powder into the glass jar.
2. Pour the ethanol over the herbs, ensuring that the liquid level is at least two inches above the herbs to cover any expansion.
3. Seal the jar tightly with its lid and store it in a cool, dark cupboard. Shake the jar daily to help the ethanol extract the active components from the herbs.
4. After six weeks, filter the mixture using cheesecloth or a fine mesh strainer into another clean jar, squeezing out as much liquid as possible.
5. Funnel the strained liquid into amber glass bottles. If possible, use bottles with droppers for easy dosage. Label each bottle clearly with the date of finalization, and any other pertinent information.

Sleep Aids

VALERIAN AND PASSIONFLOWER TINCTURE

This Valerian and Passionflower tincture is an excellent addition to your nighttime routine, helping to ease the mind and prepare the body for sleep. Recommended usage is 5 milliliters about 30 minutes before bedtime or during moments of heightened stress.

PREP TIME: 20 MINUTES   **MACERATION TIME:** 4-6 WEEKS   **YIELD:** APPROX 500 ML

INGREDIENTS

- Valerian Root: 25 grams (dried root)
- Passionflower: 25 grams (dried aerial parts)
- Alcohol (vodka or brandy, at least 40% alcohol by volume): 500 milliliters (approximately 17 ounces)

TOOLS

- Glass jar with a tight-fitting lid
- Kitchen scale (for precise herb measurement)
- Measuring cup or jug
- Fine mesh strainer or cheesecloth
- Dark glass dropper bottles for storage

INSTRUCTIONS

1. Using a kitchen scale, accurately weigh the dried Valerian root and Passionflower. Place them together in your glass jar.
2. Pour the vodka or brandy over the herbs until they are completely submerged, with an extra 2-3 inches of alcohol above the herb level to account for absorption and swelling.
3. Secure the lid on the jar and shake well to mix the ingredients thoroughly. Store the jar in a dark, cool cupboard away from direct sunlight and temperature fluctuations.
4. Let the mixture macerate for 4-6 weeks, shaking the jar every couple of days to aid the extraction process.
5. After the maceration period, filter the tincture using a fine mesh strainer or cheesecloth into another clean glass jar, ensuring all herbal residues are removed.
6. Funnel the strained tincture into dark glass bottles to preserve its potency and extend its shelf life. If possible, use bottles with droppers for easy dosage.
7. Properly label each bottle with the herb names, date of preparation, and use-by date (typically one year from the date of production).

LEMON BALM AND VALERIAN BLEND

This Lemon Balm and Valerian Root tincture is ideal for evening use, 30 minutes before bedtime, to facilitate a tranquil transition to sleep. The recommended dosage is 5 milliliters.

PREP TIME: 10 MINUTES   **MACERATION TIME:** 4-6 WEEKS   **YIELD:** ABOUT 500 MILLILITERS

INGREDIENTS

- *Lemon Balm: 25 grams (dried leaves)*
- *Valerian Root: 25 grams (dried root)*
- *High-proof Alcohol (vodka or brandy, 40-50% alcohol by volume): 500 milliliters*

TOOLS

- *Glass jar with a tight-fitting lid*
- *Kitchen scale*
- *Measuring cup*
- *Fine mesh sieve or cheesecloth*
- *Dark-colored glass dropper bottles for storage*

INSTRUCTIONS

1. Measure out the dried Lemon Balm and Valerian Root using a kitchen scale. Ensure herbs are properly dried and free from any mold or dampness.
2. Place the herbs into your clean glass jar. Pour the vodka or brandy over the herbs until they are completely submerged, with an additional two to three inches of alcohol to cover.
3. Tightly seal the jar and shake gently to mix. Store in a dark, cool cupboard away from direct sunlight for 4-6 weeks. Shake the jar every few days to aid in the extraction.

4. After maceration, filter the liquid using a fine mesh sieve or cheesecloth into another clean jar. Press or squeeze the plant material to extract as much liquid as possible.
5. Funnel the strained tincture into dark glass bottles to preserve its potency. Ensure the bottles are sterilized before use. If possible, use bottles with droppers for easy dosage.
6. Label your bottles with the herb names, date of production, and expiry date (typically one year from the date of preparation).

CALMING TINCTURE WITH CALIFORNIA POPPY AND CHAMOMILE

DOSAGE: Take 5 milliliters of the tincture diluted in a little water or directly under the tongue 30 minutes before bedtime.

PRECAUTIONS: Monitor your body's response to the tincture, particularly if combining with other sleep aids or sedatives, as herbs can potentiate the effects of pharmaceuticals.

PREP TIME: 20 MINUTES   **MACERATION TIME**: 4 TO 6 WEEKS   **YIELD:** APPROX 600 ML

INGREDIENTS

- *California Poppy: 40 grams, dried*
- *Chamomile: 40 grams, dried*
- *190-proof Ethanol: 600 milliliters (or a suitable high-proof spirit available in your region)*

TOOLS

- *Precision scale for accurate measurement*
- *Clean, dry glass jar with airtight lid (1-liter capacity)*
- *Cheesecloth or a fine mesh strainer*
- *Amber glass dropper bottles for final storage*

INSTRUCTIONS

1. Measure the dried California Poppy and Chamomile using a precision scale. Ensure the herbs are finely cut to help release the essential oils and increase the surface area for extraction.
2. Place the herbs into the glass jar.
3. Pour ethanol over the herbs, making sure that the herbs are completely submerged with a few inches of alcohol above to compensate for absorption and evaporation.
4. Seal the jar tightly with its lid and place it in a cool, dark cupboard. Shake the jar daily to mix the herbs and promote extraction.
5. After 4 to 6 weeks, filter the mixture using cheesecloth or a fine mesh strainer into another clean jar, compressing the herbs to extract as much liquid as possible.
6. Funnel the filtered tincture into amber glass bottles. If possible, use bottles with droppers for easy dosage. Label each bottle clearly with the date of finalization, and any other pertinent information.

SOOTHING TINCTURE WITH LAVENDER AND VALERIAN

DOSAGE: Administer 1 to 2 milliliters of the tincture under the tongue or in a small amount of water, 30 minutes before bedtime.

PREP TIME: 15 MINUTES

MACERATION TIME: 4 TO 6 WEEKS

YIELD: APPROX 500 ML

INGREDIENTS

- Lavender: 30 grams, dried
- Valerian Root: 30 grams, dried
- Vodka (40-50% alcohol by volume): 500 milliliters

TOOLS

- Precision scale for accurate measurement
- Clean, dry glass jar with airtight lid (1-liter capacity)
- Cheesecloth or a fine mesh strainer
- Amber glass dropper bottles for storage

INSTRUCTIONS

1. Weigh the dried Lavender and Valerian root accurately using a precision scale to ensure proper dosage.
2. Place both herbs into your glass jar.
3. Pour vodka over the herbs until they are completely submerged with an extra two inches of alcohol on top, covering them to allow for absorption and evaporation.
4. Seal the jar tightly with its lid and store it in a dark, cool cupboard. Shake the jar once daily to help with the extraction process.
5. After the maceration period, filter the liquid using cheesecloth or a fine mesh strainer into another clean glass jar, squeezing out as much liquid as possible from the herb matter.
6. Funnel the strained tincture into amber glass bottles. If possible, use bottles with droppers for easy dosage. Label each bottle clearly with the date of finalization, and any other pertinent information.

SKULLCAP AND CHAMOMILE TINCTURE

DOSAGE: Take 1 to 2 milliliters of tincture directly under the tongue or diluted in a little water, ideally 30 minutes before bedtime.

PREP TIME: 15 MINUTES   **MACERATION TIME**: 4 TO 6 WEEKS   **YIELD:** APPROX 500 ML

INGREDIENTS

- *Skullcap: 25 grams, dried*
- *Chamomile: 25 grams, dried*
- *High-proof vodka (40-50% alcohol by volume): 500 milliliters*

TOOLS

- *Precision scale for accurate measurement*
- *Clean, dry glass jar with an airtight lid (1-liter capacity)*
- *Cheesecloth or a fine mesh strainer*
- *Amber glass dropper bottles for storage*

INSTRUCTIONS

1. Weigh the dried Skullcap and Chamomile using a precision scale to maintain correct proportions for efficacy.
2. Combine both herbs in your glass jar.
3. Pour the vodka over the herbs, ensuring they are fully submerged with an additional two inches of alcohol to cover, accommodating expansion and absorption.
4. Seal the jar tightly with its lid and place it in a dark, cool location. Shake the jar daily to help mix the herbs with the alcohol and enhance the extraction process.
5. After the specified maceration period, filter the mixture using cheesecloth or a fine mesh strainer into another clean glass jar, pressing the herbs to extract as much liquid as possible.
6. Fill amber glass bottles with the strained tincture. If possible, use bottles with droppers for easy dosage. Label each bottle clearly with the date of finalization, and any other pertinent information.

Digestive Aids

SOOTHING DIGESTIVE TINCTURE

This tincture is ideal for relieving symptoms of indigestion, bloating, and stress-related gastrointestinal discomfort. Always shake the bottle before use and consider starting with small doses (1-2 droppers) to assess tolerance.

PREP TIME: 30 MINUTES   **MACERATION TIME:** 4-6 WEEKS   **YIELD:** APPROX 500 ML

INGREDIENTS

- *Lemon Balm: 20 grams (dried leaves)*
- *Peppermint: 20 grams (dried leaves)*
- *Turmeric: 10 grams (dried, sliced root)*
- *Vodka or Ethanol (40-60% alcohol by volume): 500 milliliters (approximately 17 ounces)*

TOOLS

- *Glass jar with a tight-fitting lid*
- *Kitchen scale (for precise herb measurement)*
- *Measuring cup or jug*
- *Fine mesh strainer or cheesecloth*
- *Dark glass dropper bottles for storage*

INSTRUCTIONS

1. Using a kitchen scale, accurately measure the dried herbs. Combine Lemon Balm, Peppermint, and Turmeric in your glass jar.
2. Pour vodka or ethanol over the herbs. The alcohol should completely cover the herbs by at least 2-3 inches because the herbs will expand as they absorb the alcohol.
3. Seal the jar tightly with its lid and shake to mix the herbs with the alcohol. Store the jar in a cool, dark cupboard or a pantry.
4. Let the mixture sit for 4-6 weeks, shaking the jar every few days to ensure that the herbs are effectively macerating.
5. After maceration, filter the tincture using a fine mesh strainer or cheesecloth into another clean glass jar. Ensure all solid particles are removed.
6. Funnel the strained tincture into dark glass bottles for long-term storage. If possible, use bottles with droppers for easy dosage.
7. Clearly label the bottles with the herb names, date of production, and expiration date (typically one year from the date of straining).

PREPARATION TIPS: When handling turmeric, wear gloves to avoid staining your hands.

DIGESTIVE AID TINCTURE WITH GINGER AND PEPPERMINT

This digestive tincture combines the potent digestive properties of Ginger with the soothing effects of Peppermint to help alleviate digestive discomfort, reduce bloating, and enhance overall digestion.

DOSAGE: Administer 1 to 2 milliliters of the tincture directly under the tongue or dilute in water or tea, taken before or after meals.

PREP TIME: 20 MINUTES

MACERATION TIME: 4 TO 6 WEEKS

YIELD: APPROX 500 ML

INGREDIENTS

- *Ginger: 30 grams, dried and finely chopped*
- *Peppermint: 20 grams, dried*
- *High-proof vodka (at least 40% alcohol by volume): 500 milliliters*

TOOLS

- *Precision scale for accurate measurement*
- *Clean, dry glass jar with a tight-fitting lid (1-liter capacity)*
- *Cheesecloth or a fine mesh strainer*
- *Amber glass dropper bottles for storage*

INSTRUCTIONS

1. Accurately measure the dried Ginger and Peppermint using a precision scale. This ensures effective potency and balance in your tincture.
2. Place both herbs into your clean glass jar.
3. Pour vodka over the herbs, ensuring they are completely submerged with an extra couple of inches of liquid to cover them. This accounts for absorption and expansion.
4. Securely seal the jar with its lid and store it in a dark, cool cupboard. Shake the jar daily to mix the herbs with the alcohol, which aids in the extraction process.
5. After 4 to 6 weeks, filter the liquid using cheesecloth or a fine mesh strainer into another clean jar, squeezing the herbs to extract as much liquid as possible.
6. Funnel the strained tincture into amber glass bottles. If possible, use bottles with droppers for easy dosage. Label each bottle clearly with the date of finalization, and any other pertinent information.

LICORICE ROOT AND CHAMOMILE TINCTURE

This digestive tincture blends the soothing qualities of Licorice Root with the calming effects of Chamomile, ideal for supporting a healthy digestive system and alleviating symptoms of indigestion and acid reflux.

DOSAGE: Take 1 to 2 milliliters of the tincture up to three times daily, either directly under the tongue or diluted in a small amount of water, particularly before meals to aid digestion.

PRECAUTIONS: Licorice Root should be used with caution in individuals with high blood pressure or heart conditions due to its potential effect on sodium and water retention.

PREP TIME: 15 MINUTES   **MACERATION TIME**: 4 TO 6 WEEKS   **YIELD:** APPROX 500 ML

INGREDIENTS

- *Licorice Root: 25 grams, dried and sliced*
- *Chamomile: 15 grams, dried flowers*
- *100-proof vodka: 500 milliliters*

TOOLS

- *Precision scale*
- *Clean, dry glass jar with a tight-fitting lid (1-liter capacity)*
- *Cheesecloth or a fine mesh strainer*
- *Amber glass dropper bottles for storage*

INSTRUCTIONS

1. Weigh out the dried Licorice Root and Chamomile using a precision scale to ensure accuracy in your herbal ratios.
2. Place the measured herbs into the clean glass jar.
3. Pour the vodka over the herbs until they are completely submerged with an extra inch of liquid above the herbs to allow for expansion.
4. Tightly seal the jar and store it in a dark, cool cupboard. Shake the jar once daily to promote the extraction of the herbs' beneficial properties.
5. After 4 to 6 weeks, filter the liquid using cheesecloth or a fine mesh strainer into another clean jar. Press or squeeze the herbs to extract as much tincture as possible.
6. Funnel the strained tincture into amber glass bottles. If possible, use bottles with droppers for easy dosage. Label each bottle clearly with the date of finalization, and any other pertinent information.

SAGE AND GINGER DIGESTIVE TINCTURE

This digestive tincture harnesses the potent digestive benefits of Sage, renowned for its anti-inflammatory properties, and Ginger, which is celebrated for its ability to relieve nausea and digestive discomfort.

DOSAGE: Administer 1-2 milliliters of the tincture up to three times daily. The tincture can be taken directly under the tongue or diluted in water, ideally before meals to aid with digestion.

PRECAUTIONS: Be cautious with Sage if you have conditions affected by hormonal changes, as Sage contains compounds that can influence hormone levels.

PREP TIME: 20 MINUTES

MACERATION TIME: 4 TO 6 WEEKS

YIELD: APPROX 500 ML

INGREDIENTS

- *Sage: 20 grams, dried leaves*
- *Ginger: 20 grams, fresh root, finely chopped*
- *100-proof vodka: 500 milliliters*

TOOLS

- *Precision scale*
- *Clean, dry glass jar with a tight-fitting lid (1-liter capacity)*
- *Cheesecloth or a fine mesh strainer*
- *Amber glass dropper bottles for storage*

INSTRUCTIONS

1. Weigh and prepare the dried Sage and freshly chopped Ginger using a precision scale to ensure correct dosage.
2. Place both herbs into the clean glass jar.
3. Pour the vodka over the herbs, ensuring they are completely covered by an inch of alcohol to compensate for any absorption and swelling.
4. Securely seal the jar and store it in a dark, cool cupboard. Shake the jar daily to enhance the extraction process.
5. After the maceration period, filter the tincture using cheesecloth or a fine mesh into a clean jar, pressing the herbs to extract as much liquid as possible.
6. Funnel the strained tincture into amber bottles. If possible, use bottles with droppers for easy dosage. Label each bottle clearly with the date of finalization, and any other pertinent information.

SLIPPERY ELM AND MARSHMALLOW ROOT DIGESTIVE SOOTHE TINCTURE

This digestive tincture combines the soothing properties of Slippery Elm and Marshmallow Root, both renowned for their mucilaginous content which aids in calming the digestive tract and alleviating irritation.

DOSAGE: Take 1-2 milliliters of the tincture up to three times a day. It can be taken directly or diluted in a small amount of water or tea.

PREP TIME: 20 MINUTES   **MACERATION TIME**: 4 TO 6 WEEKS   **YIELD:** APPROX 500 ML

INGREDIENTS

- Slippery Elm: 15 grams, dried bark powder
- Marshmallow Root: 15 grams, dried root
- 100-proof vodka or vegetable glycerin: 500 milliliters

TOOLS

- Precision scale
- Clean, dry glass jar with a tight-fitting lid (1-liter capacity)
- Cheesecloth or a fine mesh strainer
- Amber glass dropper bottles for storage

INSTRUCTIONS

1. Weigh the dried Slippery Elm bark powder and Marshmallow Root using a precision scale to ensure accuracy. Add both herbs to the clean glass jar.
2. Pour the vodka or glycerin over the herbs until completely submerged by at least an inch above the herb level, ensuring all parts are covered to facilitate proper extraction.
3. Tightly seal the jar with its lid and place it in a cool, dark cabinet. Shake the jar daily to mix the contents and aid in the extraction process.
4. After the maceration period, filter the contents using a cheesecloth or fine mesh strainer into another clean jar, squeezing out as much liquid as possible from the herbs.
5. Decant the clear tincture into amber glass bottles. If possible, use bottles with droppers for easy dosage. Label each bottle clearly with the date of finalization, and any other pertinent information.

CLEAVERS AND DANDELION TINCTURE

DOSAGE: Adults can take 1-2 ml of the tincture three times a day in a little water. It is best used before meals or as directed by a health care practitioner.

PRECAUTIONS: As both Cleavers and Dandelion promote diuresis, make sure to stay properly hydrated by consuming plenty of fluids during the day.

PREP TIME: 15 MINUTES   **MACERATION TIME:** 4 WEEKS   **YIELD:** APPROX 500 ML

INGREDIENTS

- Cleavers: 20 grams, dried aerial parts
- Dandelion: 20 grams, dried root
- Vodka or grain alcohol (40-50% alcohol by volume): 500 milliliters

TOOLS

- Precision scale
- Glass jar with a tight-sealing lid (at least 1-liter capacity)
- Cheesecloth or fine mesh strainer
- Dark glass dropper bottles for storage

INSTRUCTIONS

1. Accurately weigh the dried Cleavers and Dandelion using the precision scale to ensure proper ratio and potency. Place the herbs into the clean glass jar.
2. Pour the vodka or grain alcohol over the herbs until they are completely submerged, with about an inch of liquid above the top of the herbs to allow for expansion and shaking.
3. Seal the jar tightly with its lid and store it in a cool, dark cupboard. Shake the jar daily to encourage the extraction of the active constituents from the herbs.
4. After four weeks, filter the liquid using a cheesecloth or a fine mesh strainer into another clean jar. Press or squeeze the herb material to extract as much liquid as possible.
5. Funnel the strained tincture into dark glass bottles. If possible, use bottles with droppers for easy dosage. Label each bottle clearly with the date of finalization, and any other pertinent information.

JUNIPER AND PARSLEY TINCTURE

This tincture harnesses the properties of Juniper berries known for their kidney-supportive and urinary tract benefits, paired with Parsley, which is celebrated for its ability to help manage water retention naturally.

DOSAGE: For adults, take 2-3 ml diluted in water up to three times daily.

PRECAUTIONS: Stay well-hydrated while using diuretic tinctures to avoid dehydration. This tincture should be used with caution in individuals with kidney disease or those taking diuretic medications due to potential interactions and increased diuretic effect.

PREP TIME: 20 MINUTES   **MACERATION TIME**: 6 WEEKS   **YIELD:** APPROX 500 ML

INGREDIENTS

- Juniper Berries: 30 grams, dried
- Parsley: 30 grams, dried leaves
- Vodka or grain alcohol (50% alcohol by volume): 500 milliliters

TOOLS

- Precision scale
- Glass jar with a tight-sealing lid (at least 1-liter capacity)
- Cheesecloth or fine mesh strainer
- Dark glass dropper bottles for storage

INSTRUCTIONS

1. Use a precision scale to measure 30 grams each of dried Juniper berries and dried Parsley leaves.
2. Place both herbs into your clean glass jar.
3. Pour the vodka or grain alcohol over the herbs to submerge them completely, ensuring an extra inch of liquid above the herbs for proper maceration.
4. Seal the jar tightly with its lid. Store it in a cool, dark cupboard. Shake the jar daily to promote the extraction of active components from the herbs.
5. After six weeks, filter the tincture using cheesecloth or a fine mesh strainer into a clean jar. Compress the herbs to extract maximum liquid.
6. Funnel the strained tincture into dark glass bottles. If possible, use bottles with droppers for easy dosage. Label each bottle clearly with the date of finalization, and any other pertinent information.

Respiratory Health

ELECAMPANE AND MULLEIN TINCTURE

This respiratory health tincture leverages the deep lung-supporting properties of Elecampane, known for its expectorant qualities, alongside Mullein, which is revered for its soothing effect on the bronchial tubes and lungs.

DOSAGE: Adults: Take 1-2 ml of the tincture three times daily, mixed in a small amount of water.

PRECAUTIONS: Monitor for any allergic reactions, especially if you are sensitive to Asteraceae family plants.

PREP TIME: 20 MINUTES   **MACERATION TIME:** 4 WEEKS   **YIELD:** APPROX 500 ML

INGREDIENTS

- *Elecampane Root: 25 grams, dried and chopped*
- *Mullein Leaves: 25 grams, dried*
- *High-proof Vodka or Grain Alcohol (60% alcohol by volume): 500 milliliters*

TOOLS

- *Precision scale*
- *Glass jar with a tight-sealing lid (at least 1-liter capacity)*
- *Cheesecloth or fine mesh strainer*
- *Amber glass dropper bottles for storage*

INSTRUCTIONS

1. Use a precision scale to measure out 25 grams each of dried Elecampane root and dried Mullein leaves.
2. Place both the Elecampane and Mullein into your clean glass jar.

3. Pour enough vodka or grain alcohol into the jar to fully submerge the herbs, ensuring about an inch of alcohol stands above the herbs to allow for expansion.
4. Seal the jar tightly with its lid and place it in a cool, dark cupboard or a cellar. Shake the jar once daily to mix and promote extraction.
5. After four weeks, filter the tincture using cheesecloth or a fine mesh into another clean jar, pressing the plant material to extract as much liquid as possible.
6. Funnel the clear tincture to amber glass bottles. If possible, use bottles with droppers for easy dosage. Label each bottle clearly with the date of finalization, and any other pertinent information.

HYSSOP AND THYME RESPIRATORY HEALTH TINCTURE

This tincture combines the expectorant properties of Hyssop with the antimicrobial and cough-suppressant effects of Thyme, creating a robust remedy for respiratory health maintenance and support.

DOSAGE FOR ADULTS: 1-2 ml, up to three times daily. Dilute in water or tea before ingestion.

PRECAUTIONS: Hyssop should be used with caution in individuals with epilepsy or other seizure disorders as it can potentially stimulate the nervous system.

PREP TIME: 15 MINUTES   **MACERATION TIME**: 3-4 WEEKS   **YIELD:** APPROX 450-500 ML

INGREDIENTS

- *Hyssop Leaves and Flowers: 30 grams, dried*
- *Thyme: 20 grams, dried*
- *High-proof Vodka or Ethanol (40-60% alcohol by volume): 500 milliliters*

TOOLS

- *Glass jar with a tight-sealing lid (1-liter capacity)*
- *Cheesecloth or a fine mesh strainer*
- *Amber glass dropper bottles for final storage*

INSTRUCTIONS

1. Use a kitchen scale to measure the hyssop and thyme accurately.
2. Place the dried hyssop and thyme into your clean glass jar.
3. Pour the vodka or ethanol over the herbs, making sure they are completely submerged with an extra inch of liquid on top to allow for expansion.
4. Seal the jar tightly with its lid and store it in a dark, cool cupboard. Shake the jar daily to help with the extraction process.
5. After 3-4 weeks, filter the mixture using a cheesecloth or fine mesh strainer into a clean jar, squeezing out as much liquid as possible.
6. Funnel the strained liquid into amber bottles. If possible, use bottles with droppers for easy dosage. Label each bottle clearly with the date of finalization, and any other pertinent information.

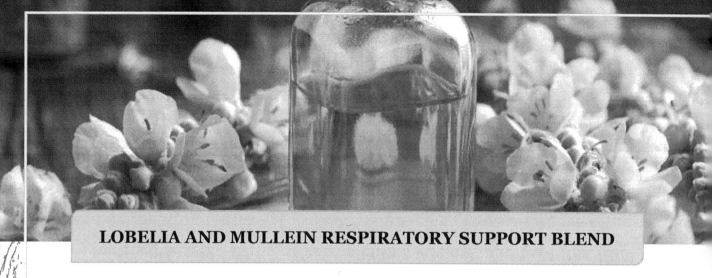

LOBELIA AND MULLEIN RESPIRATORY SUPPORT BLEND

This carefully crafted tincture combines the bronchial relaxing effects of Lobelia with the soothing properties of Mullein, creating a potent remedy for supporting respiratory health and easing breathing difficulties.

DOSAGE FOR ADULTS: 1 ml, up to three times daily, taken diluted in a glass of water or tea.

PRECAUTIONS: Due to lobelia's potent effects, start with a lower dose to assess tolerance. Lobelia is known for its use as a muscle relaxant and can significantly assist in cases of respiratory constriction but should be used cautiously due to its strength.

PREP TIME: 15 MINUTES   **MACERATION TIME**: 4 WEEKS   **YIELD:** APPROX 450-500 ML

INGREDIENTS

- *Lobelia: 15 grams, dried*
- *Mullein Leaves and Flowers: 30 grams, dried*
- *High-proof Vodka or Ethanol (40-60% alcohol by volume): 500 milliliters*

TOOLS

- *Glass jar with a tight-sealing lid (1-liter capacity)*
- *Cheesecloth or a fine mesh strainer*
- *Amber glass dropper bottles for final storage*

INSTRUCTIONS

1. Weigh out the lobelia and mullein using a digital scale to ensure accuracy.
2. Place both herbs into the clean glass jar.
3. Pour enough vodka or ethanol over the herbs to completely cover them with an extra two inches of liquid above the herbs to account for absorption and swelling.
4. Seal the jar tightly with its lid and place it in a cool, dark cupboard. Shake the jar daily to facilitate the extraction process.
5. After four weeks, filter the herbs out using a cheesecloth or fine mesh strainer, squeezing to extract as much liquid as possible.
6. Funnel the strained tincture into amber bottles. If possible, use bottles with droppers for easy dosage. Label each bottle clearly with the date of finalization, and any other pertinent information.

PEPPERMINT AND EUCALYPTUS RESPIRATORY RELIEF TINCTURE

This homemade tincture combines the cooling benefits of Peppermint with the clearing capabilities of Eucalyptus, providing a natural aid for respiratory health, particularly suitable for clearing congestion and cooling inflamed respiratory passages.

ADULT DOSAGE: Take 1-2 ml of the tincture up to three times daily. Always dilute the tincture in water or tea before ingesting.

PREP TIME: 20 MINUTES   **MACERATION TIME:** 6 WEEKS   **YIELD:** APPROX 450-500 ML

INGREDIENTS

- *Peppermint: 20 grams, dried leaves*
- *Eucalyptus: 20 grams, dried leaves*
- *High-proof Grain Alcohol (at least 60% alcohol by volume): 500 milliliters*

TOOLS

- *Glass jar with a tight-sealing lid (1-liter capacity)*
- *Cheesecloth or a fine mesh strainer*
- *Amber glass dropper bottles for storage*

INSTRUCTIONS

1. Roughly chop or crush the peppermint and eucalyptus leaves to help release the essential oils and increase the surface area for extraction. Place the chopped herbs into the sterilized glass jar.
2. Cover the herbs completely with high-proof grain alcohol, ensuring there are a few inches of alcohol above the herb level to account for absorption.
3. Tightly seal the jar with its lid and store it in a cool, dark cupboard. Shake the jar daily to help with the extraction process.
4. After six weeks, filter the mixture using cheesecloth or a fine mesh strainer. Press or squeeze the herbs to extract as much liquid as possible.
5. Funnel the strained liquid into amber bottles. If possible, use bottles with droppers for easy dosage. Label each bottle clearly with the date of finalization, and any other pertinent information.

WILD CHERRY BARK AND THYME RESPIRATORY SUPPORT TINCTURE

This tincture recipe uses the soothing properties of Wild Cherry Bark and the antiseptic benefits of Thyme, ideal for supporting respiratory health, soothing coughs, and aiding in the relaxation of respiratory muscles.

ADULT DOSAGE: Take 1-2 ml of the tincture up to three times daily, diluted in water or juice.

PREP TIME: 30 MINUTES   **MACERATION TIME:** 4-6 WEEKS   **YIELD:** APPROX 450-500 ML

INGREDIENTS

- *Wild Cherry Bark: 30 grams, dried*
- *Thyme: 15 grams, dried*
- *Vodka or Brandy (40-50% alcohol by volume): 500 milliliters*

TOOLS

- *Glass jar with a tight-sealing lid (1-liter capacity)*
- *Cheesecloth or a fine mesh strainer*
- *Amber glass dropper bottles for storage*

INSTRUCTIONS

1. Break the wild cherry bark into small pieces, and slightly bruise the thyme to release its oils.
2. Combine the wild cherry bark and thyme in the sterilized glass jar.
3. Pour the vodka or brandy over the herbs, ensuring that the liquid covers the herbs by at least two to three inches to account for absorption and swelling.
4. Secure the lid tightly and place the jar in a dark, cool cupboard. Shake the jar daily for the first week and then weekly thereafter.
5. After 4-6 weeks, filter the tincture using cheesecloth or a fine mesh strainer into a clean bowl. Compress the herbs to extract as much liquid as possible.
6. Funnel the tincture to amber glass bottles. If possible, use bottles with droppers for easy dosage. Label each bottle clearly with the date of finalization, and any other pertinent information.

Skin Conditions

CALENDULA AND ALOE VERA SKIN SOOTHING TINCTURE

This tincture combines the healing properties of Calendula and the soothing effects of Aloe Vera, making it an effective treatment for various skin conditions such as irritation, sunburn, and mild abrasions.

DOSAGE: Apply the tincture gently with a cotton pad to the affected skin area up to three times daily.

PRECAUTIONS: For sensitive skin, dilute the tincture with water before application to reduce strength.

PREP TIME: 45 MINUTES   **MACERATION TIME**: 4 WEEKS   **YIELD:** APPROX 500 ML

INGREDIENTS

- *Calendula: 40 grams, dried flower heads*
- *Aloe Vera: 20 grams, fresh gel extracted from leaves*
- *High-proof alcohol (at least 40-50% alcohol by volume, such as vodka or brandy): 600 milliliters*

TOOLS

- Glass jar with a tight-sealing lid (1-liter capacity)
- Cheesecloth or a fine mesh strainer
- Amber glass dropper bottles for storage

INSTRUCTIONS

1. Crush the dried calendula flowers to increase the surface area for better extraction. Carefully extract the gel from fresh aloe vera leaves using a spoon, ensuring to only get the clear inner gel and not the yellow latex.
2. Place the crushed calendula and aloe vera gel into the sterilized glass jar.
3. Pour the alcohol over the calendula and aloe vera, ensuring the herbs are completely submerged to prevent any potential mold growth.
4. Tighten the lid and store the jar in a dark, cool place. Shake the jar once daily for the first week to mix the contents and aid in the extraction process.
5. After 4 weeks, filter the tincture using cheesecloth or a fine mesh strainer into a clean bowl, squeezing the solids to extract as much liquid as possible.
6. Funnel the strained tincture into amber glass bottles. If possible, use bottles with droppers for easy dosage. Label each with herb names, date, and any specific usage instructions.

GOLDENSEAL AND TEA TREE SKIN HEALING TINCTURE

This tincture harnesses the potent antimicrobial properties of Goldenseal and the antiseptic benefits of Tea Tree oil, ideal for treating acne, fungal skin infections, and minor wounds.

DOSAGE: Apply the tincture sparingly with a cotton swab directly on the affected areas of the skin, no more than twice daily.

PRECAUTIONS: Due to the potency of goldenseal and tea tree oil, this tincture should be used with caution on sensitive skin areas or diluted with a carrier oil for those with sensitive skin.

PREP TIME: 30 MINUTES   **MACERATION TIME:** 6 WEEKS   **YIELD:** APPROX 450 ML

INGREDIENTS

- Goldenseal: 30 grams of dried root
- Tea Tree Oil: 10 milliliters
- High-proof alcohol (at least 40-50% alcohol by volume, such as vodka or grain alcohol): 500 milliliters

TOOLS

- Glass jar with a tight-sealing lid (1-liter capacity)
- Cheesecloth or a fine mesh strainer

- Dark glass dropper bottles for storage

INSTRUCTIONS

1. Finely chop or grind the dried goldenseal root to help release the essential oils and increase the surface area for extraction. Place the chopped goldenseal into the sterilized glass jar.
2. Carefully measure and add the tea tree oil to the jar.
3. Pour the alcohol over the goldenseal and tea tree oil, ensuring the herbs are fully submerged to avoid any potential mold growth.
4. Seal the jar tightly with its lid and store it in a cool, dark cupboard. Shake the jar daily for the first two weeks to mix the contents and enhance the extraction process.
5. After 6 weeks, filter the tincture using cheesecloth or a fine mesh strainer into a clean bowl, pressing the solids to extract as much liquid as possible.
6. Funnel the strained tincture into dark glass bottles. If possible, use bottles with droppers for easy dosage. Label each with herb names, date, and any specific usage instructions.

HORSETAIL AND CHAMOMILE SKIN SOOTHING TINCTURE

This tincture combines the silica-rich properties of Horsetail and the soothing effects of Chamomile to create a gentle remedy for skin irritations, rashes, and minor wounds.

DOSAGE: Apply the tincture directly to the skin using a clean cotton ball or pad, dabbing gently on the affected areas.

PRECAUTIONS: For sensitive skin, dilute the tincture with a carrier oil or water.

PREP TIME: 20 MINUTES   **MACERATION TIME**: 4 WEEKS   **YIELD:** APPROX 450 ML

INGREDIENTS

- *Horsetail: 40 grams of dried herb*
- *Chamomile: 30 grams of dried flowers*

- *High-proof alcohol (at least 40-50% alcohol by volume, such as vodka or grain alcohol): 500 milliliters*

TOOLS

- *Glass jar with a tight-sealing lid (1-liter capacity)*
- *Cheesecloth or a fine mesh strainer*

- *Amber glass dropper bottles for storage*

INSTRUCTIONS

1. Roughly chop the dried horsetail and chamomile to enhance the surface area.
2. Combine the chopped herbs in the sterilized glass jar.
3. Pour the alcohol over the herbs until completely submerged to prevent any mold growth.
4. Seal the jar tightly with its lid and place it in a dark, cool cupboard. Shake the jar every few days to mix the herbs and alcohol.
5. After 4 weeks, filter the mixture using cheesecloth or a fine mesh strainer into a clean bowl. Compress the herbs to extract as much liquid as possible.
6. Funnel the strained tincture into amber glass bottles. If possible, use bottles with droppers for easy dosage. Label each bottle clearly with the date of finalization, and any other pertinent information.

SARSAPARILLA AND BURDOCK ROOT SKIN PURIFYING TINCTURE

This tincture leverages the detoxifying properties of Sarsaparilla combined with the cleansing abilities of Burdock Root to create a potent remedy for skin clarity and detoxification.

DOSAGE: Apply the tincture topically with a cotton ball or pad to the affected areas of the skin.

PREP TIME: 30 MINUTES   **MACERATION TIME**: 6 WEEKS   **YIELD:** APPROX 480 ML

INGREDIENTS

- *Sarsaparilla: 50 grams of dried root*
- *Burdock Root: 50 grams of dried root*
- *High-proof alcohol (at least 40-50% alcohol by volume, such as vodka or grain alcohol): 500 milliliters*

TOOLS

- *Glass jar with a tight-sealing lid (1-liter capacity)*
- *Cheesecloth or a fine mesh strainer*
- *Amber glass dropper bottles for storage*

INSTRUCTIONS

1. Finely chop or grind the dried sarsaparilla and burdock root to increase the surface area for extraction.
2. Place the prepared herbs in the sterilized glass jar.
3. Pour the alcohol over the herbs, ensuring they are fully submerged to prevent any potential spoilage.
4. Seal the jar tightly with its lid and store it in a dark, cool cupboard. Shake the jar daily for the first week to help with the extraction process.
5. After 6 weeks, filter the tincture using cheesecloth or a fine mesh strainer into a clean container, pressing the herbs to extract maximum liquid.
6. Funnel the strained tincture into amber glass bottles. If possible, use bottles with droppers for easy dosage. Label each bottle clearly with the date of finalization, and any other pertinent information.

CLEAVERS AND CHAMOMILE SOOTHING SKIN TINCTURE

This tincture combines the lymphatic cleansing properties of Cleavers with the soothing, anti-inflammatory benefits of Chamomile to create an effective remedy for various skin conditions.

DOSAGE:

- For skin application: Dilute the tincture with water and apply to the skin with a cotton pad, particularly in areas affected by irritation or inflammation.
- As a health supplement: Take 1-2 ml of the tincture diluted in water or tea up to three times daily.

PREP TIME: 20 MINUTES   **MACERATION TIME:** 4 WEEKS   **YIELD:** APPROX 480 ML

INGREDIENTS

- *Cleavers: 40 grams of dried herb*
- *Chamomile: 40 grams of dried flowers*
- *High-proof alcohol (at least 40-50% alcohol by volume, such as vodka or grain alcohol): 500 milliliters*

TOOLS

- *Glass jar with a tight-sealing lid (1-liter capacity)*
- *Cheesecloth or a fine mesh strainer*
- *Amber glass dropper bottles for storage*

INSTRUCTIONS

1. Roughly chop the dried cleavers and chamomile to help release the essential oils and increase the surface area for extraction.
2. Place the chopped herbs into the sterilized glass jar.
3. Pour the alcohol over the herbs, ensuring they are completely submerged to avoid mold growth.
4. Seal the jar tightly with its lid and place it in a dark, cool cupboard. Shake the jar daily for the first two weeks to enhance the extraction process.
5. After 4 weeks, filter the mixture using cheesecloth or a fine mesh strainer into a clean container. Squeeze or press the herbs well to extract as much liquid as possible.
6. Funnel the strained tincture into amber glass bottles. If possible, use bottles with droppers for easy dosage. Label each bottle clearly with the date of finalization, and any other pertinent information.

Anxiolytics and Stress Relievers

LINDEN AND LEMON BALM CALMATIVE TINCTURE

This tincture blends the soothing properties of Linden with the calming benefits of Lemon Balm to create an effective remedy for managing anxiety and promoting mental well-being.

DOSAGE: Take 1-2 ml of the tincture up to three times daily, either directly under the tongue or diluted in a small amount of water or tea. Incorporate the same dosage into daily routines, especially during times of increased stress or tension.

PREP TIME: 15 MINUTES   **MACERATION TIME**: 4 WEEKS   **YIELD:** APPROX 480 ML

INGREDIENTS

- Linden: 30 grams of dried flowers
- Lemon Balm: 30 grams of dried leaves
- High-proof alcohol (at least 40-50% alcohol by volume, such as vodka or grain alcohol): 500 milliliters

TOOLS

- Glass jar with a tight-sealing lid (1-liter capacity)
- Cheesecloth or a fine mesh strainer
- Amber glass dropper bottles for storage

INSTRUCTIONS

1. Gently crush the dried Linden flowers and Lemon Balm leaves to expose more surface area without pulverizing them into a powder.
2. Place the prepared herbs into the sterilized glass jar.
3. Pour the alcohol over the herbs, ensuring that they are completely covered to prevent any mold growth.
4. Secure the lid on the jar and store it in a cool, dark cupboard. Agitate the jar daily for the first week to facilitate the extraction.
5. After 4 weeks, filter the tincture using cheesecloth or a fine mesh strainer into another clean container, pressing the herbs to extract as much liquid as possible.
6. Funnel the clear tincture into amber glass bottles. If possible, use bottles with droppers for easy dosage. Label each bottle clearly with the date of finalization, and any other pertinent information.

MOTHERWORT AND CHAMOMILE CALMING TINCTURE

This tincture combines the heart-soothing effects of Motherwort with the calming properties of Chamomile to offer relief from anxiety and support mental health.

DOSAGE: Administer 2-3 ml of the tincture under the tongue or in water, up to three times per day.

PREP TIME: 20 MINUTES   **MACERATION TIME**: 4 WEEKS   **YIELD:** APPROX 480 ML

INGREDIENTS

- *Motherwort: 25 grams of dried aerial parts*
- *Chamomile: 25 grams of dried flowers*
- *High-proof alcohol (at least 40-50% alcohol by volume, such as vodka or grain alcohol): 500 milliliters*

TOOLS

- *Glass jar with a tight-sealing lid (1-liter capacity)*
- *Cheesecloth or a fine mesh strainer*
- *Amber glass dropper bottles for storage*

INSTRUCTIONS

1. Lightly bruise the dried Motherwort and Chamomile using a mortar and pestle to increase their surface area and enhance extraction.
2. Combine the herbs in the sterilized glass jar.
3. Pour the alcohol over the herbs until fully submerged, to prevent any exposure to air which could lead to spoilage.
4. Seal the jar tightly with its lid and place it in a dark, cool cupboard. Shake the jar daily for the first week to mix the ingredients.
5. After 4 weeks, filter the mixture using cheesecloth or a fine mesh strainer into a clean container, squeezing out as much liquid as possible.
6. Funnel the strained tincture into amber glass bottles. If possible, use bottles with droppers for easy dosage. Label them with the herb names, date, and batch number for proper tracking.

PASSIONFLOWER AND LEMON BALM SOOTHING TINCTURE

This tincture blends the calming effects of Passionflower with the mood-enhancing properties of Lemon Balm to offer support for anxiety relief and mental health improvement.

DOSAGE: Take 2-3 ml of the tincture up to three times per day.

PREP TIME: 15 MINUTES   **MACERATION TIME**: 4 WEEKS   **YIELD:** APPROX 500 ML

INGREDIENTS

- Passionflower: 30 grams of dried flowers
- Lemon Balm: 30 grams of dried leaves
- High-proof alcohol (at least 40-50% alcohol by volume, such as vodka or grain alcohol): 500 milliliters

TOOLS

- Glass jar with a tight-sealing lid (1-liter capacity)
- Cheesecloth or a fine mesh strainer
- Amber glass dropper bottles for storage

INSTRUCTIONS

1. Lightly crush the dried Passionflower and Lemon Balm using a mortar and pestle to expose more surface area, which helps to extract more of the active compounds.
2. Place the crushed herbs into the sterilized glass jar.
3. Pour the alcohol over the herbs until they are completely submerged to avoid mold and oxidation.
4. Seal the jar tightly with its lid and store it in a cool, dark cupboard or a pantry. Shake the jar once daily for the first week to help with the extraction process.
5. After four weeks, filter the contents using cheesecloth or a fine mesh strainer into another clean jar. Press or squeeze the herbs to extract as much liquid as possible.
6. Funnel the strained tincture into amber glass bottles. If possible, use bottles with droppers for easy dosage. Ensure each bottle is labeled with the herb names, date of production, and batch number.

ASHWAGANDHA AND HOLY BASIL CALMING TINCTURE

This tincture combines the stress-relieving properties of Ashwagandha with the adaptogenic benefits of Holy Basil (Tulsi), creating a powerful remedy for reducing anxiety and enhancing mental clarity.

DOSAGE: Take 1-2 ml up to three times per day, depending on individual sensitivity.

PREP TIME: 20 MINUTES   **MACERATION TIME**: 4 TO 6 WEEKS   **YIELD:** APPROX 600 ML

INGREDIENTS

- Ashwagandha: 40 grams of dried root
- Holy Basil: 20 grams of dried leaves
- High-proof alcohol (at least 40-50% alcohol by volume, such as vodka or grain alcohol): 600 milliliters

TOOLS

- Glass jar with a tight-sealing lid (1-liter capacity)
- Cheesecloth or a fine mesh strainer
- Amber glass dropper bottles for storage

INSTRUCTIONS

1. Coarsely grind the Ashwagandha root and Holy Basil leaves using a mortar and pestle or a blender to enhance the extraction process.
2. Place the ground herbs into the sterilized glass jar.
3. Pour the alcohol over the herbs until they are completely submerged, ensuring all plant material is covered to prevent mold formation.
4. Seal the jar tightly with its lid and place it in a dark, cool spot, away from direct sunlight. Shake the jar once daily for the first week to encourage the extraction.
5. After the maceration period, filter the tincture using cheesecloth or a fine mesh strainer into a clean jar. Compress the herbs to extract as much liquid as possible.
6. Funnel the strained liquid into amber glass bottles, labeling each with the herb names, date, and any batch number for proper identification. If possible, use bottles with droppers for easy dosage.

WOOD BETONY AND CHAMOMILE CALMING TINCTURE

This tincture melds the neurological benefits of Wood Betony with the soothing effects of Chamomile to create a natural remedy aimed at alleviating anxiety and promoting mental well-being.

DOSAGE: Administer 1 ml of the tincture up to three times daily.

PREP TIME: 15 MINUTES   **MACERATION TIME**: 4 TO 6 WEEKS   **YIELD:** APPROX 500 ML

INGREDIENTS

- Wood Betony: 30 grams of dried aerial parts
- Chamomile: 25 grams of dried flowers
- High-proof alcohol (at least 40-50% alcohol by volume, such as vodka or grain alcohol): 500 milliliters

TOOLS

- Glass jar with a tight-sealing lid (1-liter capacity)
- Cheesecloth or a fine mesh strainer
- Amber glass dropper bottles for storage

INSTRUCTIONS

1. Gently crush the Wood Betony and Chamomile using a mortar and pestle to increase the surface area for better extraction.
2. Transfer the crushed herbs into the sterilized glass jar.
3. Pour the alcohol over the herbs, ensuring they are completely submerged to prevent any potential spoilage.

4. Close the jar securely and place it in a dark, cool cupboard. Shake the jar daily for the first week to mix the contents and aid the extraction process.
5. After the maceration period, filter the mixture using a cheesecloth or fine mesh strainer into another clean jar. Press or squeeze the plant material to extract maximum liquid.
6. Decant the clear tincture into amber glass bottles. If possible, use bottles with droppers for easy dosage. Label each bottle clearly with the date of finalization, and any other pertinent information.

VALERIAN AND LEMON BALM SOOTHING TINCTURE

This tincture brings together the powerful relaxing properties of Valerian root and the mild sedative effects of Lemon Balm to create a potent remedy aimed at reducing anxiety, easing stress, and improving overall mental health.

DOSAGE: Take 1-2 ml of the tincture 1-3 times daily.

PREP TIME: 20 MINUTES

MACERATION TIME: 4 TO 6 WEEKS

YIELD: APPROX 500 ML

INGREDIENTS

- *Valerian Root: 50 grams of dried root*
- *Lemon Balm: 40 grams of dried leaves*
- *High-proof alcohol (at least 40-50% alcohol by volume, such as vodka or grain alcohol): 500 milliliters*

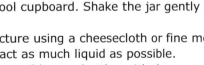

TOOLS

- *Glass jar with a tight-sealing lid (1-liter capacity)*
- *Cheesecloth or a fine mesh strainer*
- *Amber glass dropper bottles for storage*

INSTRUCTIONS

1. Roughly chop the Valerian root and Lemon Balm leaves to increase their surface area and enhance the extraction of active compounds.
2. Place the chopped herbs in the sterilized glass jar.
3. Pour the alcohol over the herbs, ensuring they are fully submerged to prevent mold and oxidation.
4. Securely seal the jar with its lid and store it in a dark, cool cupboard. Shake the jar gently once daily for the first week to help the extraction.
5. After the recommended maceration period, filter the tincture using a cheesecloth or fine mesh strainer into another clean glass jar. Compress the herbs to extract as much liquid as possible.
6. Funnel the strained tincture into amber glass bottles. If possible, use bottles with droppers for easy dosage. Ensure each bottle is labeled with the ingredients, preparation date, and batch number.

TULSI AND CHAMOMILE CALMING TINCTURE

This tincture combines the adaptogenic benefits of Tulsi (Holy Basil) with the soothing properties of Chamomile to create a powerful aid for reducing anxiety, soothing stress, and enhancing overall mental well-being.

DOSAGE: Administer 1-2 ml of the tincture up to three times daily.

PREP TIME: 15 MINUTES   **MACERATION TIME**: 4 TO 6 WEEKS   **YIELD:** APPROX 500 ML

INGREDIENTS

- *Tulsi: 40 grams of dried leaves*
- *Chamomile: 30 grams of dried flowers*
- *High-proof alcohol (at least 40-50% alcohol by volume, such as vodka or grain alcohol): 500 milliliters*

TOOLS

- *Glass jar with a tight-sealing lid (1-liter capacity)*
- *Cheesecloth or a fine mesh strainer*
- *Amber glass dropper bottles for storage*

INSTRUCTIONS

1. Coarsely chop the Tulsi leaves and Chamomile flowers to enhance their surface area, promoting better extraction of their active compounds.
2. Place the prepared herbs in the sterilized glass jar.
3. Pour the alcohol over the herbs, making sure they are completely covered to avoid mold and oxidation.
4. Seal the jar tightly with its lid and store it in a cool, dark cupboard away from direct sunlight. Shake the jar daily during the first week to mix the herbs with the alcohol.
5. After the maceration time, filter the tincture using a cheesecloth or fine mesh strainer into another clean glass jar, pressing the herbs to extract maximum liquid.
6. Funnel the strained tincture to amber glass bottles. If possible, use bottles with droppers for easy dosage. Label each bottle clearly with the date of finalization, and any other pertinent information.

ST. JOHN'S WORT AND LEMON BALM TINCTURE

This blend of St. John's Wort and Lemon Balm creates a powerful tincture that aims to improve mental clarity and reduce symptoms of anxiety and depression.

DOSAGE: Administer 3 ml when feeling anxious, up to three times per day.

PREP TIME: 20 MINUTES   **MACERATION TIME**: 4 TO 6 WEEKS   **YIELD:** APPROX 600 ML

INGREDIENTS

- *St. John's Wort: 50 grams of dried flowers*
- *Lemon Balm: 50 grams of dried leaves*
- *High-proof alcohol (at least 40-50% alcohol by volume, such as vodka or grain alcohol): 600 milliliters*

TOOLS

- *Glass jar with a tight-sealing lid (1-liter capacity)*
- *Cheesecloth or a fine mesh strainer*
- *Amber glass dropper bottles for storage*

INSTRUCTIONS

1. Gently crush the St. John's Wort flowers and Lemon Balm leaves to release their active compounds.
2. Place the herbs into your clean glass jar.
3. Pour the alcohol over the herbs until completely submerged, ensuring there are a couple of inches of alcohol above the herb level to account for absorption.
4. Seal the jar tightly with its lid and store in a dark, cool cupboard. Shake the jar every couple of days to agitate the herbs and aid in extraction.
5. After 4 to 6 weeks, filter the tincture using a cheesecloth or fine mesh strainer into another clean jar. Compress the herbs to extract as much liquid as possible.
6. Funnel the strained tincture into amber glass bottles. If possible, use bottles with droppers for easy dosage. Label each bottle clearly with the date of finalization, and any other pertinent information.

Women's Health

BLACK COHOSH AND RED CLOVER TINCTURE

This custom blend uses Black Cohosh and Red Clover, two herbs renowned for their benefits in women's health, specifically targeting menopausal symptoms, menstrual discomfort, and promoting urinary tract health.

DOSAGE:

- **Menopausal symptom relief**: Take 2-3 ml up to three times a day.
- **Menstrual discomfort**: Use 2 ml during painful periods up to three times daily.

PREP TIME: 15 MINUTES   **MACERATION TIME**: 4 TO 6 WEEKS   **YIELD:** APPROX 500 ML

INGREDIENTS

- *Black Cohosh: 30 grams of dried root*
- *Red Clover: 30 grams of dried flowers*
- *High-proof alcohol (at least 40-50% alcohol by volume, such as vodka or grain alcohol): 500 milliliters*

TOOLS

- *Glass jar with a tight-sealing lid (1-liter capacity)*
- *Cheesecloth or a fine mesh strainer*
- *Amber glass dropper bottles for storage*

INSTRUCTIONS

1. Lightly crush the Black Cohosh root and Red Clover flowers to enhance the surface area for better extraction.
2. Combine the crushed herbs in the glass jar.
3. Pour the alcohol over the herbs to completely cover them, ensuring there is enough alcohol to cover the herbs by at least two inches.
4. Seal the jar tightly with its lid and place it in a cool, dark cupboard. Shake the jar every few days to mix the herbs with the alcohol.
5. After 4 to 6 weeks, filter the liquid using a cheesecloth or fine mesh strainer into a clean jar, pressing the herbs to extract as much liquid as possible.
6. Funnel the strained tincture into amber glass bottles, label them with the date, ingredients, and any batch information. If possible, use bottles with droppers for easy dosage.

CHASTE TREE AND DONG QUAI TINCTURE

This unique tincture combines Chaste Tree and Dong Quai, two potent herbs traditionally used to manage women's health issues, including hormonal balance, menstrual irregularities, and symptoms of menopause.

DOSAGE:

- **Hormonal balance and menstrual regulation**: 2-3 ml taken in the morning.
- **Menopausal symptom relief**: 1-2 ml twice daily.

PREP TIME: 20 MINUTES

MACERATION TIME: 4 TO 6 WEEKS

YIELD: APPROX 500 ML

INGREDIENTS

- *Chaste Tree Berries: 20 grams of dried berries*
- *Dong Quai: 20 grams of dried root*
- *High-proof alcohol (at least 40-50% alcohol by volume, such as vodka or brandy): 500 milliliters*

TOOLS

- *Glass jar with a tight-sealing lid (1-liter capacity)*
- *Cheesecloth or a fine mesh strainer*
- *Amber glass dropper bottles for storage*

INSTRUCTIONS

1. Chop or lightly crush the Chaste Tree berries and Dong Quai root to maximize the extraction surface area. Place the prepared herbs into the glass jar.
2. Pour the alcohol over the herbs, ensuring they are fully submerged by about two inches of liquid to account for absorption.
3. Tightly seal the jar with its lid and store it in a dark, cool cupboard, shaking the jar every few days to facilitate the extraction process.
4. After 4 to 6 weeks, filter the tincture using cheesecloth or a fine mesh strainer, squeezing the herbs to extract as much liquid as possible.
5. Funnel the strained tincture into amber glass bottles, label them with the date and contents. If possible, use bottles with droppers for easy dosage.

RED CLOVER AND RASPBERRY LEAF TINCTURE

This specially crafted tincture combines the natural benefits of Red Clover and Raspberry Leaf, two herbs known for their supportive effects on women's health, particularly for easing menopausal symptoms and menstrual discomfort.

DOSAGE:
- **Menstrual relief**: 1-2 ml three times a day during menstrual periods.
- **Menopausal support**: 2-3 ml daily, preferably in the morning and evening.

PREP TIME: 15 MINUTES

MACERATION TIME: 4 TO 6 WEEKS

YIELD: APPROX 600 ML

INGREDIENTS

- *Red Clover: 30 grams of dried flowers*
- *Raspberry Leaf: 30 grams of dried leaves*
- *High-proof alcohol (at least 40-50% alcohol by volume, such as vodka or brandy): 600 milliliters*

TOOLS

- *Glass jar with a tight-sealing lid (1-liter capacity)*
- *Cheesecloth or a fine mesh strainer*
- *Amber glass dropper bottles for storage*

INSTRUCTIONS

1. Gently bruise the Red Clover flowers and Raspberry Leaf to increase surface area for better extraction.
2. Place the herbs into the glass jar.
3. Pour the alcohol over the herbs, ensuring they are completely submerged by about two inches of liquid to allow for expansion.
4. Close the jar tightly with its lid and store it in a cool, dark cupboard. Shake the jar every few days to mix the ingredients.
5. After the maceration period, filter the mixture using cheesecloth or a fine mesh strainer, pressing the herbs to extract all the liquid.
6. Funnel the liquid into amber glass bottles, label them with the herb names, preparation date, and any other pertinent details. If possible, use bottles with droppers for easy dosage.

DONG QUAI AND MILK THISTLE TINCTURE

This innovative tincture features a potent blend of Dong Quai and Milk Thistle, tailored to support women's health, particularly in managing symptoms related to hormonal imbalances, cystitis, and menstrual irregularities.

DOSAGE:

- **For cystitis**: Take 1-2 ml of the tincture diluted in water up to three times daily during active symptoms.
- **For menstrual and menopausal support**: Administer 2-3 ml twice daily, ideally in the morning and before bedtime.

PREP TIME: 20 MINUTES

MACERATION TIME: 4 TO 6 WEEKS

YIELD: APPROX 700 ML

INGREDIENTS

- *Dong Quai: 40 grams of dried root*
- *Milk Thistle: 40 grams of dried seeds*
- *High-proof alcohol (at least 50% alcohol by volume, such as grain alcohol): 700 milliliters*

TOOLS

- *Glass jar with a tight-sealing lid (1-liter capacity)*
- *Cheesecloth or a fine mesh strainer*
- *Amber glass dropper bottles for storage*

INSTRUCTIONS

1. Coarsely grind the Dong Quai root and Milk Thistle seeds to enhance the extraction process.
2. Combine the ground herbs in the glass jar.
3. Pour the alcohol over the herbs until fully submerged, with an extra two inches of liquid above the herb level to accommodate expansion.
4. Seal the jar tightly with its lid and place it in a dark, cool cabinet. Shake the jar every few days to agitate the herbs and ensure a thorough extraction.
5. After 4 to 6 weeks, filter the tincture using cheesecloth into a clean bowl, squeezing the herbs to extract all beneficial extracts.
6. Funnel the strained tincture into amber glass bottles, and label them clearly with the herb names, batch date, and storage instructions. If possible, use bottles with droppers for easy dosage.

Children's Health

The following recipes are designed with children's safety in mind, using glycerin instead of alcohol to create a gentle yet effective remedy for various pediatric ailments.

CALENDULA AND CHAMOMILE SOOTHING TINCTURE

This gentle tincture combines Calendula and Chamomile, both renowned for their soothing properties, making it ideal for children's health issues such as skin irritations, mild digestive upset, and aiding restful sleep.

DOSAGE:
- **For skin irritation**: Apply a small amount of tincture topically to the affected area.
- **For digestive upset**: Give 1-2 ml of the tincture, diluted in water or juice, up to twice daily.
- **For sleep aid**: Administer 1 ml 30 minutes before bedtime.

PREP TIME: 15 MINUTES   **MACERATION TIME**: 6 WEEKS   **YIELD:** APPROX 500 ML

INGREDIENTS

- *Calendula: 30 grams of dried flowers*
- *Chamomile: 30 grams of dried flowers*
- *Glycerin (vegetable-based, suitable for children): 500 milliliters*

TOOLS

- *Glass jar with a tight-sealing lid (1-liter capacity)*
- *Cheesecloth or a fine mesh strainer*
- *Amber glass dropper bottles for storage*

INSTRUCTIONS

1. Lightly crush the Calendula and Chamomile flowers to release their active compounds.
2. Place the crushed herbs in the glass jar.
3. Pour the glycerin over the herbs, ensuring they are completely submerged with an extra inch of liquid above the herbs to accommodate any absorption.
4. Seal the jar tightly with its lid and store it in a cool, dark cupboard. Gently shake the jar every few days to mix the herbs with the glycerin.
5. After 6 weeks, filter the mixture using cheesecloth into a clean bowl, pressing the herbs to extract as much liquid as possible.
6. Funnel the strained tincture into amber glass bottles, and label them with the herb names, batch date, and usage instructions. If possible, use bottles with droppers for easy dosage.

ELDERBERRY AND ECHINACEA IMMUNE BOOSTING TINCTURE

This wholesome tincture blends Elderberry and Echinacea, known for their immune-boosting properties, to create a powerful aid for enhancing children's immune responses, especially during the cold and flu season.

DOSAGE:

- **Daily immune support**: Administer 2-3 ml once daily during the cold and flu season or when exposure to illness is high.
- **During illness**: Dosage can be increased to 2-3 ml three times daily to support recovery.

PREP TIME: 20 MINUTES   **MACERATION TIME**: 6 WEEKS   **YIELD:** APPROX 600 ML

INGREDIENTS

- *Elderberry: 40 grams of dried berries*
- *Echinacea: 20 grams of dried root*
- *Non-alcoholic solvent (vegetable glycerin): 600 milliliters*

TOOLS

- *Glass jar with a tight-sealing lid (1-liter capacity)*
- *Cheesecloth or a fine mesh strainer*
- *Amber glass dropper bottles for storage*

INSTRUCTIONS

1. Gently crush the dried Elderberries and Echinacea root to increase the surface area for better extraction.
2. Place the crushed herbs in the glass jar.
3. Pour the glycerin over the herbs until fully submerged, with an extra two inches of liquid above the herb level to cover any swelling.
4. Seal the jar tightly with its lid and store in a dark, cool cupboard. Shake the jar every other day to keep the herbs well mixed with the glycerin.
5. After six weeks, filter the herbs using cheesecloth or a fine mesh strainer into a clean bowl, squeezing the herbs to extract as much liquid as possible.
6. Funnel the strained tincture into amber glass bottles. If possible, use bottles with droppers for easy dosage. Label each bottle clearly with the date of finalization, and any other pertinent information.

LEMON BALM AND CHAMOMILE CALMING TINCTURE

This gentle tincture combines Lemon Balm and Chamomile, both cherished for their soothing effects on the nervous system, making it perfect for easing restlessness and promoting a peaceful sleep in children.

DOSAGE: Give 1-2 ml in the evening or 30 minutes before bedtime.

PREP TIME: 15 MINUTES   **MACERATION TIME**: 4 WEEKS   **YIELD:** APPROX 500 ML

INGREDIENTS

- Lemon Balm: 30 grams of dried leaves
- Chamomile: 30 grams of dried flowers
- Non-alcoholic solvent (vegetable glycerin): 500 milliliters

TOOLS

- Glass jar with a tight-sealing lid (1-liter capacity)
- Cheesecloth or a fine mesh strainer
- Amber glass dropper bottles for storage

INSTRUCTIONS

1. Lightly crush the dried Lemon Balm leaves and Chamomile flowers to expose more surface area to the solvent. Combine the crushed herbs in the glass jar.
2. Pour the glycerin over the herbs ensuring they are completely submerged with a couple of inches of liquid on top to accommodate any expansion.
3. Close the jar tightly with its lid and place it in a dark, cool spot. Shake the jar daily to help the glycerin extract the active compounds from the herbs.
4. After four weeks, filter the mixture using cheesecloth or a fine mesh strainer into a clean container, compressing the herbs to extract maximum liquid.
5. Funnel the strained tincture into amber glass bottles. If possible, use bottles with droppers for easy dosage. Label each bottle clearly with the date of finalization, and any other pertinent information.

CHILDREN'S DIGESTIVE SOOTHER TINCTURE

This tincture combines the gentle digestive benefits of Fennel and Dandelion, both known for their efficacy in soothing digestive disturbances in children such as gas, bloating, and occasional stomach upset.

DOSAGE: Administer 1 ml of the tincture directly or in a small amount of water or juice after meals, up to three times per day.

PREP TIME: 15 MINUTES   **MACERATION TIME**: 4 WEEKS   **YIELD:** APPROX 500 ML

INGREDIENTS

- Fennel Seeds: 20 grams of dried seeds
- Dandelion Root: 20 grams of dried root
- Non-alcoholic solvent (food-grade vegetable glycerin): 500 milliliters

TOOLS

- *Glass jar with a tight-sealing lid (1-liter capacity)*
- *Cheesecloth or a fine mesh strainer*
- *Amber glass dropper bottles for storage*

INSTRUCTIONS

1. Lightly crush the dried Fennel seeds and chop the Dandelion root to expose more surface area.
2. Place the prepared herbs into the glass jar.
3. Pour the glycerin over the herbs, ensuring they are fully covered with an extra layer of liquid above them to allow for expansion.
4. Securely seal the jar and store it in a dark, cool cabinet. Shake the jar daily to encourage extraction.
5. After four weeks, filter the contents using a cheesecloth or a fine mesh strainer, pressing the herbs to extract as much liquid as possible.
6. Funnel the clear tincture to amber glass bottles. If possible, use bottles with droppers for easy dosage. Label each bottle clearly with the date of finalization, and any other pertinent information.

Chapter 5

Alternative Remedies without the Use of Alcohol

It is possible to make tinctures without using alcohol, using glycerin or vinegar as substitutes. These alternatives are excellent for those who avoid alcohol due to health, dietary, or personal preferences.

Glycerin Tinctures (Glycerites)

Glycerin is a sweet, syrupy substance that can extract herbal properties effectively. It is particularly good for herbs used in children's remedies because of its sweet taste.

Vinegar Tinctures

Vinegar, especially apple cider vinegar, is another popular alcohol-free solvent. It is well-suited for extracting minerals from herbs and is beneficial for digestive health.

Both alternatives have specific benefits and can be used similarly to alcohol in tincture preparations. Here's a quick guide on how to use them:

Using Glycerin:

1. Preparation: Mix one part water with two parts vegetable glycerin to create your solvent.
2. Herb-to-Solvent Ratio: Typically, use 1:5 (herb to solvent) ratio for dried herbs.
3. Maceration Time: Let the mixture sit for 4-6 weeks, shaking it periodically.
4. Strain and Store: Strain the mixture using a cheesecloth and store it in a dark, glass bottle.

Using Vinegar:

1. Preparation: Use apple cider vinegar alone as the solvent.
2. Herb-to-Vinegar Ratio: Use a 1:7 ratio for fresh herbs or 1:5 for dried herbs.
3. Maceration Time: Allow it to macerate for about 2-4 weeks, shaking daily.
4. Strain and Store: Strain and bottle similarly to the glycerin tincture.

Anti-Inflammatory

ANTI-INFLAMMATORY HERBAL GLYCERITE

PREP TIME: 10 MINUTES

MACERATION TIME: 4 TO 6 WEEKS

YIELD: APPROX 500 ML

INGREDIENTS

- Turmeric root: 50 grams, finely chopped
- Ginger root: 30 grams, finely chopped
- Black pepper: 5 grams, crushed (to enhance turmeric absorption)
- Vegetable glycerin: 400 ml
- Distilled water: 100 ml

TOOLS

- Amber glass jar with a tight lid
- Cheesecloth or fine mesh strainer
- Dark glass bottles with droppers for storage

INSTRUCTIONS

1. Thoroughly wash the turmeric and ginger roots. Peel them if not organically sourced, and finely chop to increase the surface area, which aids in the extraction process.
2. In a clean, dry amber glass jar, combine the chopped turmeric, ginger, and crushed black pepper.
3. Pour the vegetable glycerin and distilled water into the jar. Ensure the herbs are completely submerged to prevent any potential spoilage. Seal the jar tightly with its lid and shake it well to mix the contents.
4. Store the jar in a cool, dark cupboard. Shake the jar once daily to agitate the herbs and aid in the extraction.
5. After 4 to 6 weeks, filter the mixture using a cheesecloth or fine mesh strainer into a clean bowl. Press or squeeze the herbs to extract as much liquid as possible.
6. Funnel the strained glycerite into dark glass bottles. Label the bottles clearly with the date of finalization, and any other pertinent information.
7. Store the glycerite in a cool, dark place. It should last for up to 2 years if stored properly.

WHITE WILLOW HERBAL GLYCERITE TINCTURE

PREPARATION TIME: 15 MINUTES

MACERATION TIME: 4 TO 6 WEEKS

YIELD: APPROXIMATELY 500 ML

INGREDIENTS

- White Willow bark: 40 grams, finely chopped or ground
- Chamomile flowers: 25 grams
- Licorice root: 15 grams, finely chopped
- Vegetable glycerin: 350 ml
- Distilled water: 150 ml

TOOLS

- *Amber glass jar with a tight lid*
- *Cheesecloth or fine mesh strainer*
- *Dark glass bottles with droppers for storage*

INSTRUCTIONS

1. Clean all herbs thoroughly. Chop the White Willow bark and Licorice root to increase the surface area for better extraction. Ensure Chamomile flowers are free from any debris.
2. Place all the herbs in a clean, dry amber glass jar.
3. Pour the vegetable glycerin and distilled water over the herbs, making sure they are completely submerged to prevent mold and spoilage.
4. Close the jar tightly with its lid and shake well to mix the ingredients.
5. Store the jar in a cool, dark cupboard, shaking it daily to help with the extraction process.
6. After 4 to 6 weeks, filter the mixture using a cheesecloth or fine mesh strainer, pressing the herbs to extract as much liquid as possible.
7. Funnel the strained glycerite into dark glass bottles for storage.
8. Label each bottle clearly with the date of finalization, and any other pertinent information.
9. Keep the glycerite in a cool, dark location. Properly stored, it should remain potent and safe for up to 24 months.

HERBAL VINEGAR TINCTURE

PREP TIME: 20 MINUTES

MACERATION TIME: 3 TO 4 WEEKS

YIELD: APPROXIMATELY 500 ML

INGREDIENTS

- *Turmeric root: 30 grams, freshly grated*
- *Ginger root: 30 grams, freshly grated*
- *Rosemary: 15 grams, fresh or dried*
- *Apple cider vinegar: 500 ml, with the mother for added health benefits*

TOOLS

- *Glass jar with a non-metallic lid (or cover the jar with parchment paper under a metal lid to prevent corrosion)*
- *Cheesecloth or fine mesh strainer*
- *Amber or dark glass bottles for storage*

INSTRUCTIONS

1. Thoroughly wash the turmeric and ginger roots. Grate them finely to maximize the surface area exposed to the vinegar. If using fresh rosemary, gently bruise the leaves to release their essential oils.
2. Place all herbs in the glass jar.
3. Warm the apple cider vinegar slightly (do not boil), then pour it over the herbs to cover them completely. This helps to better extract their properties.
4. Seal the jar tightly with its lid and shake it well to mix the ingredients.
5. Store the jar in a cool, dark cupboard. Shake it daily to keep the herbs immersed and facilitate extraction.

6. After 3 to 4 weeks, filter the mixture using a cheesecloth or fine mesh strainer into a clean bowl. Squeeze the herbs to extract as much liquid as possible.
7. Funnel the strained vinegar into dark glass bottles. Label them clearly with the date of finalization, and any other pertinent information.
8. Store the bottles in a cool, dark place. Vinegar tinctures can last up to a year if stored properly.

CHAMOMILLE VINEGAR TINCTURE

PREP TIME: 10 MINUTES

MACERATION TIME: 4 TO 6 WEEKS

YIELD: ABOUT 480 ML

INGREDIENTS

- *Chamomile: 15 grams, dried flowers*
- *Turmeric: 14 grams, dried root, finely chopped*
- *Ginger: 14 grams, dried root, finely chopped*
- *Black pepper: 2 grams, freshly ground (to enhance turmeric absorption)*
- *Raw, unpasteurized apple cider vinegar: 480 ml*

INSTRUCTIONS

1. If using fresh turmeric and ginger, wash, peel, and chop finely. For dried herbs, ensure they are well broken down to help release the essential oils and increase the surface area for extraction.
2. In a clean glass jar, layer the chamomile, turmeric, ginger, and black pepper. Pour the apple cider vinegar over the herbs, ensuring all are fully submerged. If necessary, add more vinegar to completely cover the herbs.
3. Use a non-metallic lid or place parchment paper under a metal lid to avoid corrosion from the vinegar. Seal the jar tightly with its lid.
4. Place the jar in a cool, dark cupboard for 4 to 6 weeks. Shake the jar every few days to mix the herbs and vinegar.
5. After the infusion period, filter the mixture using cheesecloth or a fine mesh strainer into another clean jar. Press or squeeze the herbs to extract as much liquid as possible.
6. Funnel the strained tincture to clean bottles or jars. Store in a cool, dark place. The tincture can be stored for up to a year.

USAGE:
- Take 1 tablespoon (about 15 milliliters) of the tincture diluted in water or tea up to three times daily for anti-inflammatory benefits. This tincture can also be used in salad dressings or marinades to add flavor and health benefits.

Immune Boosting

ECHINACEA IMMUNE SUPPORT GLYCERITE TINCTURE

PREP TIME: 15 MINUTES

MACERATION TIME: 4 TO 6 WEEKS

YIELD: ABOUT 480 ML

INGREDIENTS

- *Echinacea: 20 grams, dried root and aerial parts*
- *Elderberry: 15 grams, dried berries*
- *Astragalus: 15 grams, dried root, finely sliced*
- *Ginger: 10 grams, dried root, finely chopped*
- *Vegetable glycerin: 360 ml*
- *Distilled water: 120 ml*

INSTRUCTIONS

1. Ensure that all herbs are thoroughly cleaned and prepared. Chop or crush the herbs slightly to increase surface area for extraction.
2. In a clean glass jar, combine the Echinacea, elderberry, astragalus, and ginger. Mix the vegetable glycerin and distilled water in a separate bowl until well blended, then pour this mixture over the herbs, making sure they are fully submerged. Add more glycerin mixture if necessary to completely cover the herbs.
3. Use a plastic lid or cover the jar with a non-metallic material to avoid any reaction with the glycerin.
4. Keep the jar in a cool, dark cupboard for 4 to 6 weeks. Shake the jar every few days to promote better infusion.
5. After the infusing period, filter the glycerite using cheesecloth or a fine mesh strainer into another clean jar, pressing the herbs to extract as much liquid as possible.
6. Pour the strained glycerite into clean, airtight bottles or jars. Store in a cool, dark place for up to a year.

USAGE:

- Take 1 teaspoon (about 5 milliliters) of the tincture daily, particularly during times when immune support is needed, such as during cold and flu season.

CAT'S CLAW GLYCERITE TINCTURE

PREP TIME: 20 MINUTES

MACERATION TIME: 4 TO 6 WEEKS

YIELD: ABOUT 480 ML

INGREDIENTS

- *Cat's Claw: 20 grams, dried bark, finely chopped*
- *Echinacea: 15 grams, dried root and aerial parts*
- *Ginger: 10 grams, dried root, finely chopped*
- *Elderberry: 15 grams, dried berries*
- *Vegetable glycerin: 360 ml*
- *Distilled water: 120 ml*

INSTRUCTIONS

1. Thoroughly clean and prepare the herbs. Finely chop the Cat's Claw bark and ginger root to enhance extraction. Ensure Echinacea and elderberries are slightly crushed to expose more surface area.
2. In a clean glass jar, layer the Cat's Claw, Echinacea, ginger, and elderberries. In a separate bowl, blend the vegetable glycerin and distilled water until well mixed, then pour this over the herbs, ensuring they are fully submerged. Adjust the glycerin mixture if necessary to cover the herbs entirely.
3. Use a plastic lid or a non-metallic material to seal the jar to avoid any reaction with the glycerin.
4. Place the jar in a cool, dark cupboard for 4 to 6 weeks. Shake the jar every few days to promote better infusion.
5. After the infusing period, filter the glycerite using cheesecloth or a fine mesh strainer into another clean jar, pressing the herbs to extract as much liquid as possible.
6. Funnel the glycerite into clean, airtight bottles or jars. Store in a cool, dark place for up to a year.

USAGE: Take 1 teaspoon (about 5 milliliters) of the tincture daily to support the immune system, particularly during times when viral illnesses are prevalent.

THYME IMMUNITY VINEGAR TINCTURE

PREP TIME: 10 MINUTES   **MACERATION TIME:** 4 TO 6 WEEKS   **YIELD:** ABOUT 500 ML

INGREDIENTS

- *Thyme: 20 grams, dried leaves*
- *Rosemary: 15 grams, dried leaves*
- *Garlic: 3 cloves, finely chopped*
- *Cayenne Pepper: 2 grams, ground*
- *Raw, unpasteurized apple cider vinegar: about 480 milliliters*

INSTRUCTIONS

1. Thoroughly clean and dry the herbs. Chop or crush the thyme and rosemary leaves slightly to release their essential oils. Peel and finely chop the garlic cloves.
2. In a clean glass jar, combine the thyme, rosemary, chopped garlic, and ground cayenne pepper. Pour the apple cider vinegar over the ingredients, ensuring they are completely submerged. Add more vinegar if necessary to cover the herbs completely.
3. Close the jar with a non-metallic lid, or place parchment paper under a metal lid to prevent corrosion from the vinegar. Seal the jar tightly.
4. Keep the jar in a cool, dark cupboard for 4 to 6 weeks, shaking it every few days to ensure the herbs are well infused.
5. After the infusion period, filter the vinegar using cheesecloth or a fine mesh strainer into another clean jar. Press or squeeze the herbs to extract as much vinegar as possible.
6. Funnel the strained vinegar into clean bottles or jars. Store in a cool, dark place. The tincture can be stored for up to a year.

USAGE: Take 1 tablespoon (about 15 milliliters) of the tincture diluted in water or tea daily, especially during cold and flu season, to help boost the immune system and provide respiratory support.

GARLIC POWER IMMUNE BOOSTER VINEGAR TINCTURE

PREP TIME: 15 MINUTES   **MACERATION TIME:** 4 TO 6 WEEKS   **YIELD:** ABOUT 500 ML

INGREDIENTS

- *Garlic: 60 grams, fresh cloves, peeled and finely chopped*
- *Horseradish: 30 grams, fresh root, peeled and finely grated*
- *Ginger: 30 grams, fresh root, peeled and finely chopped*

- *Turmeric: 15 grams, fresh root, peeled and finely chopped*
- *Black peppercorns: 2 grams, whole*
- *Raw, unpasteurized apple cider vinegar: 480 milliliters*

INSTRUCTIONS

1. Ensure all fresh ingredients are thoroughly cleaned. Peel and finely chop the garlic, horseradish, ginger, and turmeric. The finer the chopping, the more surface area is exposed for better infusion.
2. In a clean glass jar, layer the chopped garlic, horseradish, ginger, turmeric, and whole black peppercorns. Pour the apple cider vinegar over the ingredients until they are completely submerged. If necessary, add more vinegar to ensure all ingredients are covered.
3. Use a non-metallic lid, or place parchment paper under a metal lid to prevent corrosion from the vinegar. Seal the jar tightly.
4. Keep the jar in a cool, dark cupboard for 4 to 6 weeks, shaking it every few days to mix the ingredients and enhance the infusion process.
5. After the infusion period, filter the vinegar using cheesecloth or a fine mesh strainer into another clean jar. Press or squeeze the ingredients to extract as much infused vinegar as possible.
6. Funnel the strained vinegar into clean bottles or jars. Store in a cool, dark place. The tincture can be stored for up to a year.

USAGE: Take 1 tablespoon (about 15 milliliters) of the tincture diluted in water or tea daily, especially during the cold and flu season, to fight off infections.

Tonifying

ASTRAGALUS GLYCERITE TINCTURE

PREP TIME: 20 MINUTES   **MACERATION TIME:** 4 TO 6 WEEKS   **YIELD:** ABOUT 480 ML

INGREDIENTS

- *Astragalus root: 20 grams, dried root, finely sliced*
- *Ginseng: 15 grams, dried root, finely sliced*
- *Licorice root: 10 grams, dried root, finely chopped*

- *Schisandra berries: 10 grams, dried berries*
- *Vegetable glycerin: 360 ml*
- *Distilled water: 120 ml*

INSTRUCTIONS

1. Ensure all herbs are thoroughly cleaned and prepared. Finely slice or chop the roots and berries to enhance their surface area for better extraction.
2. In a clean glass jar, layer the Astragalus root, ginseng root, licorice root, and Schisandra berries. Mix the vegetable glycerin and distilled water in a separate bowl until well blended, then pour this mixture over the herbs, ensuring they are fully submerged. Adjust the glycerin mixture if necessary to cover the herbs entirely.
3. Use a plastic lid or a non-metallic material to seal the jar to prevent any reaction with the glycerin.
4. Place the jar in a cool, dark cupboard for 4 to 6 weeks. Shake the jar every few days to promote better infusion.
5. After the infusing period, filter the glycerite using cheesecloth or a fine mesh strainer into another clean jar, pressing the herbs to extract as much liquid as possible.
6. Funnel the glycerite into clean, airtight bottles or jars. Store in a cool, dark place for up to a year.

USAGE: Take 1 teaspoon (about 5 milliliters) of the tincture daily to help enhance energy levels and support the immune system.

ASHWAGANDHA ENERGY BOOST GLYCERITE TINCTURE

PREP TIME: 15 MINUTES   **MACERATION TIME:** 4 TO 6 WEEKS   **YIELD:** ABOUT 480 ML

INGREDIENTS

- *Ashwagandha root: 20 grams, dried root, finely chopped*
- *Holy Basil: 15 grams, dried leaves*
- *Rhodiola rosea: 10 grams, dried root, finely chopped*

- *Cinnamon: 2 grams, ground*
- *Vegetable glycerin: 360 ml*
- *Distilled water: 120 ml*

INSTRUCTIONS

1. Clean all herbs thoroughly. Finely chop the Ashwagandha and Rhodiola roots to enhance their surface area for better extraction. Ensure the holy basil leaves are crumbled if not already in a fine state.
2. In a clean glass jar, layer the chopped Ashwagandha, holy basil, Rhodiola, and ground cinnamon. In a separate bowl, blend the vegetable glycerin and distilled water until well mixed, then pour this over the herbs, ensuring they are fully submerged. Adjust the glycerin mixture if necessary to completely cover the herbs.
3. Use a plastic lid or cover the jar with a non-metallic material to prevent any reaction with the glycerin.
4. Keep the jar in a cool, dark cupboard for 4 to 6 weeks. Shake the jar every few days to facilitate the infusion.
5. After the infusing period, filter the glycerite using cheesecloth or a fine mesh strainer into another clean jar, pressing the herbs to extract as much liquid as possible.
6. Funnel the glycerite into clean, airtight bottles or jars. Store in a cool, dark place for up to a year.

USAGE: Take 1 teaspoon (about 5 milliliters) of the tincture daily, ideally in the morning or early afternoon, to help boost energy levels and manage stress.

GOLDEN ROOT GLYCERITE TINCTURE

PREP TIME: 20 MINUTES   **MACERATION TIME:** 4 TO 6 WEEKS   **YIELD:** ABOUT 480 ML

INGREDIENTS

- Golden Root: 15 grams, dried root, finely chopped
- Siberian Ginseng: 15 grams, dried root, finely chopped
- Holy Basil: 15 grams, dried leaves
- Green Tea: 10 grams, dried leaves
- Vegetable glycerin: 360 ml
- Distilled water: 120 ml

INSTRUCTIONS

1. Clean all herbs thoroughly. Finely chop the Golden Root and Siberian Ginseng to enhance their surface area for better extraction. Ensure that the Holy Basil and Green Tea leaves are free from any debris and slightly crushed.
2. In a clean glass jar, layer the Golden Root, Siberian Ginseng, Holy Basil, and Green Tea. In a separate bowl, mix the vegetable glycerin and distilled water until well combined, then pour this mixture over the herbs, ensuring they are fully submerged. Adjust the glycerin mixture if necessary to cover the herbs completely.
3. Use a plastic lid or cover the jar with a non-metallic material to prevent any reaction with the glycerin.
4. Place the jar in a cool, dark cupboard for 4 to 6 weeks. Shake the jar every few days to facilitate the infusion.
5. After the infusing period, filter the glycerite using cheesecloth or a fine mesh strainer into another clean jar, pressing the herbs to extract as much liquid as possible.
6. Funnel the glycerite into clean, airtight bottles or jars. Store in a cool, dark place for up to a year.

USAGE: Take 1 teaspoon (about 5 milliliters) of the glycerite daily, especially during periods of high stress or when needing a mental or physical boost.

DANDELION VINEGAR TINCTURE

PREP TIME: 15 MINUTES   **MACERATION TIME:** 4 TO 6 WEEKS   **YIELD:** ABOUT 500 ML

INGREDIENTS

- Dandelion: 30 grams, dried leaves and roots, finely chopped
- Nettle: 15 grams, dried leaves
- Burdock root: 15 grams, dried root, finely chopped
- Lemon peel: 10 grams, dried peel
- Raw, unpasteurized apple cider vinegar: about 480 ml

INSTRUCTIONS

1. Ensure all herbs and lemon peel are thoroughly dried and finely chopped to increase surface area for better extraction.

2. In a clean glass jar, layer the dandelion leaves and roots, nettle leaves, burdock root, and dried lemon peel. Pour the apple cider vinegar over the ingredients until they are completely submerged. Add more vinegar if necessary to ensure all ingredients are covered.
3. Use a non-metallic lid, or place parchment paper under a metal lid to prevent corrosion from the vinegar. Seal the jar tightly.
4. Place the jar in a cool, dark cupboard for 4 to 6 weeks, shaking it every few days to ensure the herbs are well infused.
5. After the infusion period, filter the vinegar using cheesecloth or a fine mesh strainer into another clean jar. Press or squeeze the herbs to extract as much vinegar as possible.
6. Funnel the strained vinegar into clean bottles or jars. Store in a cool, dark place. The tincture can be stored for up to a year.

USAGE: Take 1 tablespoon (about 15 milliliters) of the tincture diluted in water or tea daily to help support liver function, detoxification, and overall vitality.

Sleep Aids

SOOTHING SLEEP AID GLYCERITE TINCTURE

PREP TIME: 15 MINUTES   **MACERATION TIME:** 4 TO 6 WEEKS   **YIELD:** ABOUT 480 ML

INGREDIENTS

- *Valerian root: 20 grams, dried root, chopped*
- *Lemon balm: 15 grams, dried leaves*
- *Passionflower: 15 grams, dried flowers*
- *Lavender: 10 grams, dried flowers*
- *Vegetable glycerin: 360 ml*
- *Distilled water: 120 ml*

INSTRUCTIONS

1. Ensure that all herbs are well-cleaned and chopped if using fresh. For dried herbs, break them down slightly to help release the essential oils and increase the surface area for extraction.
2. In a clean glass jar, layer the valerian, lemon balm, passionflower, and lavender. In a separate bowl, mix the vegetable glycerin and distilled water until well combined, then pour over the herbs, ensuring all are fully submerged. Add more glycerin mixture if needed to cover the herbs completely.
3. Use a plastic or non-reactive lid to close the jar, as glycerin and herbs should not contact metal directly. Seal the jar tightly.
4. Keep the jar in a cool, dark cupboard for 4 to 6 weeks. Shake the jar every few days to help the herbs infuse into the glycerin mixture.
5. After the infusing period, filter the mixture using cheesecloth or a fine mesh strainer into another clean jar. Squeeze or press the herbs to extract as much liquid as possible.
6. Funnel the strained glycerite into clean bottles or jars. Store in a cool, dark place. The glycerite can be stored for up to a year.

USAGE: Take 1 teaspoon (about 5 milliliters) of the tincture 30 minutes before bedtime to help promote relaxation and sleep.

SKULLCAP AND HOPS GLYCERITE TINCTURE

PREP TIME: 10 MINUTES   **MACERATION TIME:** 4 TO 6 WEEKS   **YIELD:** ABOUT 480 ML

INGREDIENTS

- *Skullcap: 15 grams, dried aerial parts*
- *Hops: 10 grams, dried flowers*
- *Catnip: 15 grams, dried leaves*

- *Chamomile: 10 grams, dried flowers*
- *Vegetable glycerin: 360 ml*
- *Distilled water: 120 ml*

INSTRUCTIONS

1. Ensure that all herbs are thoroughly dried and slightly crushed to increase their surface area for better extraction.
2. In a clean glass jar, combine the skullcap, hops, catnip, and chamomile. In a separate bowl, blend the vegetable glycerin and distilled water until well integrated, then pour this mixture over the herbs. Make sure the herbs are completely submerged, adding more of the glycerin mixture if necessary.
3. Use a plastic lid or a non-reactive material to seal the jar, as glycerin should not be in direct contact with metal. Ensure the jar is tightly closed.
4. Place the jar in a cool, dark cupboard for 4 to 6 weeks. Shake the jar every few days to ensure the herbs are well infused.
5. Once the infusion period is over, filter the liquid using cheesecloth or a fine mesh strainer into another clean jar, pressing the herbs to extract as much glycerite as possible.
6. Funnel the glycerite into clean, airtight bottles or jars. Store in a cool, dark location for up to a year.

USAGE: Take 1 teaspoon (about 5 milliliters) of the tincture about 30 minutes before bedtime.

CALIFORNIA POPPY GLYCERITE TINCTURE

PREP TIME: 15 MINUTES   **MACERATION TIME:** 4 TO 6 WEEKS   **YIELD:** ABOUT 480 ML

INGREDIENTS

- *California Poppy: 20 grams, dried aerial parts*
- *Ashwagandha: 15 grams, dried root, finely chopped*
- *Linden flower: 15 grams, dried flowers*

- *Lemon Verbena: 10 grams, dried leaves*
- *Vegetable glycerin: 360 ml*
- *Distilled water: 120 ml*

INSTRUCTIONS

1. Ensure that all herbs are well-cleaned and finely chopped or slightly crushed to increase their surface area, which is particularly important for the roots and tougher materials.
2. In a clean glass jar, layer the California poppy, ashwagandha, linden flower, and lemon verbena. In a separate container, thoroughly mix the vegetable glycerin and distilled water, then pour this blend over the herbs to ensure they are fully submerged. Add more glycerin mixture if necessary to completely cover the herbs.

3. Use a plastic lid or a non-metallic material to seal the jar to prevent any reaction with the glycerin. Make sure the jar is tightly closed.
4. Keep the jar in a cool, dark cupboard for 4 to 6 weeks. Shake the jar every few days to promote infusion of the herbs into the glycerin mixture.
5. After the infusion period, filter the glycerite using cheesecloth or a fine mesh strainer into another clean jar. Press the herbs to extract as much liquid as possible.
6. Funnel the strained glycerite into clean, airtight bottles or jars. Store in a cool, dark location for up to a year.

USAGE: Take 1 teaspoon (about 5 milliliters) of the tincture about 30 minutes before bedtime to help relax and promote a restful night's sleep.

CHAMOMILE COMFORT GLYCERITE TINCTURE

PREP TIME: 10 MINUTES   **MACERATION TIME:** 4 TO 6 WEEKS   **YIELD:** ABOUT 480 ML

INGREDIENTS

- *Chamomile: 30 grams, dried flowers*
- *Lavender: 15 grams, dried flowers*
- *Spearmint: 15 grams, dried leaves*
- *Vegetable glycerin: 360 ml*
- *Distilled water: 120 ml*

INSTRUCTIONS

1. Ensure that all herbs are thoroughly dried and gently crushed to release their natural oils.
2. In a clean glass jar, layer the chamomile, lavender, and spearmint. Mix the vegetable glycerin and distilled water in a separate bowl until well combined, then pour over the herbs to ensure they are fully submerged. Adjust the glycerin mixture if necessary to cover the herbs entirely.
3. Use a non-metallic lid to seal the jar tightly to avoid any reaction with the glycerin.
4. Place the jar in a cool, dark cupboard for 4 to 6 weeks. Shake the jar every few days to help the herbs infuse into the glycerin mixture.
5. After the infusion period, filter the tincture using cheesecloth or a fine mesh strainer into another clean jar. Press or squeeze the herbs to extract as much glycerite as possible.
6. Funnel the glycerite into clean, airtight bottles or jars. Store in a cool, dark place for up to a year.

USAGE: Administer 1 teaspoon (about 5 milliliters) of the tincture 30 minutes before bedtime to help relax and encourage a restful sleep.

CAT'S CLAW SOOTHING SLEEP GLYCERITE TINCTURE

PREP TIME: 20 MINUTES

MACERATION TIME: 4 TO 6 WEEKS

YIELD: ABOUT 480 ML

INGREDIENTS

- Cat's Claw: 15 grams, dried bark, finely chopped
- Lemon Balm: 15 grams, dried leaves
- Passionflower: 15 grams, dried flowers
- Hops: 15 grams, dried flowers
- Vegetable glycerin: 360 ml
- Distilled water: 120 ml

INSTRUCTIONS

1. Thoroughly clean and prepare the herbs. The Cat's Claw bark should be finely chopped to enhance extraction. Lemon balm, passionflower, and hops can be slightly crushed to open up their structure.
2. In a clean glass jar, layer the Cat's Claw, lemon balm, passionflower, and hops. In a separate bowl, blend the vegetable glycerin and distilled water until well combined, then pour this over the herbs, ensuring they are completely submerged. Add more of the glycerin mixture if needed to fully cover the herbs.
3. Use a plastic lid or cover the jar with a non-metallic material to prevent any reaction with the glycerin.
4. Place the jar in a cool, dark cupboard for 4 to 6 weeks. Shake the jar every few days to facilitate the infusion.
5. After the infusing period, filter the glycerite using cheesecloth or a fine mesh strainer into another clean jar, squeezing the herbs to extract as much liquid as possible.
6. Funnel the glycerite into clean, airtight bottles or jars. Store in a cool, dark location for up to a year.

USAGE: Take 1 teaspoon (about 5 milliliters) of the tincture 30 minutes before bedtime to help promote a calm and restful sleep.

Digestive Aids

LICORICE ROOT GLYCERITE TINCTURE

PREP TIME: 15 MINUTES

MACERATION TIME: 4 TO 6 WEEKS

YIELD: ABOUT 480 ML

INGREDIENTS

- Licorice Root: 20 grams, dried root, finely chopped
- Peppermint: 15 grams, dried leaves
- Fennel Seeds: 10 grams
- Ginger: 10 grams, dried root, finely chopped
- Vegetable glycerin: 360 ml
- Distilled water: 120 ml

INSTRUCTIONS

1. Thoroughly clean and finely chop the licorice root and ginger. Ensure the peppermint leaves and fennel seeds are slightly crushed to release their essential oils.

2. In a clean glass jar, layer the licorice root, peppermint, fennel seeds, and ginger. Mix the vegetable glycerin and distilled water in a separate bowl until well blended, then pour this mixture over the herbs, making sure they are fully submerged. Adjust the glycerin mixture if necessary to completely cover the herbs.
3. Use a plastic lid or cover the jar with a non-metallic material to prevent any reaction with the glycerin.
4. Place the jar in a cool, dark cupboard for 4 to 6 weeks. Shake the jar every few days to ensure the herbs are well infused.
5. After the infusing period, filter the glycerite using cheesecloth or a fine mesh strainer into another clean jar, pressing the herbs to extract as much liquid as possible.
6. Funnel the glycerite into clean, airtight bottles or jars. Store in a cool, dark place for up to a year.

USAGE: Take 1 teaspoon (about 5 milliliters) of the glycerite 15 to 30 minutes before meals to help soothe the digestive tract and alleviate issues like bloating, indigestion, and occasional heartburn.

SLIPPERY ELM DIGESTIVE AID GLYCERITE TINCTURE

PREP TIME: 20 MINUTES   **MACERATION TIME:** 4 TO 6 WEEKS   **YIELD:** ABOUT 480 ML

INGREDIENTS

- *Slippery Elm: 15 grams, dried bark, finely powdered*
- *Marshmallow Root: 15 grams, dried root, finely chopped*
- *Chamomile: 15 grams, dried flowers*
- *Aloe Vera: 10 grams, dried gel powder*
- *Vegetable glycerin: 360 ml*
- *Distilled water: 120 ml*

INSTRUCTIONS

1. Ensure all herbs are thoroughly cleaned and prepared. The Slippery Elm should be in a fine powder form to maximize the release of mucilage. The marshmallow root should be finely chopped, and the chamomile flowers slightly crushed.
2. In a clean glass jar, layer the Slippery Elm, marshmallow root, chamomile, and aloe vera powder. Mix the vegetable glycerin and distilled water in a separate bowl until well combined, then pour this mixture over the herbs, making sure they are fully submerged. Adjust the glycerin mixture if necessary to cover the herbs completely.
3. Use a plastic lid or cover the jar with a non-metallic material to prevent any reaction with the glycerin.
4. Keep the jar in a cool, dark cupboard for 4 to 6 weeks. Shake the jar every few days to ensure the herbs are well infused.
5. After the infusing period, filter the glycerite using cheesecloth or a fine mesh strainer into another clean jar, pressing the herbs to extract as much liquid as possible.
6. Funnel the glycerite into clean, airtight bottles or jars. Store in a cool, dark place for up to a year.

USAGE: Take 1 teaspoon (about 5 milliliters) of the glycerite up to three times a day, particularly before meals, to help soothe the digestive system and relieve symptoms such as heartburn, indigestion, and irritation in the gastrointestinal tract.

MARSHMALLOW ROOT GLYCERITE TINCTURE

PREP TIME: 15 MINUTES   **MACERATION TIME:** 4 TO 6 WEEKS   **YIELD:** ABOUT 480 ML

INGREDIENTS

- *Marshmallow Root: 20 grams, dried root, finely chopped*
- *Licorice Root: 15 grams, dried root, finely chopped*
- *Fennel Seeds: 10 grams*
- *Peppermint: 15 grams, dried leaves*
- *Vegetable glycerin: 360 ml*
- *Distilled water: 120 ml*

INSTRUCTIONS

1. Ensure all herbs are thoroughly cleaned and prepared. Finely chop the marshmallow and licorice roots to enhance their surface area for better extraction. Crush the fennel seeds slightly and ensure the peppermint leaves are in small pieces.
2. In a clean glass jar, layer the marshmallow root, licorice root, fennel seeds, and peppermint leaves. Mix the vegetable glycerin and distilled water in a separate bowl until well blended, then pour this mixture over the herbs, ensuring they are fully submerged. Adjust the glycerin mixture if necessary to cover the herbs completely.
3. Use a plastic lid or cover the jar with a non-metallic material to prevent any reaction with the glycerin.
4. Keep the jar in a cool, dark cupboard for 4 to 6 weeks. Shake the jar every few days to ensure the herbs are well infused.
5. After the infusing period, filter the glycerite using cheesecloth or a fine mesh strainer into another clean jar, pressing the herbs to extract as much liquid as possible.
6. Funnel the glycerite into clean, airtight bottles or jars. Store in a cool, dark place for up to a year.

USAGE: Take 1 teaspoon (about 5 milliliters) of the glycerite up to three times a day, especially before meals or when experiencing digestive discomfort, to help soothe the digestive tract and alleviate symptoms like bloating and irritation.

GINGER GLYCERITE TINCTURE

PREPARATION TIME: 10 MINUTES   **MACERATION TIME:** 4-6 WEEKS

INGREDIENTS

- *Fresh ginger root, finely chopped (1 cup)*
- *Pure vegetable glycerin (2 cups)*
- *Distilled water (1 cup)*

INSTRUCTIONS

1. Combine the finely chopped ginger root in a clean glass jar.
2. Mix the vegetable glycerin with distilled water and pour over the ginger to cover it completely.
3. Seal the jar tightly and shake well. Store the jar in a cool, dark place for 4-6 weeks, shaking it daily.
4. After maceration, filter the mixture using a cheesecloth or a fine mesh into another clean glass bottle.
5. Label and store in a cool, dark place.

PEPPERMINT DIGESTIVE VINEGAR TINCTURE

PREP TIME: 10 MINUTES   **MACERATION TIME:** 4 TO 6 WEEKS   **YIELD:** ABOUT 500 ML

INGREDIENTS

- Peppermint: 30 grams, dried leaves
- Ginger: 15 grams, fresh root, finely chopped
- Fennel seeds: 10 grams
- Lemon peel: 10 grams, dried peel
- Raw, unpasteurized apple cider vinegar: 480 ml

INSTRUCTIONS

1. Ensure the peppermint leaves are thoroughly dried and the ginger root is finely chopped. Lightly crush the fennel seeds to release their oils, and ensure the lemon peel is free from any pesticides and finely chopped if fresh.
2. In a clean glass jar, layer the dried peppermint leaves, finely chopped fresh ginger, crushed fennel seeds, and dried lemon peel. Pour the apple cider vinegar over the ingredients until they are completely submerged. If necessary, add more vinegar to ensure all ingredients are covered.
3. Use a non-metallic lid, or place parchment paper under a metal lid to prevent corrosion from the vinegar. Seal the jar tightly.
4. Place the jar in a cool, dark cupboard for 4 to 6 weeks, shaking it every few days to ensure the ingredients are well infused.
5. After the infusion period, filter the vinegar using cheesecloth or a fine mesh strainer into another clean jar. Press or squeeze the ingredients to extract as much infused vinegar as possible.
6. Funnel the strained vinegar into clean bottles or jars. Store in a cool, dark place. The tincture can be stored for up to a year.

USAGE: Take 1 tablespoon (about 15 milliliters) of the tincture diluted in water or tea before meals to aid digestion and alleviate symptoms such as bloating, gas, and indigestion.

ROSEMARY DIGESTIVE VINEGAR TINCTURE

PREP TIME: 10 MINUTES   **MACERATION TIME:** 4 TO 6 WEEKS   **YIELD:** ABOUT 500 ML

INGREDIENTS

- Rosemary: 20 grams, dried leaves
- Lemon balm: 15 grams, dried leaves
- Dandelion root: 15 grams, dried root, chopped
- Coriander seeds: 10 grams
- Raw, unpasteurized apple cider vinegar: 480 ml

INSTRUCTIONS

1. Ensure that all herbs are thoroughly cleaned and dried. Lightly crush the coriander seeds and chop the dandelion root finely to enhance extraction.

2. In a clean glass jar, layer the dried rosemary leaves, lemon balm leaves, finely chopped dandelion root, and crushed coriander seeds. Pour the apple cider vinegar over the ingredients until they are completely submerged. If necessary, add more vinegar to ensure all ingredients are covered.
3. Use a non-metallic lid, or place parchment paper under a metal lid to prevent corrosion from the vinegar. Seal the jar tightly.
4. Place the jar in a cool, dark cupboard for 4 to 6 weeks, shaking it every few days to ensure the herbs are well infused.
5. After the infusion period, filter the vinegar using cheesecloth or a fine mesh strainer into another clean jar. Press or squeeze the ingredients to extract as much infused vinegar as possible.
6. Funnel the strained vinegar into clean bottles or jars. Store in a cool, dark place. The tincture can be stored for up to a year.

USAGE: Take 1 tablespoon (about 15 milliliters) of the tincture diluted in water or tea before meals to support digestion and alleviate symptoms such as bloating and indigestion.

Respiratory Health

ELECAMPANE GLYCERITE TINCTURE

PREP TIME: 20 MINUTES   **MACERATION TIME:** 4 TO 6 WEEKS   **YIELD:** ABOUT 480 ML

INGREDIENTS

- Elecampane root: 15 grams, dried root, finely chopped
- Mullein: 15 grams, dried leaves
- Thyme: 15 grams, dried leaves
- Licorice root: 10 grams, dried root, finely chopped
- Vegetable glycerin: 360 ml
- Distilled water: 120 ml

INSTRUCTIONS

1. Ensure all herbs are thoroughly cleaned and prepared. Finely chop the elecampane and licorice roots. Ensure the mullein leaves and thyme are slightly crushed to help release the essential oils and increase the surface area for extraction.
2. In a clean glass jar, layer the elecampane root, mullein leaves, thyme, and licorice root. In a separate bowl, mix the vegetable glycerin and distilled water until well combined, then pour this mixture over the herbs, ensuring they are fully submerged. Adjust the glycerin mixture if necessary to cover the herbs completely.
3. Use a plastic lid or cover the jar with a non-metallic material to prevent any reaction with the glycerin.
4. Keep the jar in a cool, dark cupboard for 4 to 6 weeks. Shake the jar every few days to promote the infusion process.
5. After the infusing period, filter the glycerite using cheesecloth or a fine mesh strainer into another clean jar, pressing the herbs to extract as much liquid as possible.
6. Funnel the glycerite into clean, airtight bottles or jars. Store in a cool, dark place for up to a year.

USAGE: Take 1 teaspoon (about 5 milliliters) of the glycerite up to three times a day during periods of respiratory distress or as part of a daily regimen during cold and flu season to support respiratory health.

HYSSOP RESPIRATORY RELIEF GLYCERITE TINCTURE

PREP TIME: 15 MINUTES　　**MACERATION TIME:** 4 TO 6 WEEKS　　**YIELD:** ABOUT 480 ML

INGREDIENTS

- Hyssop: 15 grams, dried leaves and flowers
- Eucalyptus: 15 grams, dried leaves
- Marshmallow root: 10 grams, dried root, finely chopped
- Anise seed: 10 grams
- Vegetable glycerin: 360 ml
- Distilled water: 120 ml

INSTRUCTIONS

1. Ensure all herbs are thoroughly cleaned and prepared. Slightly crush the Hyssop leaves and flowers, and Anise seeds to release their volatile oils. Finely chop the marshmallow root to enhance its mucilage extraction.
2. In a clean glass jar, layer the Hyssop, Eucalyptus leaves, marshmallow root, and Anise seeds. In a separate bowl, mix the vegetable glycerin and distilled water until well combined, then pour this mixture over the herbs, ensuring they are fully submerged. Adjust the glycerin mixture if necessary to cover the herbs completely.
3. Use a plastic lid or cover the jar with a non-metallic material to prevent any reaction with the glycerin.
4. Keep the jar in a cool, dark cupboard for 4 to 6 weeks. Shake the jar every few days to promote the infusion process.
5. After the infusing period, filter the glycerite using cheesecloth or a fine mesh strainer into another clean jar, pressing the herbs to extract as much liquid as possible.
6. Funnel the glycerite into clean, airtight bottles or jars. Store in a cool, dark place for up to a year.

USAGE: Take 1 teaspoon (about 5 milliliters) of the glycerite up to three times a day during periods of respiratory discomfort or as a preventive measure during cold and flu season to support respiratory health.

WILD CHERRY BARK GLYCERITE TINCTURE

PREP TIME: 20 MINUTES　　**MACERATION TIME:** 4 TO 6 WEEKS　　**YIELD:** ABOUT 480 ML

INGREDIENTS

- Wild Cherry Bark: 20 grams, dried bark, finely chopped
- Mullein: 15 grams, dried leaves
- Licorice Root: 10 grams, dried root, finely chopped
- Ginger: 10 grams, fresh root, finely chopped
- Vegetable glycerin: 360 ml
- Distilled water: 120 ml

INSTRUCTIONS

1. Ensure all herbs are thoroughly cleaned and prepared. Finely chop the Wild Cherry Bark and Ginger. Ensure the Mullein leaves and Licorice root are also finely chopped to maximize surface area for extraction.
2. In a clean glass jar, layer the Wild Cherry Bark, Mullein leaves, Licorice root, and Ginger. Mix the vegetable glycerin and distilled water in a separate bowl until well combined, then pour this mixture over the herbs, ensuring they are fully submerged. Adjust the glycerin mixture if necessary to completely cover the herbs.
3. Use a plastic lid or cover the jar with a non-metallic material to prevent any reaction with the glycerin.
4. Place the jar in a cool, dark cupboard for 4 to 6 weeks. Shake the jar every few days to promote the infusion process.
5. After the infusing period, filter the glycerite using cheesecloth or a fine mesh strainer into another clean jar, pressing the herbs to extract as much liquid as possible.
6. Funnel the glycerite into clean, airtight bottles or jars. Store in a cool, dark place for up to a year.

USAGE: Take 1 teaspoon (about 5 milliliters) of the glycerite up to three times a day during periods of respiratory discomfort or as a preventive measure during cold and flu season to support respiratory health.

PEPPERMINT VINEGAR TINCTURE

PREP TIME: 10 MINUTES

MACERATION TIME: 4 TO 6 WEEKS

YIELD: ABOUT 500 ML

INGREDIENTS

- *Peppermint: 30 grams, dried leaves*
- *Eucalyptus: 15 grams, dried leaves*
- *Thyme: 15 grams, dried leaves*

- *Lemon peel: 10 grams, dried peel*
- *Raw, unpasteurized apple cider vinegar: 480 ml*

INSTRUCTIONS

1. Ensure the peppermint, eucalyptus, and thyme leaves are thoroughly dried and the lemon peel is free from any pesticides and finely chopped if fresh.
2. In a clean glass jar, layer the dried peppermint leaves, eucalyptus leaves, thyme leaves, and dried lemon peel. Pour the apple cider vinegar over the ingredients until they are completely submerged. If necessary, add more vinegar to ensure all ingredients are covered.
3. Use a non-metallic lid, or place parchment paper under a metal lid to prevent corrosion from the vinegar. Seal the jar tightly.
4. Place the jar in a cool, dark cupboard for 4 to 6 weeks, shaking it every few days to ensure the ingredients are well infused.
5. After the infusion period, filter the vinegar using cheesecloth or a fine mesh strainer into another clean jar. Press or squeeze the ingredients to extract as much infused vinegar as possible.
6. Funnel the strained vinegar into clean bottles or jars. Store in a cool, dark place. The tincture can be stored for up to a year.

USAGE: Take 1 tablespoon (about 15 milliliters) of the tincture diluted in water or tea, or mix into a warm beverage for immediate relief from respiratory congestion and coughs.

Skin Conditions

CALENDULA GLYCERITE TINCTURE

PREP TIME: 15 MINUTES

MACERATION TIME: 4 TO 6 WEEKS

YIELD: ABOUT 480 ML

INGREDIENTS

- *Calendula: 30 grams, dried flowers*
- *Chamomile: 15 grams, dried flowers*
- *Plantain: 15 grams, dried leaves*
- *Lavender: 10 grams, dried flowers*
- *Vegetable glycerin: 360 ml*
- *Distilled water: 120 ml*

INSTRUCTIONS

1. Ensure all herbs are thoroughly dried and slightly crushed to increase their surface area for better extraction.
2. In a clean glass jar, layer the Calendula flowers, Chamomile flowers, Plantain leaves, and Lavender flowers. In a separate bowl, mix the vegetable glycerin and distilled water until well combined, then pour this mixture over the herbs, making sure they are fully submerged. Adjust the glycerin mixture if necessary to cover the herbs completely.
3. Use a plastic lid or cover the jar with a non-metallic material to prevent any reaction with the glycerin.
4. Keep the jar in a cool, dark cupboard for 4 to 6 weeks. Shake the jar every few days to promote the infusion process.
5. After the infusing period, filter the glycerite using cheesecloth or a fine mesh strainer into another clean jar, pressing the herbs to extract as much liquid as possible.
6. Funnel the glycerite into clean, airtight bottles or jars. Store in a cool, dark place for up to a year.

USAGE: Apply a small amount of the glycerite directly to the affected skin areas up to three times a day to soothe irritation, promote healing, and moisturize the skin.

GOLDENSEAL GLYCERITE TINCTURE

PREP TIME: 20 MINUTES

MACERATION TIME: 4 TO 6 WEEKS

YIELD: ABOUT 480 ML

INGREDIENTS

- *Goldenseal: 15 grams, dried root, finely chopped*
- *Aloe Vera: 15 grams, dried gel powder*
- *Witch Hazel: 15 grams, dried leaves*
- *Tea Tree: 5 grams, dried leaves, finely crushed*
- *Vegetable glycerin: 360 ml*
- *Distilled water: 120 ml*

INSTRUCTIONS

1. Ensure all herbs are thoroughly dried and prepared. Finely chop the Goldenseal root and crush the Tea Tree leaves to maximize their active ingredients' exposure.
2. In a clean glass jar, layer the Goldenseal root, Aloe Vera gel powder, Witch Hazel leaves, and Tea Tree leaves. Mix the vegetable glycerin and distilled water in a separate bowl until well combined, then pour this mixture over the herbs, ensuring they are fully submerged. Adjust the glycerin mixture if necessary to cover the herbs completely.
3. Use a plastic lid or cover the jar with a non-metallic material to prevent any reaction with the glycerin.
4. Place the jar in a cool, dark cupboard for 4 to 6 weeks. Shake the jar every few days to promote the infusion process.
5. After the infusing period, filter the glycerite using cheesecloth or a fine mesh strainer into another clean jar, pressing the herbs to extract as much liquid as possible.
6. Funnel the glycerite into clean, airtight bottles or jars. Store in a cool, dark place for up to a year.

USAGE: Apply a small amount of the glycerite directly to the affected skin areas up to three times a day to help treat skin infections, reduce inflammation, and promote healing.

HORSETAIL GLYCERITE TINCTURE

PREP TIME: 15 MINUTES **MACERATION TIME:** 4 TO 6 WEEKS **YIELD:** ABOUT 480 ML

INGREDIENTS

- Horsetail: 20 grams, dried aerial parts, finely chopped
- Comfrey: 15 grams, dried leaves
- Calendula: 15 grams, dried flowers
- Gotu Kola: 10 grams, dried leaves
- Vegetable glycerin: 360 ml
- Distilled water: 120 ml

INSTRUCTIONS

1. Ensure all herbs are thoroughly dried and finely chopped to maximize surface area for better extraction.
2. In a clean glass jar, layer the Horsetail, Comfrey, Calendula, and Gotu Kola. Mix the vegetable glycerin and distilled water in a separate bowl until well combined, then pour this mixture over the herbs, making sure they are fully submerged. Adjust the glycerin mixture if necessary to cover the herbs completely.
3. Use a plastic lid or cover the jar with a non-metallic material to prevent any reaction with the glycerin.
4. Keep the jar in a cool, dark cupboard for 4 to 6 weeks. Shake the jar every few days to promote the infusion process.
5. After the infusing period, filter the glycerite using cheesecloth or a fine mesh strainer into another clean jar, pressing the herbs to extract as much liquid as possible.
6. Funnel the glycerite into clean, airtight bottles or jars. Store in a cool, dark place for up to a year.

USAGE: Apply a small amount of the glycerite directly to the affected skin areas up to three times a day to support skin healing, improve elasticity, and enhance overall skin health.

CHAMOMILE VINEGAR TINCTURE

PREP TIME: 10 MINUTES   **MACERATION TIME:** 4 TO 6 WEEKS   **YIELD:** ABOUT 500 ML

INGREDIENTS

- *Chamomile: 30 grams, dried flowers*
- *Lavender: 15 grams, dried flowers*
- *Witch Hazel: 15 grams, dried leaves*
- *Cucumber peel: 10 grams, dried peel*
- *Raw, unpasteurized apple cider vinegar: 480 ml*

INSTRUCTIONS

1. Ensure the chamomile and lavender flowers, witch hazel leaves, and cucumber peel are thoroughly dried. This will help preserve their natural properties and prevent mold growth in the tincture.
2. In a clean glass jar, layer the dried chamomile flowers, lavender flowers, witch hazel leaves, and dried cucumber peel. Pour the apple cider vinegar over the ingredients until they are completely submerged. If necessary, add more vinegar to ensure all ingredients are covered.
3. Use a non-metallic lid, or place parchment paper under a metal lid to prevent corrosion from the vinegar. Seal the jar tightly.
4. Place the jar in a cool, dark cupboard for 4 to 6 weeks, shaking it every few days to ensure the ingredients are well infused.
5. After the infusion period, filter the vinegar using cheesecloth or a fine mesh strainer into another clean jar. Press or squeeze the ingredients to extract as much infused vinegar as possible.
6. Funnel the strained vinegar into clean bottles or jars. Store in a cool, dark place. The tincture can be stored for up to a year.

USAGE: Dilute 1 tablespoon (about 15 milliliters) of the tincture in 1 cup (240 milliliters) of water and use as a soothing facial rinse or applied with a cotton pad to affected areas of the skin up to twice daily. This can help reduce skin inflammation, soothe irritations, and promote healing.

Anxiolytics and Stress Relievers

LINDEN GLYCERITE TINCTURE

PREP TIME: 15 MINUTES   **MACERATION TIME:** 4 TO 6 WEEKS   **YIELD:** ABOUT 480 ML

INGREDIENTS

- *Linden flowers: 20 grams, dried flowers*
- *Lemon Balm: 15 grams, dried leaves*
- *Passionflower: 15 grams, dried flowers*
- *Chamomile: 10 grams, dried flowers*
- *Vegetable glycerin: 360 ml*
- *Distilled water: 120 ml*

INSTRUCTIONS

1. Ensure all herbs are thoroughly dried and slightly crushed to increase their surface area for better extraction.
2. In a clean glass jar, layer the Linden flowers, Lemon Balm leaves, Passionflower, and Chamomile. Mix the vegetable glycerin and distilled water in a separate bowl until well combined, then pour this mixture over the herbs, ensuring they are fully submerged. Adjust the glycerin mixture if necessary to cover the herbs completely.
3. Use a plastic lid or cover the jar with a non-metallic material to prevent any reaction with the glycerin.
4. Place the jar in a cool, dark cupboard for 4 to 6 weeks. Shake the jar every few days to promote the infusion process.
5. After the infusing period, filter the glycerite using cheesecloth or a fine mesh strainer into another clean jar, pressing the herbs to extract as much liquid as possible.
6. Funnel the glycerite into clean, airtight bottles or jars. Store in a cool, dark place for up to a year.

USAGE: Take 1 teaspoon (about 5 milliliters) of the glycerite up to three times a day during times of stress or anxiety, or before bedtime to promote relaxation.

ST. JOHN'S WORT GLYCERITE TINCTURE

PREP TIME: 20 MINUTES   **MACERATION TIME:** 4 TO 6 WEEKS   **YIELD:** ABOUT 480 ML

INGREDIENTS

- *St. John's Wort: 20 grams, dried flowers and leaves*
- *Valerian Root: 15 grams, dried root, finely chopped*
- *Skullcap: 15 grams, dried aerial parts*
- *Lemon Verbena: 10 grams, dried leaves*
- *Vegetable glycerin: 360 ml*
- *Distilled water: 120 ml*

INSTRUCTIONS

1. Ensure all herbs are thoroughly dried and prepared. The St. John's Wort and Skullcap should be slightly crushed to release their active compounds. Finely chop the Valerian root to enhance extraction.
2. In a clean glass jar, layer the St. John's Wort, Valerian root, Skullcap, and Lemon Verbena. Mix the vegetable glycerin and distilled water in a separate bowl until well combined, then pour this mixture over the herbs, ensuring they are fully submerged. Adjust the glycerin mixture if necessary to cover the herbs completely.
3. Use a plastic lid or cover the jar with a non-metallic material to prevent any reaction with the glycerin.
4. Place the jar in a cool, dark cupboard for 4 to 6 weeks. Shake the jar every few days to promote the infusion process.
5. After the infusing period, filter the glycerite using cheesecloth or a fine mesh strainer into another clean jar, pressing the herbs to extract as much liquid as possible.
6. Funnel the glycerite into clean, airtight bottles or jars. Store in a cool, dark place for up to a year.

USAGE: Take 1 teaspoon (about 5 milliliters) of the glycerite three times a day during times of heightened anxiety or stress, or as directed by a healthcare provider.

PRECAUTIONS: Be aware that St. John's Wort may interfere with a range of medications, such as antidepressants, contraceptives, and others.

WOOD BETONY GLYCERITE TINCTURE

PREP TIME: 15 MINUTES **MACERATION TIME:** 4 TO 6 WEEKS **YIELD:** ABOUT 480 ML

INGREDIENTS

- *Wood Betony: 20 grams, dried aerial parts*
- *Holy Basil: 15 grams, dried leaves*
- *Lemon Balm: 15 grams, dried leaves*
- *Rose petals: 10 grams, dried petals*
- *Vegetable glycerin: 360 ml*
- *Distilled water: 120 ml*

INSTRUCTIONS

1. Ensure all herbs are thoroughly dried and slightly crushed to increase their surface area for better extraction.
2. In a clean glass jar, layer the Wood Betony, Holy Basil, Lemon Balm, and Rose petals. Mix the vegetable glycerin and distilled water in a separate bowl until well combined, then pour this mixture over the herbs, ensuring they are fully submerged. Adjust the glycerin mixture if necessary to cover the herbs completely.
3. Use a plastic lid or cover the jar with a non-metallic material to prevent any reaction with the glycerin.
4. Keep the jar in a cool, dark cupboard for 4 to 6 weeks. Shake the jar every few days to promote the infusion process.
5. After the infusing period, filter the glycerite using cheesecloth or a fine mesh strainer into another clean jar, pressing the herbs to extract as much liquid as possible.
6. Funnel the glycerite into clean, airtight bottles or jars. Store in a cool, dark place for up to a year.

USAGE: Take 1 teaspoon (about 5 milliliters) of the glycerite up to three times a day during times of stress or anxiety to help calm the mind and ease nervous tension.

CHAMOMILE VINEGAR TINCTURE

PREP TIME: 10 MINUTES **MACERATION TIME:** 4 TO 6 WEEKS **YIELD:** ABOUT 5000 ML

INGREDIENTS

- *Chamomile: 30 grams, dried flowers*
- *Lavender: 15 grams, dried flowers*
- *Lemon Balm: 15 grams, dried leaves*
- *Mint: 15 grams, dried leaves*
- *Raw, unpasteurized apple cider vinegar: 480 ml*

INSTRUCTIONS

1. Ensure the chamomile, lavender, lemon balm, and mint are thoroughly dried to prevent mold growth during infusion.
2. In a clean glass jar, layer the dried chamomile flowers, lavender flowers, lemon balm leaves, and mint leaves. Pour the apple cider vinegar over the herbs until they are completely submerged. If necessary, add more vinegar to ensure all ingredients are covered.

3. Use a non-metallic lid, or place parchment paper under a metal lid to prevent corrosion from the vinegar. Seal the jar tightly.
4. Place the jar in a cool, dark cupboard for 4 to 6 weeks, shaking it every few days to ensure the ingredients are well infused.
5. After the infusion period, filter the vinegar using cheesecloth or a fine mesh strainer into another clean jar. Press or squeeze the ingredients to extract as much infused vinegar as possible.
6. Funnel the strained vinegar into clean bottles or jars. Store in a cool, dark place. The tincture can be stored for up to a year.

USAGE: Take 1 tablespoon (about 15 milliliters) of the tincture diluted in water or tea up to three times a day to help reduce anxiety and promote relaxation.

Women's Health

BLACK COHOSH GLYCERITE TINCTURE

PREP TIME: 20 MINUTES   **MACERATION TIME:** 4 TO 6 WEEKS   **YIELD:** ABOUT 480 ML

INGREDIENTS

- Black Cohosh: 15 grams, dried root, finely chopped
- Red Clover: 15 grams, dried flowers
- Chaste Tree Berry: 10 grams, dried berries
- Dong Quai: 10 grams, dried root, finely chopped
- Vegetable glycerin: 360 ml
- Distilled water: 120 ml

INSTRUCTIONS

1. Ensure all herbs are thoroughly dried and finely chopped to help release the essential oils and increase the surface area for extraction. This step is particularly important for tough roots like Black Cohosh and Dong Quai.
2. In a clean glass jar, layer the Black Cohosh, Red Clover, Chaste Tree Berry, and Dong Quai. Mix the vegetable glycerin and distilled water in a separate bowl until well combined, then pour this mixture over the herbs, ensuring they are fully submerged. Adjust the glycerin mixture if necessary to cover the herbs completely.
3. Use a plastic lid or cover the jar with a non-metallic material to prevent any reaction with the glycerin.
4. Keep the jar in a cool, dark cupboard for 4 to 6 weeks. Shake the jar every few days to promote the infusion process.
5. After the infusing period, filter the glycerite using cheesecloth or a fine mesh strainer into another clean jar, pressing the herbs to extract as much liquid as possible.
6. Funnel the glycerite into clean, airtight bottles or jars. Store in a cool, dark place for up to a year.

USAGE: Take 1 teaspoon (about 5 milliliters) of the glycerite up to twice a day to help manage symptoms associated with menopause, such as hot flashes, night sweats, and hormonal imbalances.

PRECAUTIONS: Black Cohosh should be used with care, as it may interact with certain medications and is not recommended for everyone, especially those with liver issues. Always consult with a healthcare provider before beginning any new herbal regimen.

MILK THISTLE LIVER SUPPORT GLYCERITE TINCTURE

PREP TIME: 15 MINUTES   **MACERATION TIME:** 4 TO 6 WEEKS   **YIELD:** ABOUT 480 ML

INGREDIENTS

- *Milk Thistle: 20 grams, dried seeds, finely ground*
- *Dandelion Root: 15 grams, dried root, finely chopped*
- *Turmeric: 10 grams, dried root, finely chopped*

- *Peppermint: 10 grams, dried leaves*
- *Vegetable glycerin: 360 ml*
- *Distilled water: 120 ml*

INSTRUCTIONS

1. Ensure all herbs are thoroughly dried. Grind the Milk Thistle seeds to a fine powder to maximize the extraction of silymarin, its active compound. Finely chop the Dandelion Root and Turmeric for better extraction. Crush the Peppermint leaves slightly to help release their essential oils.
2. In a clean glass jar, layer the ground Milk Thistle seeds, chopped Dandelion Root, Turmeric, and Peppermint leaves. Mix the vegetable glycerin and distilled water in a separate bowl until well combined, then pour this mixture over the herbs, ensuring they are fully submerged. Adjust the glycerin mixture if necessary to cover the herbs completely.
3. Use a plastic lid or cover the jar with a non-metallic material to prevent any reaction with the glycerin.
4. Place the jar in a cool, dark cupboard for 4 to 6 weeks. Shake the jar every few days to promote the infusion process.
5. After the infusing period, filter the glycerite using cheesecloth or a fine mesh strainer into another clean jar, pressing the herbs to extract as much liquid as possible.
6. Funnel the glycerite into clean, airtight bottles or jars. Store in a cool, dark place for up to a year.

USAGE: Take 1 teaspoon (about 5 milliliters) of the glycerite up to twice a day to support liver function and promote hormonal balance.

DONG QUAI GLYCERITE TINCTURE

PREP TIME: 20 MINUTES   **MACERATION TIME:** 4 TO 6 WEEKS   **YIELD:** ABOUT 480 ML

INGREDIENTS

- *Dong Quai: 15 grams, dried root, finely chopped*
- *Red Raspberry Leaf: 15 grams, dried leaves*
- *Vitex Berry: 10 grams, dried berries*

- *Nettle: 10 grams, dried leaves*
- *Vegetable glycerin: 360 ml*
- *Distilled water: 120 ml*

INSTRUCTIONS

1. Ensure all herbs are thoroughly dried and finely chopped or ground to increase their surface area for better extraction.

2. In a clean glass jar, layer the Dong Quai, Red Raspberry Leaf, Vitex Berry, and Nettle. Mix the vegetable glycerin and distilled water in a separate bowl until well combined, then pour this mixture over the herbs, making sure they are fully submerged. Adjust the glycerin mixture if necessary to cover the herbs completely.
3. Use a plastic lid or cover the jar with a non-metallic material to prevent any reaction with the glycerin.
4. Place the jar in a cool, dark cupboard for 4 to 6 weeks. Shake the jar every few days to promote the infusion process.
5. After the infusing period, filter the glycerite using cheesecloth or a fine mesh strainer into another clean jar, pressing the herbs to extract as much liquid as possible.
6. Funnel the glycerite into clean, airtight bottles or jars. Store in a cool, dark place for up to a year.

USAGE: Take 1 teaspoon (about 5 milliliters) of the glycerite up to twice a day to support hormonal balance, menstrual health, and overall reproductive health.

PRECAUTIONS: Dong Quai should not be used during pregnancy.

CHASTE TREE GLYCERITE TINCTURE

PREP TIME: 20 MINUTES

MACERATION TIME: 4 TO 6 WEEKS

YIELD: ABOUT 480 ML

INGREDIENTS

- *Chaste Tree Berry: 20 grams, dried berries*
- *Black Cohosh: 15 grams, dried root, finely chopped*
- *Dandelion Root: 15 grams, dried root, finely chopped*
- *Licorice Root: 10 grams, dried root, finely chopped*
- *Vegetable glycerin: 360 ml*
- *Distilled water: 120 ml*

INSTRUCTIONS

1. Ensure all herbs are thoroughly dried and finely chopped or ground to maximize their surface area for better extraction. Crushing the Chaste Tree berries slightly can help release their active compounds.
2. In a clean glass jar, layer the Chaste Tree berries, Black Cohosh root, Dandelion root, and Licorice root. Mix the vegetable glycerin and distilled water in a separate bowl until well combined, then pour this mixture over the herbs, ensuring they are fully submerged. Adjust the glycerin mixture if necessary to cover the herbs completely.
3. Use a plastic lid or cover the jar with a non-metallic material to prevent any reaction with the glycerin.
4. Keep the jar in a cool, dark cupboard for 4 to 6 weeks. Shake the jar every few days to promote the infusion process.
5. After the infusing period, filter the glycerite using cheesecloth or a fine mesh strainer into another clean jar, pressing the herbs to extract as much liquid as possible.
6. Funnel the glycerite into clean, airtight bottles or jars. Store in a cool, dark place for up to a year.

USAGE: Take 1 teaspoon (about 5 milliliters) of the glycerite daily, particularly in the morning, to help regulate menstrual cycles and address symptoms of hormonal imbalances such as PMS and menopausal symptoms.

PRECAUTIONS: Note that Chaste Tree may affect hormonal medications, such as birth control pills.

Synergistic Use of Tinctures and Other Herbal Products

The art of herbal medicine is deeply rooted in understanding the synergistic effects that different herbal products can have when used together. Tinctures, with their concentrated extracts, play a pivotal role in this interplay, offering enhanced therapeutic benefits when combined with other herbal forms such as teas, capsules, and topical preparations.

1. Complementary Combinations

The synergy between tinctures and other herbal products lies in their ability to complement each other's therapeutic properties. For instance:

- **Tinctures and Teas**: Combining tinctures with herbal teas can enhance the bioavailability of water-soluble compounds. For example, a chamomile tea might be paired with a valerian root tincture to augment its soothing effects, ideal for promoting relaxation and sleep.

- **Tinctures and Capsules**: This combination can be particularly effective when immediate and sustained effects are needed. A capsule containing a slow-releasing herbal extract like milk thistle might be used in conjunction with a tincture of dandelion to support liver health, providing both immediate and extended benefits.

2. Layering Effects for Enhanced Efficacy

Layering different forms of herbal products can target multiple pathways in the body, enhancing the overall efficacy of the treatment protocol. This strategy involves:

- **Sequential Dosing**: Administering a tincture for quick absorption followed by a longer-lasting herbal form like a capsule ensures that the therapeutic effect is initiated quickly and sustained over time. For instance, an echinacea tincture could be taken at the onset of cold symptoms, followed by echinacea capsules throughout the day to maintain immune support.

- **Topical and Internal Use**: In cases where both internal and external relief is needed, tinctures can be taken orally while a corresponding herbal cream or salve is applied externally. This is especially useful in the treatment of conditions like eczema or arthritis, where a turmeric tincture might reduce inflammation internally while a turmeric-based cream provides topical relief.

3. **Maximizing Bioavailability and Absorption**

The use of tinctures in conjunction with other herbal products can also maximize the bioavailability of active ingredients, ensuring that they are absorbed more effectively into the bloodstream.

- **Lipophilic and Hydrophilic Compound Matching**: Tinctures, often alcohol-based, can extract and preserve both water-soluble and fat-soluble compounds. By matching these with herbal teas or oils that extract different types of compounds, one can ensure a fuller spectrum of the plant's medicinal properties is utilized.

- **Herb Pairings**: Certain herbs, when taken together, can enhance each other's absorption and efficacy. For example, pairing a peppermint tincture with a ginger capsule can enhance digestive relief more effectively than using either alone.

4. **Safety and Interaction Considerations**

While the synergistic use of tinctures with other herbal products offers many benefits, it is crucial to consider potential safety and interaction issues:

- **Consultation with a Healthcare Provider**: Always recommend consulting with a healthcare professional, particularly for individuals with underlying health conditions or those taking prescription medications, to avoid adverse interactions.

- **Allergy and Sensitivity Checks**: Ensure compatibility between different herbal forms, particularly for users with allergies or sensitivities to specific herbs.

If you're eager to expand your knowledge about the preparation of other herbal remedies beyond tinctures—including teas, capsules, extracts, poultices, balms, essential oils, and much more—check out my book, "The Healing Power of Ancient Remedies." It offers a thorough exploration of numerous healing modalities, packed with valuable tips and a wide array of effective remedies.

HERE IS YOUR BONUS!

"Herbal Tincture Workbook"

Your Essential Printable Workbook to keep track your tincture preparation, dosages, and results and personalize your healing journey

SCAN HERE TO DOWNLOAD IT

HERBAL TINCTURE WORKBOOK

Keep Track of Your Herbal Experimentation and
Successes Day By Day.

Mix, Test and Refine your Remedies
Tailored to Your Needs

SCAN HERE!

Made in the USA
Las Vegas, NV
13 November 2024

11772893R00105